Environmental Justice and Soy Agribusiness

Environmental justice research and activism predominantly focus on openly conflictive situations; claims making is central. However, situations of injustice can still occur even if there is no overt conflict. *Environmental Justice and Soy Agribusiness* fills this gap by applying an environmental justice incommensurabilities framework to reveal the mechanisms of why conflicts do not arise in particular situations, even though they fall within classic environmental justice schemes.

Empirically, the case study focus is on the remote soy frontier in Northwest Argentina, particularly the town of Las Lajitas as the nucleus of soy production. This represents an excellent example of the recent expansion of the soy agribusiness industry in Latin America. First, a classic environmental justice analysis is carried out. Second, and drawing on the epistemological works of Ludwik Fleck, an alternative analytical framework is proposed, visualising locals' thought styles on change, effects and potential conflict in relation to soy agribusiness. Here, visceral elements and the application of a jazz methodology are vital for a more holistic form of multisensory cognition. Third, incommensurabilities among the classic and alternative approach are uncovered, arguing for the importance of temporal and spatial contexts in environmental justice research.

Robert Hafner is a postdoctoral researcher, funded by the Post-DocTrack Pilot Program of the OeAW, and a member of the Work Group Development Studies and Sustainability Research, the Institute of Geography, Innsbruck University, Austria.

Other books in the Earthscan Food and Agriculture Series

For further details please visit the series page on the Routledge website:
www.routledge.com/books/series/ECEFA/

Environmental Justice and Soy Agribusiness

Robert Hafner

LONDON AND NEW YORK

from Routledge

First published 2018 by Routledge

2 Park Square, Milton Park, Abingdon, Oxfordshire OX14 4RN
52 Vanderbilt Avenue, New York, NY 10017

Routledge is an imprint of the Taylor & Francis Group, an informa business

First issued in paperback 2020

British Library Cataloguing-in-Publication Data
A catalogue record for this book is available from the British Library

Library of Congress Cataloging-in-Publication Data
A catalog record has been requested for this book

ISBN: 978-0-8153-8535-6 (hbk)
ISBN: 978-0-367-50855-5 (pbk)

Typeset in Bembo
by Wearset Ltd, Boldon, Tyne and Wear

Contents

Figures

Tables

Boxes

Preface and acknowledgements

I like odd statistics.

Up to this point, I have spent 1,509 days working on this book, which means I have been writing about 80 words per day on average.

Most of the pages were generated in St. Wolfgang im Salzkammergut in Austria, at the house of my parents, Sonja and Reinhold. They always – much like my sister Iris – supported me in any way possible, helped me push through difficult stages and put things in perspective when necessary. I am very grateful to them for that.

The second highest number of pages (and the majority of the figures and maps) came together in Innsbruck, sitting in the office of our Work Group Development Studies and Sustainability Research at the Institute of Geography, Innsbruck University, in Austria. Thank you for the input, particularly relating to the figures and maps, but especially for tolerating my antics of writing on 3/7 of all the windows. Not just moral support from my family *in situ* was personified by my aunt. Thanks for always being there for me, Elfriede.

The third highest number of pages were written in San Miguel de Tucumán in Argentina, at the *Instituto Superior de Estudios Sociales*, Universidad Nacional de Tucumán. Thank you for offering me a desk and (especially moral) support during my fieldwork phase.

Speaking of fieldwork organisation, I have spent 14 months in Argentina, made two round-trip transatlantic flights, travelled 22,000 km by bus, carried out fieldwork twice by car (thank you, Pablo Paolasso, for showing me around on my first trip) and once with a pickup truck. I have slept in 15 different types of accommodation, including hostels, hotels, floors and truck beds, a private house (thank you, Isabel and Hugo Karplus, for your great hospitality and friendship over the years; without you, I would not have discovered so many facets of Argentina and Buenos Aires), or private rooms. Thank you, Soledad, José María, Julia, Olga and the people from the *Vecinos Autoconvocados del Río Juramento*.

However, there are also dark sides to fieldwork. During my stay, two birds were hit by our car, and approximately 20 cockroaches as well as seemingly 100,000 mosquitos killed.

On a more pleasant note, the suckling pig that was grilled for us by Pablo in Coronel Mollinedo was delicious (thanks to the whole Sánchez family, for letting us stay at your house and giving us insights into local structures).

Some 167 interviews were conducted, 120 caught on tape (leaving me with 176 hours, 33 minutes and 30 seconds of audio material) and 47 not recorded. Thank you all for using your precious time to talk to me. You were a great help.

Some 15 workshops were conducted with the local youth. Thank you very much to all of you for participating enthusiastically, opening a window of cognition that would have otherwise remained eternally shut. Thanks also go to the teachers, headmistresses and headmasters for letting us carry out our activities with their students.

Most of the fieldwork (particularly the workshops), was carried out with my colleague, Julieta Krapovickas. Thank you, Julieta, for your awesome input; together, we made a great team!

There is no dissertation without a supervisor. Martin Coy, thank you for putting up with my sometimes off-the-norm ideas and approaches, but (almost) always encouraging me to venture forth.

Special thanks goes to Gerhard Rainer, thank you for your input, critiques and your willingness to read the *whole thing*. Roman Ossner, you always had a keen eye on my figures and maps, thanks for that. Walter Kraus, an excellent proof-reader, it is beyond my understanding how you work so efficiently, I owe you big time. And Simone Sandholz, even though our offices are no longer next to each other, thanks for letting me bug you with anything and everything, at any time.

Money makes the world go round. So in order for *me* to go around the world, I'd like to thank Innsbruck University for granting me both the Doctorate Scholarship for Young Researchers (DOC-UIBK) and the Scholarship for Short-Term Studies Abroad (KWA, Innsbruck University) at the *Instituto Superior de Estudios Sociales, Universidad Nacional de Tucumán*, Argentina. Thank you OeAD GmBH for awarding me a 12-month Marietta Blau Scholarship (OeAD, Austria) at the *Instituto Superior de Estudios Sociales, Universidad Nacional de Tucumán*, Argentina. And thanks to the Austrian Academy of Science for a three-year DOC Fellowship of the Austrian Academy of Science at the Institute of Geography, Innsbruck University, Austria.

And finally, I want to thank you, dear reader, for your openness and willingness to engage with a somewhat unusual book and its underlying, new approaches towards cognition.

Abbreviations

Term	Spanish	English
AACREA	Asociación Argentina de Consorcios Regionales de Experimentación Agrícola	Argentinian Association of Regional Consortia for Agricultural Experimentation
AAPRESID	Asociación Argentina de Productores en Siembra Directa	Argentinian Direct Tillage Producers Association
ARS		Argentinian peso
ASC		Local administrations, support and control institutions. Those actors range from local politicians, members of the public sector, representatives of the police, environmental enforcement groups as well as representatives of INTA.
BRL		Brazilian Real
CEPRONAT	Centro de Protección a la Naturaleza	Centre for the Protection of Nature
CONICET	Consejo Nacional de Investigaciones Científicas y Técnicas	National Commission of Scientific and Technical Research
DTM		digital terrain model
EDU		Schools and education entities. This category comprises representatives of schools, i.e. headmasters, teachers and librarians.
EFSA		European Food Safety Authority
EJ		environmental justice

Term	Spanish	English
EJIF		environmental justice incommensurabilities framework
EJOLT		Environmental Justice Organisations, Liabilities and Trade
EOEA		Executive Office of Environmental Affairs (USA)
FARN	Fundación Ambiente y Recursos Naturales	Foundation for the Environment and Natural Resources
GM		genetically modified
GMO		genetically modified organism
GRR	Grupo de Reflexión Rural	Group of Rural Reflection
INTA	Instituto Nacional de Tecnología Agropecuaria	National Institute of Agriculture and Livestock Technology (Argentina)
IPV	Instituto Provincial de Vivienda	Provincial Institute of Housing
LULU		locally undesired land use
MEMSIS		Framework for Assessing the Sustainability of National Resource Management Systems (Spanish acronym)
Mercosur	Mercado Común del Sur	Southern Common Market
MNCI – Vía Campesina	Movimiento Nacional Campesino Indígena	National Campesino-Indigenous Movement
NEA	Noreste Argentino	North-east Argentina
NGO		non-governmental organisation
NOA	Noroeste Argentino	North-west Argentina
NPA		National Park Administration
OECD		Organisation for Economic Cooperation and Development
PE★ (total); PEL (Las Lajitas); PEM (Coronel Mollinedo); PER (regional)		Local perception actors. This group comprises locals I have spent significant amounts of time with and thus gained insights into their ways of thinking and acting.

Term	*Spanish*	*English*
REDAF	Red Agroforestal	Agroforestal Network
RTRS		Round Table on Responsible Soy
SAB		Soy agribusiness. The majority of the members of this group are farmers, members of *pooles de siembra* and/or agroservice providers.
SENASA	Servicio Nacional de Sanidad y Calidad Agroalimentaria	National Service for Health and Quality of Agrifoods
SOC		Social entities. Members of social entities are considered hospital staff (both administrative and medical), members of health centres, social workers, who work directly 'in the field', visiting households, or heads of religious organisations with social projects in the region (e.g. soup kitchens).
TIN		Triangulated Irregular Network
TSDF		treatment/storage/disposal facility
UAC	Unión de Asambleas Ciudadanas	Union of Citizen Assemblies
UNSA	Universidad Nacional de Salta	National University of Salta (Argentina)
UPOV		International Union for the Protection of New Varieties of Plants
US EPA		US Environmental Protection Agency
US FDA		US Food and Drug Administration
WHO		World Health Organisation

1 Introduction

Have you ever applied environmental justice in obviously conflicting settings and nothing happened?

Environmental justice conflicts are omnipresent. By October 2017, 2,252 cases worldwide had been reported to the Environmental Justice Atlas (EJOLT 2016), covering topics ranging from nuclear to mineral ores, waste and water management, infrastructure, to biodiversity conservation, biomass and land conflicts. Soy agribusiness-related conflicts are an under-represented part of this list, even though they encompass central issues like new globalisation processes, land grabbing and far-reaching environmental problems, deforestation, GMO and fumigation and the exclusion of indigenous groups, as well as fairness and fair trade.

The potential is there, research is missing. Adding a small part to the manageable corpus of literature, this book will focus on the particular setting of the third-largest soy producer worldwide: Argentina (FAOSTAT 2014). The core area of soy production lies in the Argentine Pampas Region, a traditional agricultural region, where – through the application of heavy machinery, fertilisers and pesticides/herbicides – vast areas of soy monocultures have developed. Based on the increasing international demand for soy and its derivatives over the last three decades, a spatial expansion of the producing area towards the North-west of Argentina (NOA) is observed (cf. Reboratti 2010, p. 65). This traditionally peripheral region with economic and infrastructural deficits and above-average proportion of the population living below the poverty line, is now being transformed to an area of large-scale, externally financed and export-oriented soy fields (Bolsi 1997; Reboratti 2001; Bolsi and Paolasso 2009; Rivas and Natera Rivas 2009). Thus, the integration of the North-west into the processes of globalised soy agribusiness, particularly the accompanying structural and procedural changes, is generating socio-spatial fragmentation and conflicts among local actors, among actors on different scalar levels and among different interest groups. Such topics have already been studied in my research area (e.g. Hufty 2008; Izquierdo and Grau 2009; Silva *et al.* 2010; Venencia *et al.* 2012; Goldfarb and Zoomers 2013; Piquer-Rodríguez *et al.* 2015).

Three observations stand out: first, no explicit reference to the concept of environmental justice has been made so far, neither from an activist nor a scientific perspective. Second, locals living in urban areas (i.e. the villages and small towns) make up the majority of the population in the Chaco Salteño; they are affected by both the environmental change of their surrounding environments (e.g. through deforestation or fumigation) as well as by social effects (e.g. related to health, work, crime) thereof; but their thought styles (i.e. processes, circulations of ideas and social practices from which the style-appropriate conditioning of perception, thinking and acting of actors emerge) have not yet been the focus of social-environmental research. And, finally third, very little (meta-) research has been carried out (an exception is Davoudi and Brooks 2014) on the prequel to environmental justice conflicts, i.e. the focus on the asking (and subsequent questioning) of the 'right' questions.

Hence, with this book I aim to tackle those three central themes, go off the beaten path and introduce new forms of thinking (Schopenhauer 1851, p. 93) about environmental justice and soy agribusiness at the frontier in North-west Argentina.

Theoretically, I show that environmental justice activism/research – with few exceptions – has too narrow a perspective, leaving the pre-conflict stage and creation of different realities out of sight. Hence, my book 'fills a much-needed gap'[1] by focusing on the blank spaces of thought style incommensurabilities that hinder the understanding among actors.

Empirically, I focus on the most remote soy frontier in North-west Argentina, particularly the town of Las Lajitas as the nucleus of soy production. My aim here is to go beyond a classic stakeholder analysis and visualise the thought styles of locals (no extensive work has been done here so far) on change, effects and conflict (potentials) in relation to the soy agribusiness.

Finally, I show that context matters, both from a theoretical (i.e. which theoretical line of thought do I follow?), as well as an empirical perspective (i.e. what sort of questions, methods and findings do I use?).

Structure of the book

Research on environmental justice allows room for experimentation with research designs (Funderburg and Laurian 2015; Hodges and Stocking 2015). This book falls into this category. It is highly influenced by two elements: perspective and jazz. While the former draws heavily on the thinking of Ludwik Fleck (1980) and his thought styles and thought collectives (i.e. a group of people with similar backgrounds who share the same codes and rationalities as well as context) to obtain an understanding of the underlying dimensions that ultimately lead to the construction of differing realities (thus he can be considered a proto-constructivist), the latter resembles the methodological approximations that I have used to design both my fieldwork as well as post-processing, applying the attributes of this musical genre as a strong metaphor (Chapter 3).

This book, while maintaining the spirit of alternative research designs, is divided into three parts. Part I focuses on the meta-contextualisation of the research process and the epistemologies of cognition that become relevant throughout the empirical analysis. Here, Chapter 2 on thought styles and incommensurabilities, two terms highly influenced by Ludwik Fleck, lays the foundation for Chapter 3, dealing with the method(olog)ical consequences of Fleck's forms of thinking. Viscerality, jazz and the translation of those two concepts into the research process are put to the foreground. Thus, understanding the epistemology of my thinking, as I argue, is the first step towards the understanding of my perspectives, my thought styles and ways of thinking.

Part II deals with the contextualisation of the two main themes of this book. In Chapter 4, the notion of justice is conceptualised and analysed according to its origins and forms of normative interpretation, as well as dimensions. Consequently, those considerations hold true for the debate on environmental justice (EJ), a concept that has undergone major shifts in foci over the last year. Chapter 5 highlights the thematic, temporal and spatial contexts of the soy agribusiness in Argentina. In so doing, strategic reasoning for expanding the soy frontier to the North-west of Argentina is revealed, which will be of particular importance for the in-depth analysis of the case study in Chapter 8.

Part III re-contextualises both the thematic as well as the spatial configurations presented in Part II. Chapter 6 embeds the debate on environmental justice in a Latin American context, highlighting the challenges that come with the concept in this particular setting. Going more into detail in Chapter 7, the Chaco Salteño research area located in the North-west of Argentina is used to combine and adapt classic environmental justice concepts discussed in Chapter 4. Here I take up one aspect that has not yet been studied: EJ incommensurabilities, or why environmental justice activism/research does not work under certain circumstances. Taking up this omission, I develop an environmental justice incommensurabilities framework (EJIF). However, unlike those concepts' focus on openly conflictive situations, the starting point of my approach is pre-conflict, thus particularly designed for cases where all conditions for EJ activism are given, but still nothing happens, no conflict arises. Chapter 8 relies on the new framework and takes up different realities and readings (CLASSIC, ALTERNATIVE and the COMPLETE, see the next section) of local facts in the town of Las Lajitas located in the nucleus of soy production in the Chaco Salteño.

Finally, Chapter 9 ties all the loose ends together, answering the questions posed in three different readings as well as giving a contextualisation of the whole method applied.

As you like it: a guide to three different perspectives

In line with the two themes of perspective and jazz, I propose three different readings in this book. They are based on three perspectives towards environmental justice (Table 1.1): the CLASSIC, the ALTERNATIVE and the

Table 1.1 Three perspectives discussed in the book

THE CLASSIC ENVIRONMENTAL JUSTICE ACTIVISM/SCIENCE PERSPECTIVE	THE ALTERNATIVE BEYOND ENVIRONMENTAL JUSTICE AND WHAT 'REALLY' MATTERS
The first reading focuses on a narrow perspective of environmental justice, greatly influenced by the early stages of environmental justice (particularly phase 1; cf. Chapter 4) in general and distributional justice in particular. The thought style is framed deductively, i.e. the research area is viewed explicitly theoretically informed, applying environmental justice methodologies to identify conflict potentials.	The ALTERNATIVE approach goes the opposite way to the CLASSIC one. A theoretical embeddedness in environmental justice discussions is – though important – not primarily the key aspect and induction central here. The main objective is to construct thought styles of local actors first, identifying their concerns and claims, highlighting underlying dimensions that can or cannot lead to conflicts in the research area.[1]
Thus, the main questions in this field are:	Here, the central questions are:
What forms of social-environmental conflicts are observed in Las Lajitas?	*Who are the core actors in the research area?*
• Where are those conflicts located? • Who are the actors in the conflict? • How are environmental goods and bads distributed?	• What are their thought styles in relation to the soy agribusiness, regional development and social-environmental interaction? • What types of social-environmental problems are identified? • How far are claims made, against whom, and why (not)?
The requirements for an analysis of this sort are relatively low; little time for fieldwork is necessary to identify conflicts, interactions can be kept to a minimum by identifying and working with key actors.	This exploratory approach has the great advantage – by means of long-term fieldwork and by being 'more than just physically "there"' (Atkinson, 2015, p. 39) – to obtain a broader picture of local structures and elements of (thought style) powers.

THE COMPLETE
ENVIRONMENTAL JUSTICE INCOMMENSURABILITIES
The last perspective is a combination and comparison of the CLASSIC and the ALTERNATIVE approach. Here, the cognitive interest is of a more abstract nature: The incommensurabilities (i.e. the blind spots that hinder the understanding among the thought collectives) of the different thought styles' realities will be revealed. The central question is:

What consequences arise from environmental justice incommensurabilities?

• What differences and similarities of results show the CLASSIC and ALTERNATIVE perspective on environmental justice?
• How and why are they manifested in the way they are?

Note
1 While four different actor groups are identified, I have placed the main focus on the locals' perception, since very little research has been carried out on that topic so far.

COMPLETE. Each perspective has different – thought-style-dependent – research questions. Here, the concept of 'methodological drag', 'a perform-ance in which qualitative methodologists convincingly masquerade as situated within epistemological, theoretical, and methodological frameworks, even those that they may not situate themselves in personally or professionally' (Nordstrom and Happel-Parkins 2016, p. 149) becomes important. Counter-discourses beyond the familiar are deliberately shown to unearth new forms of cognition and allow for the creation of 'space[s] of curiosity' (Phillips 2014). So, based on the thought styles, certain contextual information is pro-vided, ultimately leading to the construction of different realities. Each chapter is (or not), marked according to its inclusion/exclusion in the respec-tive perspective.

Note

1 This is part of an alleged quote by Moses Hadas (cf. The Quotations Page 2015).

References

Bolsi, A.S.C., ed., 1997. *Problemas agrarios del Noroeste argentino: Contribuciones para su inventario*. San Miguel de Tucumán: Instituto de Estudios Geográficos, Universidad Nacional de Tucumán.

Bolsi, A.S.C. and Paolasso, P., eds., 2009. *Geografía de la pobreza en el Norte Grande argentino*. Tucumán.

Davoudi, S. and Brooks, E., 2014. When does unequal become unfair? Judging claims of environmental injustice. *Environment and Planning A*, 46 (11), 2686–2702.

EJOLT, 2016. *Environmental Justice Organizations, Liabilities and Trade* [online], EJOLT. Available at: www.ejolt.org/ (accessed 25 April 2016).

FAOSTAT, 2014. Available at: http://faostat.fao.org/site/567/DesktopDefault. aspx?PageID=567#ancor (accessed 12 November 2015).

Fleck, L., 1980. *Entstehung und Entwicklung einer wissenschaftlichen Tatsache: Einfuhrun-gen. in der Lehre von Denkstil und Denkkollektiv*. Frankfurt am Main: Suhrkamp.

Funderburg, R. and Laurian, L., 2015. Bolstering environmental (in)justice claims with a quasi-experimental research design. *Land Use Policy*, 49, 511–526.

Goldfarb, L. and Zoomers, A., 2013. The drivers behind the rapid expansion of geneti-cally modified soya production into the Chaco region of Argentina. In Z. Fang, ed. *Biofuels – Economy, Environment and Sustainability*. Rijeka, Croatia: InTech.

Hodges, H.E. and Stocking, G., 2015. A pipeline of tweets: environmental move-ments' use of Twitter in response to the Keystone XL pipeline. *Environmental Pol-itics*, 25 (2), 223–247.

Hufty, M., 2008. Pizarro protected area: a political ecology perspective on land use, soybeans and Argentina's nature conservation policy. In: M. Galvin and T. Haller, eds. *People, Protected Areas and Global Change: Participatory Conservation in Latin America, Africa, Asia and Europe*. Bern: NCCR North-South, Swiss National Centre of Competence in Research North-South, University of Bern, pp. 145–173.

Izquierdo, A.E. and Grau, H.R., 2009. Agriculture adjustment, land-use transition and protected areas in Northwestern Argentina. *Journal of Environmental Manage-ment*, 90 (2), 858–865.

Nordstrom, S.N. and Happel-Parkins, A., 2016. Methodological drag: subversive performances of qualitative methodologist and pedagogical practices. *Qualitative Inquiry*, 22 (2), 149–153.

Phillips, R., 2014. Space for curiosity. *Progress in Human Geography*, 38 (4), 493–512.

Piquer-Rodríguez, M., *et al.*, 2015. Effects of past and future land conversions on forest connectivity in the Argentine Chaco. *Landscape Ecology*, 30 (5), 817–833.

Reboratti, C., 2001. Cambio y persistencia en el agro argentino. Paper presented at conference Actas del VII Encuentro de Geógrafos de América Latina. Available at: http://ffyl1.uncu.edu.ar/IMG/pdf/REBORATTI_C._Cambio_y_persistencia_en_ el_agro_argentino.pdf

Reboratti, C., 2010. Un mar de soja: la nueva agricultura en Argentina y sus conse- cuencias. *Revista de Geografía Norte Grande*, 45, 63–76.

Rivas, A.I. and Natera Rivas, J.J., 2009. La distribución de la tierra en el Norte Grande Argentino: persistencias y cambios. *Baetica*, 31, 91–113.

Schopenhauer, A., 1851. *Parerga und Paralipomena: Kleine Philosophische Schriften*. Berlin: A. W. Hayn.

Silva, A., *et al.*, 2010. *Desmontar Pizarro*. Salta, Argentina.

The Quotations Page, 2015. Quotation #664 [online]. Available at: www.quotations page.com/quote/644.html (accessed 14 August 2016).

Venencia, C.D., Correa, J.J., Del Val, V., Buliubasich, C. and Seghezzo, L., 2012. Conflictos de tenencia de la tierra y sustentabilidad del uso del territorio del Chaco Salteño. *Avances en Energías Renovables y Medio Ambiente*, 16, 105–112.

Part I

Meta–contextualisation

2 Thought styles and incommensurabilities

Writing in the realms of science presupposes the possession of a certain conception of science itself. The epistemology of thinking, i.e. the membership in particular thought collectives, interactions and experiences of and among researchers, the articles and books read; all those elements are influential for the thinking process of an individual (Egloff 2005). Thus, context matters, be it (inter-, intra-, multi-, or trans-) disciplinary, outside the walls of academic institutions, i.e. in the field while doing research, or after results have been compiled and are being transmitted to the audience. This context also influences the way of how to do science, which questions are to be asked and which conclusions are drawn (see Ginev 2015). Nevertheless, as Das (2015, p. 39) highlights, most of the studies do not reveal their epistemological perspective for research question framing or how the data collected is applied in answering the questions posed. I fully agree with Das and therefore have the obligation/privilege to uncover the meta-theoretical and meta-contextual background of this book. In this sense, I find the writings of Ludwik Fleck highly enlightening; his ideas and thoughts have deeply influenced my way of doing science.

Ludwik Fleck, a physician and biologist, sees science not as a formal construct but rather as a task carried out by communities of scientists. His writings on the philosophy of science and logology are (as yet) little known, even though they had a great influence on Thomas S. Kuhn and his *The Structure of Scientific Revolutions* (1971), where he mentions that Fleck had actually anticipated many of his own ideas; but beyond this comment, he does not make the references to Fleck explicit (ibid., pp. 6–7).

Kuhn's terminology in his (1971) model of change was an eye-opener in the 1960s and 1970s, particularly for many geographers, even though years later, Kuhn (1991) himself argued that his model was not suitable for disciplines in the pre-paradigmatic stage:

> A paradigm is an academic culture, a means of operating whereby the adherents … agree on issues of epistemology, ontology and methodology within a defined sphere of academic activity – usually a sub-discipline rather than an entire discipline, as Kuhn made clear in his later writings.
>
> (Johnston 2004, p. 267)

Thus, this discrepancy of the use of paradigms and Kuhn's original intention will be used as a starting point to compare Fleck and Kuhn, allowing for a better understanding of the overall context (Table 2.1).

The core difference between Fleck and Kuhn is based on the fact that the former works on a very small-scale level, focusing on practical applicability and thus developed a well-described and named methodology for the generation of knowledge in different and plural contexts. The latter wants to reflect the bigger picture deriving from the history of physics (Werner and Zittel 2011, p. 15) and thus striving for very high levels of abstractions. This feature had been highly criticised by Fleck (before Kuhn even published *The Structure of Scientific Revolutions*) as being methodically outdated (Werner and Zittel 2011, p. 12).

For the purposes of this book, I favour Fleck's approach of an open epistemology (cf. Borck 2004) and his considerations of fluidity and evolution

Table 2.1 Differences between Ludwik Fleck's and Thomas S. Kuhn's philosophies of science

Category	Ludwik Fleck★	Thomas S. Kuhn
Central concept for common thinking	*Denkstil* (thought style)	Paradigm
Change of ideas	*Denkstilumwandlung* *Denkstilumänderung* (transformation of thought style)	Paradigm shift
Occurrence of change of ideas	often	Very rarely
Type of change of ideas	Fluid, transformation-like	Radical; Kuhn mentions up to four examples for paradigm shifts, such as Copernicus
Discipline of origin	Medicine, microbiology	Physics
Origin of thinking	From praxis, i.e. scientific communication	Large-scale theoretical changes
Type of approach	Bottom-up	Top-down
Scalar focus	Small-scale occurrences	Large-scale epochs
Reach of philosophy of science	Beyond the scientific community	Remains predominantly within scientific community
Understanding of history and sociology of ideas	Fluid, context-loaded and historically influenced	Properly developed and established patent and received structure

Note
★ Most of Ludwik Fleck's work has been written in German and is therefore read in the original language. Translations of the terms applied by Fleck derive from the work of Graf and Mutter (2006), who compiled the *Flecksikon*, a list of key words and concepts used by Ludwik Fleck in German that are translated into French and English. (own elaboration based on Kuhn 1971, Fleck 1980, Kuhn 1991, cf. Babich 2003, p. 88, Fleck 2008, 2011f, 2011g, 2011b, 2011a, 2011c, 2011e, 2011d, Werner and Zittel 2011, p. 16).

rather than revolution. Thus, the following pages briefly describe the core elements of Fleck's ideas.

Thus, thought styles[1] are neither methods nor fixed forms of thinking; they do not represent an epoch, worldview or ideology and they do not characterise any individuals, social groups or institutions; they are processes, circulations of ideas and social practices, out of which the style-appropriate conditioning of perception, thinking and acting of researchers emerge (Werner and Zittel 2011, p. 19). Or, as Fleck writes, '[t]he style is, then, a limited entity, a closed organism, and there is no possibility to obtain access through a common human, i.e. "logical" or "rational" way' (2008, p. 92; my translation).

The interrelation of science with praxis is crucial: 'Science is not a flower from the greenhouse, cultivated in absolute isolation from the world' (Fleck 2011f, p. 328). Each scientist is influenced by her/his socio-cultural surrounding, which consequently influences the form of how to approach scientific work, and vice versa (Stuckey *et al.* 2015). Thus, Fleck talks about the three components of cognition (both in everyday life and in science): Besides the *subject* and the *object* as the first two elements, the third is considered the *collective* (Fleck 2011b, p. 411), later termed *community*, defined as being 'creative like a subject, stubborn like an object and dangerous like an elemental force' (Fleck 2011a, pp. 470–471; my translation). His main objective here is to humanise science (particularly natural sciences), with the proposed advantage that the gap between theory and praxis in scientific life would disappear, leading to less hypocrisy. New ideals would develop, bringing the natural sciences and humanities closer together, allowing scientific conventions to become more transparent and explicable (ibid., p. 471). In a certain way, Fleck has already argued strongly (though implicitly) for the incorporation of transdisciplinary research, highlighting the democratic attribute of open as well as citizen science in order to validate 'truth' by the community rather than the elite (Fleck 2008, p. 98).

The three components of cognition have far wider-reaching consequences than just bringing together different strands and standards of science and the community. The interrelatedness of science and non-science mean that scientific achievements are not the outcome of individuals but produced by collectives (Fleck talks about *thought collectives*; Fleck 1980) during complex exchange processes (Werner and Zittel 2011, p. 18). This, again, has two subsequent effects:

1   Personalised thought styles, such as 'Galileo Galilei's thought style', or 'Nicolaus Copernicus' thought style'[2] cannot exist, since they too were involved in and influenced by their surroundings, be it supportive, accepting, critical or hostile (ibid., p. 21).
2   Thinking and cognition are both social and collective activities, expressed both in the form of ideas but also materialised in scientific practices; the scientific objects of the communication of thoughts are not only thought

but also made (Schlünder 2005, p. 60). Only the pre-acquired knowledge in the background allows the cognition of particular forms (both material and immaterial); or as Fleck puts it, '[t]he sentence "Jan has recognized the phenomenon" is incomplete: One has to add "within the thought style of S", possibly "from epoch E"' (Fleck 2008, p. 89). In order to deal with cognition, thus, clear contextualisation – both in terms of thought style as well as temporality – is pivotal. Fleck argues that every individual does have her/his personal reality/realities related to individual experiences and preferences. Part of individual incommensurabilities (though not explicitly named as such) is the aspect that one can belong to contradictory thought styles (Fleck 2011g, pp. 53–54): professional, private, religious, political, etc. For example, a person can be both a physicist and deeply religious.

It is established that the role of thought collectives is paramount for thinking and cognition (cf. Egloff 2011). Fleck further elaborates on the definition of a thought collective as a 'community of people that are in thought exchange or interplay of thinking' and thus becomes the 'carrier of a historical development of the area of thought, a certain stock of knowledge and culture, i.e. a particular thought style' (Fleck 1980, pp. 54–55). A thought collective is established when two or more people share ideas, which can be of a temporal nature (*momentary thought collectives*) or (relatively) *stable thought collectives*, which form particularly around organised social groups (ibid., pp. 135–136).

The advantage of thought collectives is that they allow a better understanding and comparison of particular groups of scientists without having to separate science and the social context (Werner and Zittel 2011, p. 21). Thought collectives, however, have to be able to be pinned down and therefore be concrete elements; nations, ethnic or age groups cannot form a thought collective per se, since all members should participate in a particular area of knowledge (including language and specific terms) (Fleck 1980, p. 141). Fleck then argues that particular technical terms within a thought collective have meaning beyond their logical definition, which is shaped by the collective interaction, creating an *'eigenartigen Denkzauber'* ('peculiar magic of thought'; ibid., p. 91; my translation). Thus, in order to understand a particular thought style, one has to be initiated; only the members are able to identify the particular colouring of styles (Werner and Zittel 2011, p. 19). Nevertheless, another characteristic of thought collectives is their openness to other members and thus allowing heterogeneity and fluidity within a collective (Fehr 2005, p. 26). It goes without saying that people do belong to different thought collectives – with different roles and degrees of involvement in them. Fleck (2008, pp. 93–94, 2011e, p. 199) distinguishes between two groups: (1) an *esoteric circle*, i.e. those who directly participate in the production of an idea within a thought collective; they are experts and specialists in the field of the idea and are at the core and thus considered the elite; and (2) the *exoteric circle*, i.e. those who are lay persons in the field of the idea and thus considered on the periphery of the thought collective and are called the crowd. They are only part of the collective through the mediation of those who are in group (1); popular knowledge of the idea is key; barriers to enter the thought collective's exoteric circle are very low. The interrelation between esoteric and exoteric circles is not unidirectional, since every expert in one thought collective is a lay person in another one; an aspect that is considered fundamentally democratic for Fleck. Additionally, since people can be part of non-connected thought collectives, people can leave one thought collective and enter another one. In so doing, they take all their experiences with them. Those external influences on the respective collectives have the potential to spark new ideas and thus move the collective's thought style in new directions.

Entering and creation of a thought style and thought collective

> In order to see, you first have to know.
>
> (Fleck 2011b, p. 390)

Fleck (ibid.) distinguishes between looking, seeing and knowing: to look is an activity without context and background, which makes it difficult if not impossible to make sense of what you look at (Figure 2.1).

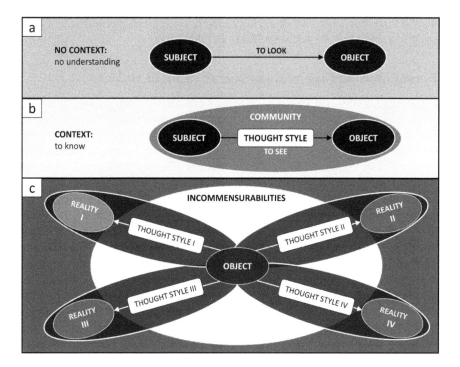

Figure 2.1 Thought styles, cognition and incommensurabilities.

The next stage is, then, to see, i.e. you have to know what is relevant or irrelevant, what lies in the foreground and what in the background and which category it belongs to. From an epistemological point of view, you first have to have knowledge in order to know and to be able to contextualise, you have to forget part of your knowledge in order to make sense, that is to develop a focused willingness to see. To visualise this thought, Fleck uses the metaphor of the alphabet: 'A child learning the alphabet painstakingly conquers the knowledge that an adult has to forget for most of its parts' (ibid., p. 396; my translation). Further exemplifying that a practitioner does make different observations in a crowd of people than a fashion-oriented person, it becomes clear for Fleck that seeing comprises an intrinsically collective[3] notion, depending on the socialisation of the individual who looks: 'We look with our own eyes, we see with the eyes of the collective' (ibid., p. 397; my translation). Thus, the question arises, to what point are results of observations justified in being used for the creation of universal descriptions? Fleck (2011c, pp. 217–219) argues that every observation has – theoretically – the potential to do so, but then continues that a specific part of the observation results cannot be verbalised or visualised at all, which, in turn, depends once again on the type of thought collective one is part of. Consequently, universal results are only possible if everybody has: (1) the same education and training; and (2) the same experiences and background. The inversion of the argument then stipulates that two researchers with their thought styles far apart do not share a common object of observation, even though the physical object they are researching may be the same (ibid., p. 220).

Foreignness and the comparison of thought styles

It has been established that thought styles are highly context-based, both in terms of content, region and time/epoch, but also formed by members of the thought style's thought collective. Fleck approaches gaps of understanding by acknowledging barriers between different disciplines, particularly between 'soft' humanities and 'hard' natural sciences. Then, he takes the considerations one step further. The epistemological foreignness not only occurs across disciplines, but even more so within them, particularly when varying ethnic contexts demand comparisons (Griesecke 2008, p. 24). How are the thoughts and actions of a Chinese practitioner different from a European one, how do a Japanese philologist, an Indian biologist or a Brazilian physicist go about their work (Fleck 1980, p. 142)? I argue more explicitly that the spatial component is equally as important as the temporal one, or the thought style, for that matter. Particularly when considering societal relationships with nature (Becker and Jahn 2006), the specific attributes of physical settings are shaped by and actively shape human behaviour, actions and reactions inasmuch as the particular time parameter does have an influence on the spatiality and content of context-related thought styles and materialisations thereof.

Beyond all criticism of Fleck's theory of being inconsistent, fluid and non-specific, he himself considers this feature to be absolutely positive and uses this inconsistency as a way to apply contradictory practices to free himself from too narrow perspectives and, in so doing, expand the horizon of his perception (Schlünder 2005, pp. 59–60). The generation of new questions rather than the confirmation of already existing ones lies at the foreground of this thinking and acting. This automatically leads to a forced leaving of one's comfort zone and unsettling of individual securities. As a result, foreign thought styles are central to Fleck's theory of cognition, or in the words of Griesecke (2008, p. 24; my translation): 'No epistemology without the experience of foreignness.' Fleck does not make a normative ranking of different thought styles but rather focuses on the collection of different perspectives for comparison. This methodological approach has gained much critical attention, culminating in long-standing controversies with Izydora Dąmbska, who argues that Fleck builds on anthropologically uniform empirical basic structures, which goes against his context-based claims for doing research (ibid., p. 36).

Other critical remarks focus on the implied common basis of universal rationality, or how Fleck talks about context-driven and closed thought styles that are incommensurable for others but he still tries to achieve comparisons of different systems – a thought to be critically considered as self-contradictory. As seen, the overall point of criticism lies in neglecting normativity while Fleck – himself not liberated from particular thought styles – establishes a form of comparison of thought styles and is thus – without wanting to do so – put above other thought styles; something that Griesecke calls 'performative auto-contradiction' (ibid., p. 33; my translation). Here it becomes obvious that Fleck denies core axioms of scientific praxis and encourages lateral thinking beyond pre-given structures. He rejects the idea that a scientific character can be identified by a catalogue of criteria; it is rather intertwined with social practices and the community, more fluid than stable. The aim of Fleck's comparison of different perspectives is not to establish an 'objective or synthetic overall picture, but leads to a parallel existence of contradicting, non-fitting pictures' (Werner and Zittel 2011, p. 25; my translation). It comes as no surprise that Fleck himself does not speak about truth in scientific processes in the form of an axiom (see Herrnstein Smith 2000). He uses 'truth' instead as a temporary tool to make a thought style researchable (Fleck 2008, p. 107). He focuses on the process of verification of earlier discoveries, which are then, inherent in the process, altered and ultimately become – in evolutionary rather than revolutionary terms – outdated: 'Much that has been proven will be shown to be unproven and much unproven to be superfluous' (Fleck 2011g, p. 63; my translation).

In so doing, Fleck also undermines a global fundamental of logical thinking and the empirical basic structure of perception; he does not intend to be more 'scientific', more 'rational', more objective than the thought styles he researches (Griesecke 2008, p. 37). Thus, what makes Fleck stand out from the crowd is his striving not for certainty but his discovery of incommensurabilities, gaps and perspectives that previously were non-existent or overlooked, which ultimately forces researchers not just to unearth foreign thought styles but also to engage in critical self-reflection on individual socialisations in respective thought styles, leading to a '"relativization" of scientific thinking' (Graf 2008, p. 176). In this vein, he talks about a developing science rather than a developed science; 'every solution is part of a new problem inasmuch as every problem already contains part of its solution' (Fleck 2011g, p. 61; my translation).

Summing up (see Figure 2.1c), Fleck – here considered to be a proto-constructivist – argues that every researcher, every person, looks at an object, sees different things based on the thought style(s) (s)he possesses and thus creates different realities. The process towards cognition, as well as cognition itself, can be absolutely coherent within those thought styles. The different realities, however, may not share many, if any, commonalities, creating the sensation of foreignness.

The underlying causes of foreignness are unearthed – and thus going back to the inner circle – in the form of incommensurabilities of thought styles. Becoming aware of those gaps and finding a way of putting them into perspective, that is the ultimate aim of Ludwik Fleck.

Notes

1 While the term *style* may connote different meanings nowadays, I want to refer to Zittel (2012) who historically contextualises its meaning of the 1920s and 1930s and I want to highlight the differences of understanding between now and then. Translated to the discipline of geography Schlottmann and Hannah (2016) highlight the difficulty of *style* by comparing it to the – often seen as troubled – concept of 'landscape' (*Landschaft*).
2 The scheme itself can be and has been expanded to other groups of people as well, e.g. Schnelle (2005).
3 As Kołtan (2008, p. 129) notes, the term '*Kollektiv*' (i.e. collective) may be outdated and, particularly in the Polish language, associated with the institutionalised language of the totalitarian regime as well as processes of forced collectivisation. Fleck's use of the term, however, seems to be quite distant from the ideas of Communism and socialism and its strict political-economic context. This is partly due to the fact that many of his writings appear before the introduction of Communism.

References

Becker, E. and Jahn, T., eds., 2006. *Soziale Ökologie: Grundzüge einer Wissenschaft von den gesellschaftlichen Naturverhältnissen*. Frankfurt am Main: Campus.

Borck, C., 2004. Message in a bottle from 'the crisis of reality': on Ludwik Fleck's interventions for an open epistemology. *Studies in History and Philosophy of Science Part C: Studies in History and Philosophy of Biological and Biomedical Sciences*, 35 (3), 447–464.

Das, U., 2015. Toward methodological precision: linking qualitative meta-theories and methods to environmental justice research design. *Environmental Justice*, 8 (2), 39–46.

Egloff, R., ed., 2005. *Tatsache – Denkstil – Kontroverse: Auseinandersetzungen mit Ludwik Fleck.* Zürich: Collegium Helveticum.

Egloff, R., 2011. Evolution des Erkennens. In: B. Pörksen, ed. *Schlüsselwerke des Konstruktivismus.* Wiesbaden: VS Verlag für Sozialwissenschaften, pp. 60–77.

Fehr, J., 2005. Vielstimmigkeit und der wissenschaftliche Umngang damit. Ansätze zu einer Fleck'schen Philologie. In: R. Egloff, ed. *Tatsache – Denkstil – Kontroverse: Auseinandersetzungen mit Ludwik Fleck.* Zürich: Collegium Helveticum, pp. 25–37.

Fleck, L., 1980. *Entstehung und Entwicklung einer wissenschaftlichen Tatsache: Einführung in der Lehre von Denkstil und Denkkollektiv.* Frankfurt am Main: Suhrkamp.

Fleck, L., 2008. Das Problem einer Theorie des Erkennens. In: E.O. Graf and B. Griesecke, eds. *Ludwig Flecks vergleichende Erkenntnistheorie.* Berlin: Parerga, pp. 63–108.

Fleck, L., 2011a. Krise in der Wissenschaft. Zu einer freien und menschlicheren Wissenschaft. In: S. Werner and C. Zittel, eds. *Denkstile und Tatsachen: Gesammelte Schriften und Zeugnisse.* Berlin: Suhrkamp, pp. 466–474.

Fleck, L., 2011b. Schauen, Sehen, Wissen. In: S. Werner and C. Zittel, eds. *Denkstile und Tatsachen: Gesammelte Schriften und Zeugnisse.* Berlin: Suhrkamp, pp. 390–418.

Fleck, L., 2011c. Über die wissenschaftliche Beobachtung und die Wahrnehmung im allgemeinen. In: S. Werner and C. Zittel, eds. *Denkstile und Tatsachen: Gesammelte Schriften und Zeugnisse.* Berlin: Suhrkamp, pp. 211–238.

Fleck, L., 2011d. Über einige spezifische Merkmale des ärztlichen Denkens. In: S. Werner and C. Zittel, eds. *Denkstile und Tatsachen: Gesammelte Schriften und Zeugnisse.* Berlin: Suhrkamp, pp. 41–51.

Fleck, L., 2011e. Wie entstand die Bordet-Wassermann-Reaktion und wie entsteht eine wissenschaftliche Entdeckung im allemeinen? In: S. Werner and C. Zittel, eds. *Denkstile und Tatsachen: Gesammelte Schriften und Zeugnisse.* Berlin: Suhrkamp, pp. 181–210.

Fleck, L., 2011f. Wissenschaft und Umwelt. In: S. Werner and C. Zittel, eds. *Denkstile und Tatsachen: Gesammelte Schriften und Zeugnisse.* Berlin: Suhrkamp, pp. 327–339.

Fleck, L., 2011g. Zur Krise der „Wirklichkeit". In: S. Werner and C. Zittel, eds. *Denkstile und Tatsachen: Gesammelte Schriften und Zeugnisse.* Berlin: Suhrkamp, pp. 52–69.

Ginev, D., 2015. Ways and dynamics of reception of Ludwik Fleck's work in the social sciences. *Social Science Information,* 54 (2), 192–210.

Graf, E.O., 2008. Die Verstörung des „gesunden Menschenverstandes" durch die Sozialisierung des Denkens. Zur Kontroverse von Ludwik Fleck mit Izydora Dąmbska. In: E.O. Graf and B. Griesecke, eds. *Ludwig Flecks vergleichende Erkenntnistheorie.* Berlin: Parerga, pp. 175–194.

Griesecke, B., 2008. Vergleichende Erkenntnistheorie. Einführende Überlegungen zum Grundkonzept der Fleckschen Methodologie. In: E.O. Graf and B. Griesecke, eds. *Ludwig Flecks vergleichende Erkenntnistheorie.* Berlin: Parerga, pp. 9–59.

Herrnstein Smith, B., 2000. Netting truth. *PMLA* [online], 115 (5), 1089–1095. Available at: www.jstor.org/stable/463280 (accessed 1 September 2016).

Johnston, R., 2004. Disciplinary change and career paths. In: R. Lee and D. M. Smith, eds. *Geographies and Moralities: International Perspectives on Development, Justice, and Place.* Malden, MA: Blackwell, pp. 265–283.

Kołtan, J., 2008. Kommentar zur deutschen Übersetzung von Ludwik Flecks Das Problem einer Theorie des Erkennens und der anschließenden Debatte zwischen Ludwik Fleck und Izydora Dąmbska. In: E. O. Graf and B. Griesecke, eds. *Ludwig Flecks vergleichende Erkenntnistheorie.* Berlin: Parerga, pp. 127–132.

Kuhn, T. S., 1971. *The Structure of Scientific Revolutions.* 2nd edn. Chicago: Chicago University Press.

Kuhn, T. S., 1991. The natural and the human sciences. In: D.R. Hiley, J. Bohman and R. Shusterman, eds. *The Interpretive Turn: Philosophy, Science, Culture.* Ithaca, NY: Cornell University Press, pp. 17–24.

Schlottmann, A. and Hannah, M., 2016. Fragen des Stils/Questions of style. *ACME: An International E-Journal for Critical Geographies,* 15 (1), 81–103.

Schlünder, M., 2005. Flüchtige Körper, instabile Räume, widersprüchliche Theorien: Die produktive Vagheit der Erkenntnistheorie Ludwik Flecks und die Geschichte der Reproduktionsmedizin. In: R. Egloff, ed. *Tatsache – Denkstil – Kontroverse: Auseinandersetzungen mit Ludwik Fleck.* Zürich: Collegium Helveticum, pp. 57–62.

Schnelle, T., 2005. Die Moderation von Verständigungsprozessen in und zwischen Organisationen: Wie man zwischen Denkstilen und lokalen Rationalitäten quer zu den Funktionen vermittelt. In: R. Egloff, ed. *Tatsache – Denkstil – Kontroverse: Auseinandersetzungen mit Ludwik Fleck.* Zürich: Collegium Helveticum, pp. 85–95.

Stuckey, M., *et al.*, 2015. The philosophical works of Ludwik Fleck and their potential meaning for teaching and learning science. *Science & Education,* 24 (3), 281–298.

Werner, S. and Zittel, C., 2011. Einleitung: Denkstile und Tatsachen. In: S. Werner and C. Zittel, eds. *Denkstile und Tatsachen: Gesammelte Schriften und Zeugnisse.* Berlin: Suhrkamp, pp. 9–38.

Zittel, C., 2012. Ludwik Fleck and the concept of style in the natural sciences. *Studies in East European Thought,* 64 (1–2), 53–79.

3   Method(olog)ical consequences

The meta-theoretical considerations described above are crucial for the understanding of my post-structural method(olog)ical approach. The consequences of a more praxis-driven and – some may argue inconsistent – data collection and analysis process entail the possibility of actively including non-rational elements in the evaluation of thought style-based cognition of respective actors (including the author and the consumers of this written account). In order to avoid methodological arbitrariness, the following sections focus on one form of conceptualising Ludwik Fleck's fluidity of perspectives.

Viscerality

Slowly, but steadily, visceral elements make their way into the discussion of new forms of doing geographies. Price sees great potential insofar as the intrinsic connection between the 'intimate mapping of the human body' and the 'mutually constitutive of place, landscape, … and … culture' (2014, p. 515) is made. The main aim of the visceral is to go beyond the classic forms of the written and visualised and highlight a 'sensory engagement with the material and discursive environments in which we live' (Longhurst *et al.* 2009, p. 334). Sound, smell, taste, touch and sight are considered to be equally important for experiencing a more holistic form of comprehension (cf. Mears 2014). Or, as Rodaway (1994, p. 3) puts it, '[t]he sensuous – the experience of the senses – is the ground base on which a wider geographical understanding can be constructed'. This aspect, however, also leads to an opposition to the popular conception of 'visceral', being emotional, purely biological and non-intellectual. Various research has shown that viscerality goes much deeper, is much more complex and multi-faceted (Butler 1993; Nash 2000; cf. Hayes-Conroy and Hayes-Conroy 2010, p. 1273).

The term 'visceral' is increasingly applied to go beyond dualistic approaches (cf. Latour 1993, p. 11) in order to better visualise 'realit[ies] that emphasize the capacity of mind and body to judge, think and perform' (Hayes-Conroy and Martin 2010, p. 269). The road to visceral cognition, then, has proven to be filled with a lot of passion; the major downfall for a 'traditionally scientific thinking' lies with the lack of straightforwardness of thinking about the body

(Hayes-Conroy and Hayes-Conroy 2008, p. 464). Or, as Probyn highlights, 'we cannot capture the body within categories … we still do not know what a body is capable of' (2000, p. 132), since 'these internal or visceral … may be seen to shape (and be shaped by) all manner of socio-political actions' (Hayes-Conroy and Hayes-Conroy 2008, p. 464). 'The visceral, then, is about feeling, but it [*sic*] also about the relational and the random' (Longhurst *et al.* 2009, p. 335).

Following McWhorter (1999) inasmuch as the body is also understood as a minded-body, the 'visceral realm necessarily includes the cognitive mind and biological brain, but should not be understood as exclusively mediated through the brain; the visceral is an internal relation of mind and body, not sequential from one to the other' (Hayes-Conroy and Martin 2010, p. 270). Continuing this train of thought, Hayes-Conroy and Martin (ibid., p. 272), highly influenced by feminist theory, relational social philosophy and affect geography, identify five different characteristics of the 'visceral':

1   *Sensory perception:* The first characteristic deals with the question of how the human body *experiences* the world. In so doing, particular case-relevant activities are scrutinised and analysed according to the way how those activities feel. 'Gut reactions' or 'heartfelt' are elements that are actively given a place in the analysis, highlighting the relevance of the subjective sensory in relation to the 'objective and measurable'.

2   *Biosocial process:* Here, the connection and interaction between biological as well as social forces are made clear. The objective is, rather than seeing the biological and the social as rivals, a discontinuation of the natural-social divide (e.g. Mansfield 2008).

3   *Relationality:* Directly deriving from the previous characteristic, the bio-social is relational. '[N]either ideas nor matter are immutable, passive or pre-known' (Hayes-Conroy and Martin 2010, p. 272); both the cellular/chemical as well as the discursive/intellectual go hand in hand and only come to existence through their interaction (cf. Colls 2007).

4   *Developmental:* The human body undergoes continuous development, based on individual experiences, physical, emotional or intellectual influences. The individually different biosocial context, for that matter, is highly important here and lays the foundation for the creation of different – and often incommensurable – realities (cf. Fleck 1980).

5   *Heterogeneity:* Visceral tendencies are considered heterogeneous and – implicitly – inconsistent, something that Murdoch (2006, pp. 56–57) has called the 'space of heterogeneous association'. This means that each form of influence – be it 'a headache, a spoken word, the weather, a memory, a pat on the back' (Hayes-Conroy and Martin 2010, p. 272) – has context-related significance on the individual's feeling, the outcome of a process or the process itself.

Visceral geographies, so far, have mostly focused on – predominantly in feminist geography-affine surroundings – thematic issues of (slow) food

(Hayes-Conroy and Hayes-Conroy 2008; Hayes-Conroy and Martin 2010), migration and food (Longhurst *et al.* 2008), health (Mansfield 2008), (non-) fluid embodied geographies (Misgav and Johnston 2014), violence and planning (Sweet and Ortiz Escalante 2015), or racial microaggression (Joshi and McCutcheon 2015). The areas of interest are still very limited; nevertheless the potential of visceral approaches seems quite promising. Still maintaining a certain level of abstraction, the approach offers a number of different – if not new – perspectives on already established forms of thinking:

- *Focus over boundary:* The overarching goal of visceral methodologies lies in the holistic way of approaching the human body, both from a biological as well as a social angle. In so doing, the borders or boundaries – much as in the tradition of feminist geographies they are drawn back (but not necessarily torn down) to make way for a form of cognition that goes beyond the dualist dichotomy of mind/body or representation/non-representation (cf. Hayes-Conroy and Hayes-Conroy 2010, p. 1274).
- *Inconsistency becomes method:* The logical continuation of the last aspect leads to the manifestation of inconsistencies among different thought styles, such as not totally neglecting structuralist ways of doing science but also including post-structuralist forms of thinking and acting.
- *Interaction is key:* As already highlighted, relationality does play a major role in visceral geographies; the form of (non)interaction among actors is thereby nuancedly studied through the inclusion of visceral – and previously omitted – elements often termed as 'gut level'.

Thus, I follow Hayes-Conroy and Hayes-Conroy, who maintain that 'addressing the visceral realm – and hence the catalytic potential of bodily sensations – has the potential to increase political understanding of how people can be *moved* or *mobilized* either as individuals or as groups of social actors' (2008, p. 469). They also continue that '[m]emory, perception, cognitive thinking, historical experience, and other material relations and immaterial forces all intersect with individuals' sensory grasp of the world, complicating one's visceral experience' (ibid., p. 465).

Reflections, critique and outlook on engaging with the visceral

While the idea of visceral geography does have strong legs to stand on theoretically, the question remains to what extent the visceral can be analysed and visualised inasmuch as to be able to fully grasp the context-driven biosocial processes.

Writing in the field of visceral geography it goes without saying that the methods applied have to be – at least to some extent – sensory-based, they have to take into account inconsistency and interaction (i.e. the social web). Thus, the main focus – and criticism – of the works previously published in this field have to do with their method(olog)ical approaches. Until now, the visceral has been an access point to new forms of cognition, however, only up until the pre-point of dissemination of results. The visceral, thus, has only been part of the analysis – or in other words, the analysis has been based on the sensual aspects of the biosocial processes. The actual presentation of findings, then, excludes the viscerality of the receptive audience, i.e. the reader(s). This aspect resembles a profound form of discontinuity.

Though not proclaiming to have a solution for this conceptual dilemma, the methodological approach in this work attempts to pursue focus, interaction and inconsistency to the next level, inviting the consumer(s) to leave (possible) comfort zones of doing science and to join a (temporary) thought collective of multi-sensory forms of consuming scientific outcomes, which should be actively influenced by the visceral. The main objective is to multiply perspectives and unearth spaces of incommensurability in the Flecksian sense by not just introducing new forms of wording but also including elements of foreignness (cf. Schnelle 2005, p. 89) by engaging with this book both through reading the text and listening to the music proposed.

All those considerations above lead to the elaboration of a metaphor that will be placed within the overall thought style of post-modernism, touching upon visceral geography (though not necessarily explicitly feminist), while still maintaining the hybridity of structural/post-structural forms of doing science (cf. Murdoch 2006). In so doing, a strong metaphor is needed to bridge the theoretical ideal with putting it in praxis through the deconstruction and re-arrangement of (existing) methods: jazz.

Jazz methodology

Including music in geography is not a new demand made by researchers, particularly since Smith (1997) has articulated a call to geographers to go beyond the visible and include the audible in their studies. This particular feature does follow the vein of current trends, for example, taking into account the works of Paterson (2009) and his understanding of haptic geographies, or more closely related to music and methodology, as seen in Morton (2005), Wood *et al.* (2007), or Gallagher and Prior (2014). Another interesting approach has been elaborated by Kanngieser (2012), who focuses on the more-than-words-impact of sonority on the context and content. However, as Gallagher and Prior (2014, p. 271) so aptly point out, the sonic output is often reduced to the transcriptive; the more-than-representational remains under-analysed. Taking this pitfall into account, I answer Smith's call for more inclusion of music in geographic research differently and focus on one aspect only implicitly touched upon: The actual processing of sound and music viscerally, i.e. not just focusing on sound when applying methods of data collection, but even more so when focusing on the output in the form of the written word. The consequent step for Smith (1997) would have been to present her findings not just in the form of a paper but also include a guide for beyond-visual experiencing of the results. I take up this quest and encourage the consumer of the following pages to be open-minded to the experience of jazz.

The metaphoric power of jazz

The use of metaphors goes beyond the mere literary or linguistic; the 'term itself becomes a metaphor for a cognitive process and a particular way of "seeing" the world around and within us' (Salner, cited in Purser and Montuori 1994, p. 29). Seeing is considered to be looking at something with a contextual background in order to obtain cognition. The power of such metaphors in changing perceptions and even actions, as Purser and Montuori (1994, p. 29) pinpoint, should not be underestimated. However, the attempt here with the jazz metaphor is to expand the image-based metaphors of 'perspective', 'theoretical lens', or 'framing' (Gallagher and Prior 2014, p. 275) towards a more sensory-open, but still audio-minded symbolism.

A great advantage of a jazz metaphor is grounded in the fact that the term itself does not represent a unified articulation of one single matter. The term 'jazz' has – since its coming to life at the beginning of the twentieth century – often been used in different forms and variations. It made its first appearance through baseball in California to describe an unpredictable throw of the ball by Ben Henderson, i.e. Ben's Jazz Curve (Dickson and McAfee 2009, p. 466). At that time, jazz music had already been played but not named as such. This is very much emblematic of this style of music, as Hatch states: 'Jazz happens. It is an activity not just an abstract category. As an activity, jazz is something to be entered into, participated in, experienced' (1999, p. 82). The holistic form of taking in jazz is seen as a form of 'liberating pursuit of aesthetic experience' (Oakes 2009, p. 469) and thus strengthens and/or romanticises the aspect of freedom of performers and fans.

Laying the metaphor bare, I use jazz on different levels in this book:

1   As a meta-theoretical understanding of context-based ad hoc flexibility in relation to data collection: allowing improvisation.
2   As an explanatory model for the application of mixed methods: giving structure.
3   As an empowering tool for the reader: embracing viscerality.

Allowing improvisation

> 'You can't improvise on nothin', man', he'd said, shaking his head at the shambles around him.
> 'You gotta improvise on somethin.'
> (Charles Mingus, cited in Dyer 2009, p. 119)

This quote already highlights one of the most important issues in relation to improvisation: It cannot be done out of thin air, but rather needs a lot of training in order to be flexible and able to give an ad hoc response to a given situation.

Structures have to be learned first in order to be forgotten later on. This feature is opposite to the 'popular misconception … that jazz players are untutored geniuses who play their instruments as if they are picking notes out of thin air' (Barrett 2012, p. 7). Even the *Oxford Dictionary* (2016) defines improvisation as an action to 'create and perform (music, drama, or verses) spontaneously or without preparation', highlighting the element of luck or talent for the creation of success. However, as Barrett (2012, p. 7) continues, 'the art is very complex – *the result of a relentless pursuing of learning and disciplined imagination*'. This ultimately leads to the understanding of creative improvisation as the creation of the unforeseen, yet unheard, but still within the framework of a particular song (Montuori 2003, p. 239).

Much like jazz improvisation, doing (exploratory) fieldwork marks the necessity for methodological adaptations *on the fly*, depending on the people you encounter, their willingness to cooperate with you, or the time slots you are given for your research. However, embracing improvisation in the scientific field does have a negative aspect of not being coherent in applying methods, and the results are therefore often not considered to be reproducible.

The question of how improvisation actually got a bad reputation has been widely studied in the field of music, being fundamental to most forms of music worldwide (Bailey 1993). Two temporal categories can be drawn up (Montuori 2003, pp. 247–248):

- pre-1800s: Improvisation was central to any musician; it was embraced. Mozart, Chopin or Beethoven had the reputation of being great improvisers; Franz Liszt clearly favoured musical performance over the visualisation in the form of transcripts.
- post-1800s: A major shift occurred from the 'genius performer' to the 'genius composer'. Improvisation was limited since it was expected that the visions of the composer would be carried out rather than focusing on the interpretative power of the moment of performance. Furthermore, with the elimination of improvisation, it became easier to evaluate the performance of a musician, since structure in the form of sheet music exists.

Very similar to the exact execution of sheet music, the application of scientific methods is more often than not subject to scrutiny on how closely those methods have been executed. Plans and structures are key elements for evaluation, which is

> dreadfully limited and limiting, since it leaves out so much of who we are, originating as it did in a time when for science to be science, the author's individuality and subjectivity had to be eliminated in favour of universality and objectivity.
>
> (Montuori 2003, p. 253)

However, as Barrett so strikingly writes, '[b]usinesses have plans for everything' and continues, 'the only plan that's missing, it often seems, is the one for things as they actually happen' (2012, p. 1). This leads to the second use of the jazz metaphor: giving structure.

Giving structure

> Jazz is not just, 'Well, man, this is what I feel like playing.'
> It's a very structured thing that comes down from a tradition and requires a lot of thought and study.
>
> (Marsalis, cited in Berliner 1994, p. 63)

Improvisation and structure are intrinsically linked. Particularly when performing jam sessions, there is always a minimal form of consensus on the music they want to perform; '[t]hey know the rules, but do not have to think about them' (Montuori 2003, p. 249). This feature sets a counterpoint to improvisation mentioned before: While it is vital to be creative and able to perform ad hoc reactions, transparency should not be given up in return. The key challenge, therefore, is to combine both objectivity and subjectivity at the same time, while still going beyond the pre-defined notions of doing science. In other words, '[r]esearch is both discovery and creation, an ongoing dialogue between subject and object' (ibid., p. 253).

Thus, jazz entails an 'implicit structure' – which is not necessarily sacred (Hatch 1999, pp. 83–84). The same goes for jazz methodology. 'Jazz works because the process is designed around small patterns, minimal structures that allow freedom to embellish – a system that balances between too much autonomy and too much consensus' (Barrett 2012, p. 71). Consequently, since no major frameworks are relied upon, but rather small portions, core patterns that are reduced to the simplest level, it is easier to find connectors between the different fragments (Kamoche and Cunha 2001). This thought has been exercised and tested throughout my entire fieldwork: splitting up methods into their core parts and reassembling them – with the help of colleagues, locals and parties involved – to achieve previously unexperienced combinations of methods flexible enough to adapt to the different realities on site.

The components of minimal structure are as follows (Barrett 2012, pp. 73–74):

- *Clear basic constraints detached from the actors involved*: Those constraints are seen as artistic and almost axiomatic guidelines for playing. A common agreement on those constraints without discussion is already set. Transferring this category to scientific methods, the common ground is to fulfil ethical standards, or to give as much transparency as possible.
- *Interaction around the patterns agreed upon*: Information is passed on as music is being played. Comping, i.e. active listening, leading and following, action and reaction, leads to the creation of a – at least temporary – thought collective.

- *Punctuation of constraining patterns*: Here, the reinterpretation of the clear basic restraints through punctuation or off-beat becomes relevant. The previous structures are once again broken up, but not totally neglected – a paradox in itself. However, through the different contextualisation, new meanings and rearrangements of patterns are likely to occur: New perspectives (not just in the visual sense) are given space to be further developed.

Embracing viscerality

Jazz is not just music; it is a lifestyle, forming a thought collective on how to interact even though – or just because – the structurality of non-structure is embraced. 'Jazz is crowdsourcing. Jazz shares. It trades. In the marketplace of what gets played and remembered, jazz also votes' (Barrett 2012, p. 117). In this book, the visceral element of jazz is taken further than in any other scientific publication: It should not stop at the analytical level, but be forwarded to the reader of those lines. In so doing, each sub-heading is linked to some piece of audio that gives the experience of internalising, subjectivising, but also feeling the results in a different way than without music. Since every consumer comes with individual contextual background, the factual as well as normative results are then, once again, individually (re-)interpreted, leading to empowerment over the topic at hand.

Translation into methods

The next step is to translate the elements of viscerality and jazz methodology into more workable methodological packages (cf. Ciorba and Russell 2014). In the course of the research process, I have experimented with 16 different methods, 12 of which provided data that was useful for the narrowed-down focus of this book. In the spirit of jazz, I focused on re-thinking the application of the different methods, adapting them to the case-sensitive context and problems that I wanted to tackle.

In other words, I gave one possible answer to Schopenhauer's call, stating that "the task is not just to see what nobody has seen before, but to think like nobody has thought before on what everybody sees" (Schopenhauer 1851, p. 93; my translation). The methods (either partly or fully) applied were my choice of tools to stimulate new ways of thinking the research topic. In the following section, they will be briefly presented.

Literature review/archive work

This book is deliberately based on a wide array of cross-disciplinary, if not to say post-disciplinary, influences. Focusing on the problem rather than the discipline, my first steps were to familiarise myself with the development of soy production in Argentina, relying on previous works compiled by anthropologists, sociologists, geographers, biologists, and economists and spanning a time frame from the early twentieth century to the present. Archive work, though very little in comparison to the other methods applied, was carried out both at the National Library of the Argentine Republic (which proved to be more a study on absence rather than presence), as well as several private collections on the topic by both scientists and economists from Buenos Aires and Salta. The aim was to capture the genesis of soy production in Argentina in order to 'get a feeling' (in the sense of viscerality) of the soy-related thought collectives and to understand why soy production had moved to the north-west of Argentina, as that was my research area.

Socio-spatial analysis

Since the majority of the fieldwork was carried out *in situ* applying ethnographic methods, GIS and descriptive statistics played a fundamental role to contextualise the findings, validate the statements of the locals and keep track of my whereabouts.

Descriptive statistics

The main source of statistics was the Sistema Integrado de Información Agropecuaria (SIIA), an official site for statistics for agricultural purposes in Argentina. Scrutinising the sources I used (as some official data bases lack validity), I was advised by Argentine colleagues to use this source of data as a reliable provider of information. Furthermore, particularly for the early soy production quantities, before official statistics were compiled, I relied on informal reports and technical bulletins. At this point it has to be mentioned that my focus does not lie on the exact date and quantity of production but rather to show a trend of development in Argentina, contextualising the current state of the art.

GIS

Geoinformatics is used in three different forms. First, at a macro-meso level, data from remote sensing is applied to visualise the advance of deforestation and soy production in the research area, abstracting the development to visualise the new soy frontier. Furthermore, spatial calculations have been made to visualise researchers' evaluation of land tenure conflict (potentials) in the Chaco Salteño. Second, almost all my movements during the fieldwork were recorded with a small GPS logger in my pocket (Duncan and Regan 2016). This allowed the geotagging of the many photos and videos I took (using GpicSync), but also permitted me to combine interview data and locations with those photos and the physical space. This proved particularly useful when carrying out Jane's Walks when there was no time to set individual GPS points to particular points (or pathways) of interest. By means of the time stamps in the GPS paths and the voice recordings, the walks could be re-created post-fieldwork for a deeper contextual analysis.

Localisation is central here. Localisation of vision, in the sense of 'what the human eye is physiologically capable of seeing' (Rose 2012, p. 2), always dependent on the seer's thought style, as well as localisation of actions. While the first form of using GIS had an as close as possible representation of the physical environment in mind, the second one emphasises the localisation of points of interest and social interactions.

Ethnography

In search of a methodological approach that goes hand in hand with viscerality and jazz methodology, but also takes into account the current in vogue more-than-human discussion in human geography (Dowling *et al.* 2016), I consider an ethnographic angle most suitable. Highlighting this feature, Crang and Cook pinpoint this very sensation by stating that 'the most fascinating aspect of ethnographic research … [is] what you don't expect to discover' (2007, p. 17), explicitly arguing against the 'three-stage read-*then*-do-*then*-write model for … academic research' (2007, p. 2) and cherishing elements of surprise as well as serendipity (Rivoal and Salazar 2013). Improvisation – and in jazz methodology's terms, comping –are not just a necessary evil of fieldwork but rather the positive core, making it 'simultaneously interesting, relevant and doable' (Crang and Cook 2007, p. 17). Going along with this theme, '[w]e cannot predict, and should not prescribe in advance, the precise methods that we will need to use in any one ethnographic research project' (Pink 2013, p. 49), cherishing the benefits of an 'ethnography on an awkward scale' (Comaroff and Comaroff 2003). The non-linear, interactive and cyclical nature of ethnographic fieldwork is also highlighted by Atkinson: '[It] is rarely based on predetermined research designs or tightly formulated research hypotheses. It is rarely conducted in the manner of hypothesis-testing, deductive research. Its guiding spirit has always been an exploratory one' (2015, pp. 34–35), 'which is more suited to the generation of ideas than the testing of hypotheses' (ibid., p. 45).

Thus, I follow the definition of Hammersley and Atkinson, who say that ethnography is considered

> a particular method or set of methods that involves the ethnographer participating, overtly or covertly, in people's daily lives for an extended period of time, watching what happens, listening to what is said, asking questions – in fact, collecting whatever data are available to throw light on the issues that are the focus on the research.
>
> (1995, p. 1)

Participant observation and interviews are two core methods. Crang and Cook see the former as central, defining ethnography 'as participant observation *plus* any other appropriate methods/techniques/etc. including statistics, modelling and/or archive work if they are appropriate for the topic' (2007, p. 35), while Atkinson warns of reduction of ethnography to the 'enactment of a series of interviews, however "active" or exploratory they may be' (2015, p. 34). He also criticises today's diluted understanding of ethnographic work, arguing for long-term stays in the field and a mix of methods.

> We can and should move *between* different versions of local reality, in order to move our analysis to the *generic* level, developing concepts – even models – that capture recurrent features of social life across a range of social situations of cultural domains.
>
> (Ibid., p. 14)

Ethnographic analysis

The analysis of research data is often presented as a multi-stage roadmap, creating the illusion of disentanglement and straightforward methodology. However, as Pink so clearly highlights, 'it is more beneficial to take a broader and more flexible approach to how, where and when analysis occurs and what it involves' (2013, p. 143). She thus defines 'analysis as a process of abstraction, which serves to connect the phenomenology of experienced reality into academic debate or policy recommendations' (ibid., p. 142) and then makes a distinction based on temporality and spatiality:

1   Analysis within the process of fieldwork as an 'implicit element of ethnographic fieldwork … as a way of knowing engaged in by the researcher during the research' focusing on the process of on-the-fly 'relating forms of ethnographic learning and knowing and theoretical ideas' (ibid., p. 143).
2   Analysis spatially and temporally detached from the fieldwork: Here, the sensory connection to the materials and the forms of knowing has to be actively (re-)constructed, creating the 'ethnographic place as a new event' (ibid., p. 143). Consequently, 'the analysis itself should be situated *in relation to* the phenomenological context of the production of the materials' (ibid., p. 143).

Here, it has to be borne in mind that the analytical framework cannot be divorced from the research process (Atkinson 2015, p. 10).

Ethnographic methods

The following section shows the variety of ethnographic methods that I have applied in the field and found their way in one form or another into the book.

1 PARTICIPANT OBSERVATION

(Participant) observation is defined as the systematic capturing and interpretation of sensory behaviour at the time of occurrence (Atteslander 2010, p. 64). Two forms are identified: quantitative and qualitative observations. The former is strongly led by theoretical and structural considerations, where representativeness, variability and reliability are crucial (ibid., p. 76). The latter is more focused on an interpretative-cognitive process where numerical analyses move to the background and leave space for contextual interpretations of happenings (Reuber and Pfaffenbach 2005, p. 107). Since this book focuses on the creation and interaction of thought collectives and their thought styles, the latter form of observation prevails. Exploratory research and theory development lie at the forefront of cognitive interest (Flick 2011, p. 27).

2 INTERVIEWS

Interviews play a fundamental role in this book. I want to highlight from the start that no pure form of interview types like expert, problem-centred or narrative interviews have been used. The core interest when talking to people was to focus on the data and pieces of information needed, based on the interview partner and the situation (Hafner 2014, p. 69).

Since context is vital, it goes without saying that I follow an interactionist (rather than an instrumentalist) as well as idealist (i.e. where interview data allow for the envisioning of multiple realities; Pink 2013, p. 73) approach towards interviews.

The actual process of interviewing was highly influenced by visceral elements and jazz. First, preparation was carried out to get as much background information on the interview partner beforehand. However, since many valuable situations have turned up to be spontaneous, on-the-fly improvisation became a standard tool for me. Second, particularly in delicate interviewing situations, I deliberately played with the power of silence (cf. Jaworski 1993), i.e. allowing interview phases where no word is spoken. While such situations are often considered major mistakes caused by the interviewer, I argue that those moments have generated the most valuable output of my interviews. This technique resembles that of John Steinbeck (1999), which he crafted to perfection in *A Russian Journal*: Instead of asking too many questions, an invisible battle between the interviewer and interviewee over who can stand the longest period of silence is fought, where feelings of disgust or revulsion can indeed lead to the extraction of valuable information (Longhurst *et al.* 2008).

As observed in Table 3.1, a large number of interviews were carried out over the total period of fieldwork (14 months). In Chapter 8, extracts from the interviews are presented, with the abbreviation and number following indicating the group and number of interview, e.g. SAB11. In order to retrieve the information necessary for each stage of analysis, three different

Table 3.1 Aggregated list of interviews

Forms of information	Types of data (ranking)	Number of interviews	
		Not recorded	Recorded
Interviews with professionals (access to their expertise)	1 (b) 2 (a) 3 (c)	6	47
Interviews indirectly related to soy agribusiness (context)	1 (a) 2 (b)	12	9
Perception interviews	1 (c)	29	64

Notes
a …background data.
b …structural data.
c …perspectivist data.

types of data are identified (Hafner 2014, pp. 70–71): (a) background; (b) structural; and (c) perspectivist data.

(a) *Background data*: As a first step, I got in contact with local scientists working on the subject of soy frontiers in Argentina. In my first two-month field stay, I conducted unstructured interviews with key persons (through the snowball principle), as well as informal talks with locals in the greater region of my research area. This openness allowed great improvisatory and thematic liberty, vital for exploratory research stages (Atteslander 2010, p. 134). These bits of data were used to get a first idea of the local context. Based on those results, a clearer picture of potential research questions and key actors could be achieved.

(b) *Structural data*: Already more focused, the idea behind structural data collection is to gain factual information on the genesis of soy production in Argentina. Interview partners ranged from scientists, members of agricultural unions, soy agribusiness and high-level political representatives. The interviews had a semi-structured character with basic outlines on thematic issues to be covered (Reuber and Pfaffenbach 2005, p. 129; Atteslander 2010, p. 133).

(c) *Perspectivist data*: One central theme of this book is the unearthing of thought styles and subsequent understanding of varying realities. Thus, interviews (among other methods) have been used to identify the different ways of thinking *in situ*. The degree of structure as well as the context, duration (from 20 minutes to eight hours) and place (from offices, public places, soy fields to private homes) of the interviews varied greatly, reflecting the very idea of jazz's comping. For this particular category, the amount of time spent with my interview partners proved to be crucial in order to contextualise and validate the perspectives presented. Or as Crang and Cook highlight: 'First, second and third impressions can often be wrong because members of the research community may well be just playing on their expectations of the researcher's expectations to wind her/him up to provoke a reaction' (2007, p. 45). Being aware of this pitfall, one interview with an elderly couple first turned out to be perfectly fitting in the classic environmental justice themed frame (see Chapter 8). The couple first lived in the forest, then were forcefully resettled to the village and now they live there with no basic means of living. However, after some hours of talking, a different story emerged: the couple had always lived in the village and had not suffered major changes of lifestyle described before. When asked about those incommensurabilities, the reaction was: 'Oh, they have us exposed!' (PEL12). So I found it very useful 'to keep in mind the fact that few people, including the researcher, are ever 100% (dis) honest, earnest, flippant, sure what they think, consistent in what they say across all contexts or anything else' (ibid., p. 45).

The majority of the interviews and informal talks were 'like participant observation with a tape recorder switched on' (ibid., p. 45). Since I exclusively used my smartphone to record conversations, even I sometimes forgot that the conversations were recorded. Thus, also bearing in mind the quantity of recordings, it comes as no surprise that I ended up with 176 hours, 33 minutes and 30 seconds of audio material on my hard drive.

When operationalising the transcription in the post-processing phase, I opted for a variation of the open-code-based transcription (cf. Corbin and Strauss 2008, pp. 195–203). Passages from the recordings were directly and fully transcribed in case they met categories within the Environmental Justice Incommensurabilities Framework (EJIF). At this point it is important to note that this was a non-linear process, circulating between the creation of EJIF categories, dismantling them in the process of interview coding, and re-establishing different foci, a process so accurately described by Marshall and Rossman as 'real research [that] is often confusing, messy, intensely frustrating, and fundamentally non-linear' (1989, p. 21).

Other pieces of information were either summarised or left out of the transcription process. The rationale behind this approach was goal-oriented: The majority of the interviews were used to define the four different thought styles presented in Chapter 8, and to carry out an analysis on the thematic issue of (non-)claims making. At this point it is vital to mention that all transcriptions were done by me, since I was the one conducting the interviews, knowing the setting and the context behind the spoken word, i.e. I was the only one able to re-contextualise nuances and the non-spoken elements between the lines, getting a fuller picture of the persons and situations. If I had not done that, 'the recording itself becomes evocated of the environment in which the interview took place' (Pink 2013, p. 152).

3 VISUAL ETHNOGRAPHY

Visual elements have a strong position in the formation of geographic knowledge. However, due to their prominence, they can in turn create blind spots of cognition that still remain undertheorised (Schlottmann and Miggelbrink 2009, p. 13). Photographs, as much as videos, are neither 'objective visual documents' nor 'photographic truth', but they have the potential to identify perspectives (Schwartz 1992, p. 14) with underlying and contextual nuances of cognition (Roberts 2013). This holds particularly true when collaborative photographic and video activities are taken. They, in this sense, have great potential to be viewed as 'mobile ethnographic method[s], a process of making images as we go through the world, accompanied by others, … [focusing] on the idea of photographing and viewing as we move through and in and as part of environments' (Pink 2013, p. 91). Or in almost lyrical terms:

> [K]nowledge is grown along the myriad paths we take as we make our ways through the world in the course of everyday activities, rather than assembled from information obtained from numerous fixed locations. Thus it is by walking along from place to place, and not by building up from local particulars, that we come to know what we do.
>
> (Ingold 2010, pp. 121–122)

4 PHOTOGRAPHY

Taking photographs during fieldwork has become quite a standard procedure and has to be distinguished from images that were found rather than specifically made for the research purpose. Thus, it is important to bear in mind that 'these are not visual objects that simply illustrate some aspects of the research project' (Rose 2007, p. 297). Avoiding the trap highlighted by Marcus Banks, that photographs are used as a 'largely redundant visual representation of something already described in the text' (2001, p. 144), I agree with Rose (2012, pp. 298–299) that photographs share a strong sense of perceptive representation and have the power to transport more information than the textuality of the written word: '[T]hey can convey something of the feel of … places, space and landscapes, … they can suggest the layout, colour, texture, form, volume size and pattern of the built environment … [capturing] something of the sensory richness' (ibid., p. 298).

In order to take advantage of those characteristics, I applied the concept of shooting scripts (Collier and Collier 1986; Rothstein 1986) for Chapter 8, elaborating a visual representation of my – deliberately narrowing – perspective of somebody doing research with the tool of environmental justice (activism), cherishing the thought style-based bias of the selection of *what* and *how* to photograph to focus on the effects of perspective on the outcomes of research. *In situ* I followed Charles Suchar (1997, pp. 37–40) in his – I argue, not so – grounded theory approach to using shooting scripts:

1 *Establishing the initial shooting script*: A particular set of questions are defined as a guideline on what and where to take pictures. Here, the first major bias is identified. Rather than *looking* at the space of research interest, the researcher already engages in high levels of pre-interpretation, *seeing* what is – to some extent – expected to be seen (Fleck 2011).

2 *Writing descriptive narratives (open coding)*: The consequence of thought style-bound pre-interpretation of photos is that the photographs 'do not speak for themselves' (Rose 2012, p. 302; see also Fleck 2011), having to contextualise them with an added story by the photographer. Based on the information provided, codes are assigned to be able to compare the pictures and to approximate answers to the research questions posed before the drafting of the shooting script.

3 *Reformulating the shooting script*: The third step is a reiteration and adaptation of (1), based on the additional information gathered from (2), catering to answer new (sub-)questions and adding contextual information.

The implications of shooting scripts hold great potential for a critical visual engagement in research processes. The risk is, however, that without a thorough discussion (much like what has been done by Suchar 2006) one only 'creat[es] photographs that appear simply illustrative' (Rose 2012, p. 304).

5 VIDEOGRAPHY

The inclusion of videos in the research process can take a great variety of forms and methodical approaches. I have applied videography for two purposes: first, in similar ways as described with photography, with two major advantages to the latter. Videos allow greater stimulation of the senses through the inclusion of audio as well as giving movement to the still image. Additionally, videos allow a broader, viewer-dependent contextualisation of the content, since fewer filters (of course, depending on the post-processing of the videos by the editor) are being applied. Second, I recorded every workshop, particularly the presentations of results by the children and young adults. Those clips were – although having had official permission for filming in classrooms – from the beginning exclusively designed for the documentation and post-workshop analyses rather than for publication purposes.

6 SENSORY ETHNOGRAPHY: WORKSHOPS AND YOUTH PARTICIPATION

Doing participatory research, workshops are a helpful way to engage with locals on a more structured and focused level. During my fieldwork phase Julieta Krapovickas, a PhD candidate from NW Argentina working on similar topics, and I conducted 15 workshops with children (aged approximately ten years old) and young adults (predominantly 14–16 years of age). The rationale was threefold. First, the mix of a female Argentine with teaching experience and a male foreigner proved to be very productive in handling particular situations in class as well as balancing out each other's weaknesses. Second, schools give a direct access to a certain age group of people. Additionally, since the area of Las Lajitas does not support private schools, the whole socio-economic spectrum could be covered. Third, before starting my research project, one of my objectives was not just to 'go out, do research and come back', but to actually engage with locals, learn from them and give back data and information.

Finding formats to get children and young adults actively involved in the research process was one of the big challenges. One approach is to apply the concept of 'sensescape', defined as 'the idea that the experience of the environment, and of the other persons and things which inhabit that environment, is produced by the particular mode of distinguishing, valuing and combining the senses in the culture under study' (Howes 2005, p. 143). The objective, thus, is to grasp local 'ways of sensing', a challenge that particularly anthropology and geography of the senses are concerned with. Ethnography comes in handy, as O'Dell and Willim put forward: '[E]thnography can be seen as a process consisting of multimodal and sensuous practices, leaving room for possible connections between ethnography and creative practices like art and design', highlighting 'the possibilities created if we jumble our metaphors or reimagine how we conceptualize ethnographic work' (2015, p. 316).

Answering Atkinson's complaint that 'too many studies are based on single-method designs, and on single forms of data' (2015, p. 38), as well as embracing children's and young adults' creativity, I used a variety of different interactive methods during workshops. The aim was to explore their sensescape of Las Lajitas, and express their results both textually (questionnaires and reports), visually (drawings), orally (in presentations of their experience), as well as haptically (through walks and experiences of touch).

Four methods and the subsequent analyses have made it into the final version of this book: (a) questionnaires and participatory interviewing; (b) mental maps; (c) Jane's Walks; and (d) the method of the five senses:

(a) *Questionnaires and participatory interviewing*: In order to increase the credibility of the results from my interviews, short questionnaires were used. I want to highlight that the whole process from designing the questions to the presentation of preliminary results was based on workshops with young adults: first, the overall idea behind the questionnaires was discussed with them. In a second step, small groups were assembled to work on possible themes of questions to be included. Third, the questions were agreed upon and matched to the research interests of my colleague and me. Fourth, we finalised the questionnaires and arranged methodical sessions with the young adults on how to conduct interviews. The aim was to give them the tools necessary to be able to conduct their proper interviews based on the questionnaires. Fifth, the actual task of interviewing was left to the young adults, getting to know their families' histories as well as perceptions of the village. The great advantage here is the close emotional proximity of the interviewers and the interviewees, removing a barrier of providing opinions to a foreign person. Sixth, the results from the interviews were then presented by the students in class, commenting on the content as well as the procedure of interviewing, including what they have learned.

(b) *Mental maps*: Several workshops with 10-year-old children were conducted under the theme of 'my village and my surroundings', focusing on the place where they lived, both urban and rural. After I had given a short presentation of where I come from, what my home town and the natural environment there looked like, the good and the bad things happening there, the children were asked to do the same thing. However, the aim here was not to verbalise their responses, but to visualise them on a piece of paper. During the drawing period, my colleague and I talked with the young artists to get additional contextual information on why they were drawing what they were drawing. Those conversations were both video-recorded (DSRL camera in one corner of the classroom), as well as audio-recorded (via mobile phones) for a couple of drawings and conversations in the post-processing phase. Finally, the resulting mental maps were presented in front of the class, using it as an exercise in free speaking (a requirement by the teachers).

(c) *Jane's Walks*: Jane's Walks are a method referring to the works of the writer and activist Jane Jacobs (e.g. 1992), 'open[ing] the ideas of modernist city planning and building … [focusing on] a new vision of diverse, fine-grained cities made for and by ordinary people' (Storring 2014). The Jane's Walks' project motto is 'Everyone knows something about where they live', organising walks in urban spaces, guided by locals and providing their particular perspectives. One of the ten big ideas of the initiative, funded by the Tides Canada Initiatives Society, is the commitment to citizen science, drawing on locals' knowledge and their conversational distribution of it (ibid.). In an exploratory session with young adults, I transplanted the urban setting of traditional Jane's Walks to the rural-urban setting and gave them the task of organising a socio-environmental tour through the village (and beyond). Approximately 10–15 people joined the afternoon tour that took about three to four hours of walking and talking. It proved to be an excellent method of adding new perspectives, enriched by contextual background of stories and narratives, to my previous walks through the village.

(d) *Method of the five senses*: The method of the five senses was designed to approach the content of the exercise with mental maps in an alternative way. One major difference was that the students were given the task of experiencing their village and surrounding environments (urban and rural) with all the senses, primarily using vision, sound and smell and, if possible, haptics and taste. In one week's time, the continuation of the workshop included both a table of individual sensory experiences as well as presentations of the results in front of the class. The idea behind this approach was to obtain a different angle on how the region was perceived by the young adults, what the core perception foci are, as well as how far those perceptions are reproduced from the results obtained from the interviews and questionnaires of local adults.

7 AUTOETHNOGRAPHY

Autoethnography, defined as a 'self-centred ethnographic writing, in which the central narrative threads are the selves of researchers and/or researched' (Crang and Cook 2007, p. 167), is a particularly useful meta-method here to unearth the importance of the researcher's membership in thought collectives and thought styles. While some researchers critically assess autoethnography – for example, Pile and Thrift fear that 'the writer's subject becomes the writer's object and the writer's object slides gently away' (1995, p. 16) – Crang and Cook (2007, p. 168), referring to Ellis and Bochner (2000), relativise those concerns by arguing that there is little difference between ethnography and autoethnography. The only difference is that greater focus is placed on three questions (Crang and Cook 2007, p. 168):

(a) The reasons for selecting a particular research topic.
(b) How the topic is changed in the course of the research process (great resemblance to Flecksian thought style expansions is seen).
(c) How the parties involved (researcher, researched *and* the reader) can be involved in the interpretation process of findings.

I read the accounts of Crang and Cook (2007) a year after the last fieldwork phase and I was baffled (and glad) to have found a thorough debate on the forms and effects of autoethnography that showed a lot of resemblance to my quests for understanding my role in the whole research process. Particularly question (c) is of great importance for me to be able to base my ideas of active reader (listener) involvement in the (re-)interpretation of the empirical findings, influenced by visceral (including sonic) elements during this process.

References

Atkinson, P., 2015. *For Ethnography*. London: Sage.
Atteslander, P., 2010. *Methoden der empirischen Sozialforschung*. 13th edn. Berlin: Schmidt.
Bailey, D., 1993. *Improvisation: Its Nature and Practice in Music*. New York: Da Capo Press.

Banks, M., 2001. *Visual Methods in Social Research*. London: Sage.

Barrett, F., 2012. *Yes to the Mess: Surprising Leadership Lessons from Jazz*. Boston, MA: Harvard Business Press.

Berliner, P., 1994. *Thinking in Jazz: The Infinite Art of Improvisation*. Chicago: University of Chicago Press.

Butler, J., 1993. *Bodies that Matter: On the Discursive Limits of 'Sex'*. New York: Routledge.

Ciorba, C.R. and Russell, B.E., 2014. A proposed model of jazz theory knowledge acquisition. *Journal of Research in Music Education*, 62 (3), 291–301.

Collier, J. and Collier, M., 1986. *Visual Anthropology: Photography as a Research Method*. Albuquerque, NM: University of New Mexico Press.

Colls, R., 2007. Materialising bodily matter: intra-action and the embodiment of 'Fat'. *Geoforum*, 38 (2), 353–365.

Comaroff, J. and Comaroff, J., 2003. Ethnography on an awkward scale: postcolonial anthropology and the violence of abstraction. *Ethnography*, 4 (2), 147–179.

Corbin, J.M. and Strauss, A.L., 2008. *Basics of Qualitative Research: Techniques and Procedures for Developing Grounded Theory*. 3rd edn. Thousand Oaks, CA: Sage.

Crang, M. and Cook, I., 2007. *Doing Ethnographies*. London: Sage.

Dickson, P. and McAfee, S., 2009. *The Dickson Baseball Dictionary*. 3rd edn. New York: W.W. Norton & Co.

Dowling, R., Lloyd, K. and Suchet-Pearson, S., 2016. Qualitative methods II: more-than-human methodologies and/in praxis. *Progress in Human Geography*, 41 (6). Available at: http://journals.sagepub.com/doi/abs/10.1177/0309132516664439

Duncan, D.T. and Regan, S.D., 2016. Mapping multi-day GPS data: a cartographic study in NYC. *Journal of Maps*, 12 (4), 668–670.

Dyer, G., 2009. *But Beautiful: A Book about Jazz*. New York: Farrar, Straus and Giroux.

Ellis, C. and Bochner, A., 2000. Autoethnography, personal narrative, reflexivity: researcher as subject. In: N.K. Denzin and Y. Lincoln, eds. *Handbook of Qualitative Research*. 2nd edn. London: Sage, pp. 733–768.

Fleck, L., 1980. *Entstehung und Entwicklung einer wissenschaftlichen Tatsache: Einführung. in der Lehre von Denkstil und Denkkollektiv*. Frankfurt am Main: Suhrkamp.

Fleck, L., 2011. Schauen, Sehen, Wissen. In: S. Werner and C. Zittel, eds. *Denkstile und Tatsachen: Gesammelte Schriften und Zeugnisse*. Berlin: Suhrkamp, pp. 390–418.

Flick, U., 2011. *Qualitative Sozialforschung: Eine Einführung*. Reinbek bei Hamburg: Rowohlt-Taschenbuch Verlag.

Gallagher, M. and Prior, J., 2014. Sonic geographies: exploring phonographic methods. *Progress in Human Geography*, 38 (2), 267–284.

Hafner, R., 2014. *handlung | macht | raum: Urbane Materialsammler-Kooperativen und ihre Livelihoods-Strategien in Buenos Aires*. Berlin: LIT.

Hammersley, M. and Atkinson, P., 1995. *Ethnography: Principles in Practice*. 2nd edn. London: Routledge.

Hatch, M.J., 1999. Exploring the empty spaces of organizing: how improvisational jazz helps redescribe organizational structure. *Organization Studies*, 20 (1), 75–100.

Hayes-Conroy, A. and Hayes-Conroy, J., 2008. Taking back taste: feminism, food and visceral politics. *Gender, Place & Culture*, 15 (5), 461–473.

Hayes-Conroy, A. and Martin, D.G., 2010. Mobilising bodies: visceral identification in the Slow Food movement. *Transactions of the Institute of British Geographers*, 35 (2), 269–281.

Hayes-Conroy, J. and Hayes-Conroy, A., 2010. Visceral geographies: mattering, relating, and defying. *Geography Compass*, 4 (9), 1273–1283.

Howes, D., 2005. Sensation in cultural context. In: D. Howes, ed. *Empire of the Senses: The Sensual Culture Reader*. New York: Berg, pp. 143–146.

Ingold, T., 2010. Footprints through the weather-world: walking, breathing, knowing. *Journal of the Royal Anthropological Institute*, 16, S121–S139.

Jacobs, J., 1992. *The Death and Life of Great American Cities*. New York: Vintage Books.

Jaworski, A., 1993. *The Power of Silence: Social and Pragmatic Perspectives*. Newbury Park, CA: Sage.

Joshi, S. and McCutcheon, P., 2015. Visceral geographies of whiteness and invisible microaggressions. *ACME: An International E-Journal for Critical Geographies* [online], 14 (1), 298–323. Available at: http://ojs.unbc.ca/index.php/acme/article/view/1152 (accessed 22 October 2015).

Kamoche, K. and Cunha, M.P.E., 2001. Minimal structures: from jazz improvisation to product innovation. *Organization Studies*, 22 (5), 733–764.

Kanngieser, A., 2012. A sonic geography of voice: towards an affective politics. *Progress in Human Geography*, 36 (3), 336–353.

Latour, B., 1993. *We Have Never Been Modern*. Cambridge, MA: Harvard University Press.

Longhurst, R., Ho, E. and Johnston, L., 2008. Using 'the body' as an 'instrument of research': Kimch'i and Pavlova. *Area*, 40 (2), 208–217.

Longhurst, R., Johnston, L. and Ho, E., 2009. A visceral approach: cooking 'at home' with migrant women in Hamilton, New Zealand. *Transactions of the Institute of British Geographers*, 34 (3), 333–345.

Mansfield, B., 2008. Health as a nature-society question. *Environment and Planning A*, 40 (5), 1015–1019.

Marshall, C. and Rossman, G.B., 1989. *Designing Qualitative Research*. Newbury Park, CA: Sage.

McWhorter, L., 1999. *Bodies and Pleasures: Foucault and the Politics of Sexual Normalization*. Bloomington, IN: Indiana University Press.

Mears, A., 2014. Seeing culture through the eye of the beholder: four methods in pursuit of taste. *Theory and Society*, 43 (3–4), 291–309.

Misgav, C. and Johnston, L., 2014. Dirty dancing: the (non)fluid embodied geographies of a queer nightclub in Tel Aviv. *Social & Cultural Geography*, 15 (7), 730–746.

Montuori, A., 2003. The complexity of improvisation and the improvisation of complexity: social science, art and creativity. *Human Relations*, 56 (2), 237–255.

Morton, F., 2005. Performing ethnography: Irish traditional music sessions and new methodological spaces. *Social & Cultural Geography*, 6 (5), 661–676.

Murdoch, J., 2006. *Post-Structuralist Geography: A Guide to Relational Space*. London: Sage.

Nash, C., 2000. Progress reports, performativity in practice: some recent work in cultural geography. *Progress in Human Geography*, 24 (4), 653–664.

Oakes, S., 2009. Freedom and constraint in the empowerment as jazz metaphor. *Marketing Theory*, 9 (4), 463–485.

O'Dell, T. and Willim, R., 2015. Transcription and the senses. *The Senses and Society*, 8 (3), 314–334.

Oxford Dictionary, 2016. Improvise [online]. Available at: www.oxforddictionaries.com/definition/english/improvise (accessed 3 September 2016).

Paterson, M., 2009. Haptic geographies: ethnography, haptic knowledges and sensuous dispositions. *Progress in Human Geography*, 33 (6), 766–788.

Pile, S. and Thrift, N.J., 1995. Mapping the subject. In: S. Pile and N.J. Thrift, eds. *Mapping the Subject: Geographies of Cultural Transformation*. New York: Routledge, pp. 13–51.

Pink, S., 2013. *Doing Visual Ethnography*. 3rd edn. Thousand Oaks, CA: Sage.

Price, P.L., 2014. Culture. In: R. Lee, *et al*., eds. *The SAGE Handbook of Human Geography*. Thousand Oaks, CA: Sage , pp. 505–521.

Probyn, E., 2000. *Carnal Appetites: Foodsexidentities*. London: Routledge.

Purser, R.E. and Montuori, A., 1994. Miles Davis in the classroom: using the jazz ensemble metaphor for enhancing team learning. *Journal of Management Education*, 18 (1), 21–31.

Reuber, P. and Pfaffenbach, C., 2005. *Methoden der empirischen Humangeographie: Beobachtungen und Befragung*. Braunschweig: Westermann.

Rivoal, I. and Salazar, N.B., 2013. Contemporary ethnographic practice and the value of serendipity. *Social Anthropology*, 21 (2), 178–185.

Roberts, E., 2013. Geography and the visual image: a hauntological approach. *Progress in Human Geography*, 37 (3), 386–402.

Rodaway, P., 1994. *Sensuous Geographies: Body, Sense, and Place*. New York: Routledge.

Rose, G., 2012. *Visual Methodologies: An Introduction to Researching with Visual Materials*. 3rd edn. Thousand Oaks, CA: Sage.

Rose, N.S., 2007. *Politics of Life Itself: Biomedicine, Power, and Subjectivity in the Twenty-First Century*. Princeton, NJ: Princeton University Press.

Rothstein, A., 1986. *Documentary Photography*. Boston: Focal Press.

Schlottmann, A. and Miggelbrink, J., 2009. Visuelle Geographien – ein Editorial. *Social Geography*, 4 (1), 13–24.

Schnelle, T., 2005. Die Moderation von Verständigungsprozessen in und zwischen Organisationen: Wie man zwischen Denkstilen und lokalen Rationalitäten quer zu den Funktionen vermittelt. In: R. Egloff, ed. *Tatsache – Denkstil – Kontroverse: Auseinandersetzungen mit Ludwik Fleck*. Zürich: Collegium Helveticum, pp. 85–95.

Schopenhauer, A., 1851. *Parerga und Paralipomena: Kleine Philosophische Schriften*. Berlin: A.W. Hayn.

Schwartz, D., 1992. *Waucoma Twilight: Generations of the Farm*. Washington, DC: Smithsonian Institution Press.

Smith, D.M., 1997. Geography and ethics: a moral turn? *Progress in Human Geography*, 21 (4), 583–590.

Steinbeck, J., 1999. *A Russian Journal*. New York: Penguin Books.

Storring, N., 2014. *Ten Big Ideas* [online], Jane's Walk. Available from: http://janeswalk.org/files/3614/6064/8739/Jane_Jacobs_One_Pager_1.pdf (accessed 9 August 2016).

Suchar, C.S., 1997. Grounding visual sociology in shooting scripts. *Qualitative Sociology*, 20 (1), 33–55.

Suchar, C.S., 2006. The physical transformations of Metropolitan Chicago: Chicago's central area. In: J.P. Koval, ed. *The New Chicago: A Social and Cultural Analysis*. Philadelphia, PA: Temple University Press, pp. 56–76.

Sweet, E.L. and Ortiz Escalante, S., 2015. Bringing bodies into planning: visceral methods, fear and gender violence. *Urban Studies*, 52 (10), 1826–1845.

Wood, N., Duffy, M. and Smith, S.J., 2007. The art of doing (geographies of) music. *Environment and Planning D: Society and Space*, 25 (5), 867–889.

Part II

Contextualisation

This Part offers two contextualisations: on a more theoretical level, the debate on justice and environmental justice is unrolled, highlighting the short-comings of the current form of how to apply concepts of environmental justice in diverse settings. The second contextualisation is of a thematic and regional nature, focusing on the soy agribusiness in Argentina from a them-atic, temporal and spatial point of view.

4 (Environmental) justice

Literature on justice is vast; almost every possible aspect of it has been studied and written about. However, I argue that one form of differentiation and ultimately understanding of justice has rarely – if at all – been touched upon: the actual categorisation of justice (and subsequent notions of social, environmental, ecological justice, to name but a few) according to the understanding of being a theory, concept, or conception. I find this particularly relevant, since this simple trick to explicitly position the width and depth, as well as scope of 'justice' in particular contexts of the discussion. Henceforth, I suggest the following brief guidelines:

- A theory is an account of certain axiomatic and abstract principles and views for the basic underlying structure (or non-structure, for that matter).
- A concept is part of a theory and represents an operationalisation of the theory's abstract principles by making the connection to empirical cases. I consider the creation of concepts to be more deductively closer to theoretical debates rather than empirical findings.[1]
- A conception, then, represents an interpretation of the process and/or outcome of the concept. It is perception-based and can vary according to different points of view.

Now focusing on justice, it is a hub of normativity and best understood when not defined (see Weidner 2005). The *Oxford English Dictionary* (2015) defines justice as 'just behaviour or treatment' as well as 'the quality of being fair and reasonable'. This calls for two observations: first, the definition of justice incorporates the word itself in the definition, leading to a circular relationship and the assumption of pre-existing knowledge. Second, it stresses certain forms of *being* (passive) and *acting* (active) generally considered fair (another term to be critically analysed) under the assumption of rationality. Leaving aside that fairness is even less theorised about than justice, the definition explicitly requires some alignment within certain framework of norms agreed upon; context is key. The definition, however, matters, since 'different groups … resort to different conceptions of justice to bolster their position' (Harvey 1996, p. 398).

Justice and distribution

Put all the political theorists' discussions on justice together and you end up talking about distribution in approximately 95 per cent of cases (cf. Schlosberg 2009, p. 11). By the mere numbers of papers published on distributional justice, it seems safe to say that it is a central part of the overall debate and very important. Several distinctions about distributive justice can be made.

First, the procedural-mechanistic focus circles around rule-making of how to reach justice (e.g. Barry 2005). Second, deontological-substantive approaches have a pre-set notion of what a society has to look like. Thus, generally speaking, actions can have certain intrinsic good or bad attributes. Third, utilitarian standpoints concentrate on the outcome of distributive processes. Here, the Benthamite principle has the greatest happiness of the greatest number of people at its core, while the rights-based approach sets minimum standards to be enjoyed by everybody (Schofield 2006; Blaikie and Muldavin 2014).

At an operational level (moving from theories towards concepts of distributive justice), the different concepts range from the focus on principles of governing distribution (while still remaining in the procedural realm) to the other end towards the objects, rights and goods to be distributed. Having identified the three different groups of distribution, John Rawls (1973) suggests that a just society equally distributes 'fair' shares of resources available. Rawls – being very fond of liberal ideals – follows a utilitarian approach of fairness. He focuses on welfare issues arguing in favour of inequalities as long as they are 'to the greatest benefit of the least advantaged members of society' (Rawls 1993, p. 293). This 'pro-poor approach' thus implies that individuals who are disadvantaged in today's unequal societies have to be prioritised in the distribution process in order to fulfil their needs (Cohen 2009). The ultimate goal for Rawls is to reach the empirical reflection of a theoretically ideal situation of society. He does not see his theory of justice as a 'description of ordinary meanings', but rather focuses on the distributional principles that make societies' structures work (Rawls 1973, p. 10).

Fairness, in Rawlsian terms, is intrinsically linked to the nation state and its political as well as its legal institutions. Additionally, Rawls himself points out, '[j]ustice as fairness is framed for a democratic society' (2001, p. 39). So, his ideal situation in his theory of justice shows the following characteristics: first, a democratic society has to be in place and functioning; social cooperation, rather than social coordination, has to be found. This feature implies that every member of society respects and follows the rules (procedural fairness), since one's membership means an improvement in one's own standing (ibid., p. 6). Second, every member follows rational principles for decision-making; thus, emotions, tradition or normative aspects of justice are left in the background. These aspects can be seen in two ways:

1   As a great strength, since Rawls has developed – to his way of thinking – a fair form of how to reach his two principles of justice. The starting point is

the 'original position' behind a 'veil of ignorance'. This veil has been designed to ignore all strengths and weaknesses of the actors involved, stripping down the case to the minimum set of variables. Additionally, the position of all actors remains undisclosed. Consequently, this *tabula rasa* approach allows the removal of particular emotional, cultural, ideological settings and preconceived notions of hierarchy and forces a concentration on the rationality of facts. In such an ideal situation, the finding of consensus can be pragmatically reduced to the weighing up of facts and thus can be streamlined. Right at the heart of liberal justice theory, fair distribution then means the reduction of substantial fairness and focus on procedural fairness of distribution, since context is hidden behind the 'veil of ignorance'. This focus on the technicality of distributive procedure is possibly the most widespread conception (i.e. the interpretation) of justice, since the image of objectivity is created, attempting to reduce normativity through the establishment of rules of distributive justice (Schlosberg 2009, p. 13).

2   The last point, however, also highlights the great weakness of Rawls' approach: The question of how the creation of an ideal situation is helpful in understanding (real-life) non-ideal situations. Hence, the question is how far a close-knit framework can be stretched in a *theory* of justice.[2] Once we are dealing with non-ideal situations, the 'original position' is abandoned; so are the cornerstones of the theory. From a pragmatic-empirical point of view, this does not present major difficulties; the most significant change occurs inasmuch as the operationalisation level is reached and justice is being treated as a concept. Here, the role of principles of justice in distributive matters is under scrutiny. The concept itself becomes more flexible and adaptable to specific contexts, breaking up the universalist character of the *Theory of Justice*.

Summing up justice and distribution, I have relied heavily on the ideas of John Rawls, who was one of the most influential writers on the subject. As mentioned, I have two distinct criticisms of Rawls' *Theory of Justice*. First, his interpretation of justice has a universal character, implying that there is only one way to conceive of justice, particularly through distribution. While this works in a theoretical scenario, going as far as ideal-typesque, recognition does not play a role in here, meaning that in different socio-cultural settings other principles of justice may be applicable and thus this destroys Rawls' cornerstones of his theory of justice. Thus, I favour a more open form of interpretation of distribution beyond procedure and outcome, including the objects subject to distribution as well as principles of governing those goods based on entitlement, deserving case and need (ibid., p. 13). Second, and even more important, questions of scale are not touched upon in Rawls' theory. My argument here is that while the two principles of justice are placed on a society-level, this does not necessarily mean that the implications of the principles (i.e. the operationalisation and interpretation) are the same at the local level as they are on the national level.

Combining recognition, elements of substantial fairness and scale, I agree with Susan Owens, who argues that 'siting conflicts are unlikely to be resolved by changing procedures alone' and highlights that they are often 'misconstrued (or misrepresented) as conflicts between "national need" and "local interests"' (2004, p. 102).

Justice beyond distribution

Brian Barry (1999) clearly highlights the intrinsic interrelation between justice and distribution; without the latter, he argues, one cannot talk about justice but rather only make the distinction between right or wrong. Mostly embedded in liberal theories, interpretations of distributive justice are 'concerned with the just redistribution of resources and how they are channelled from those who have to those who have not' (Davoudi and Brooks 2014, p. 2688). This standpoint is particularly opposed by Marxist critics due to the strong reliance on the individual rather than the structural, including the omission of class struggles (Simpson 1980). Starting in the 1990s in particular, the de facto standard position of distribution began to be challenged. Mainly feminists like Iris Young (2011a, 2011b) or Nancy Fraser (1997, 2009), but also Axel Honneth (1996, 2001) or Charles Taylor (1994) criticised the mere focus on distribution and tried to put the 'underlying causes of maldistribution' (Schlosberg 2009, p. 14) at the centre of analysis. Stanley, in a feminist political theory's perspective repeating Young (2011a), even goes so far as to propose a 'displace[ment of] distribution as the analytic focus of justice' (2009, p. 1000). Four points of critique of the distributive paradigm's dominance when discussing issues of (social) justice are revealed:

1   Most discussions on justice start from the physical aspect of distribution; Young, however, marks a clear counter-statement: 'The concepts of domination and oppression, rather than the concept of distribution, should be the starting point for a conception of social justice' (Young 2011a, p. 16). On purpose or not, Young's statement positions her understanding of (social) justice as a conception, thoroughly embedded in the context of openness towards different perspectives on justice. 'Distribution', as well as 'domination and oppression' are termed concepts, implying the theory-induced understanding thereof. To put it simply: unlike Rawls' understanding of justice, justice is not considered to be at the level of a theory but rather at the other end, at the conception.

2   Young's further criticism is that '[t]he distributive paradigm defines social justice as the morally proper distribution of social benefits and burdens' (ibid., p. 16) and thus directly challenges Rawls' 'conception of justice as providing in the first instance a standard whereby the distributive aspects of the basic structure of society are to be assessed' (Rawls 1973, p. 9). The social context, according to Young, is mistakenly ignored.

3   Young's point of critique pinpoints the pattern focus of the distributive paradigm. It is, in her opinion, too output-oriented, leading to the evaluation of justice according to the 'end-state pattern of persons and goods that appear on the social field' (Young 2011a, p. 18). In this respect, her major concern deals with the implicit assumption of society being static, ignoring the institutional context as well as misinterpreting the logic of distribution when it comes to non-tangible goods.

4   Finally, Young in her pragmatic-fluid and context-based approach towards justice criticises distributive theories' structuralist and static definition of goods. In going beyond descriptive measures of distribution, Young is more interested in 'what *determines* poor distribution' (Schlosberg 2009, p. 15) and follows Michael Walzer inasmuch as the latter proposes a 'shift … [of] attention from distribution itself to conception and creation' (1983, p. 7).

Recognition

Schlosberg (2009, p. 24) clarifies that no rejection of distribution has been made in the literature on recognition. The main difference between representatives of the distribution and the recognition thought style lies in the starting point. While the later focus on the *why* of injustice thus starts from the non-ideal and conflictive situation, this highlights the creation of ideal frameworks and processes of justice within liberal and democratic societies. Both have valid points and their full right of existence; a combination of both, however, allows an even broader way to look at matters in hand. As Fraser points out '[j]ustice today requires *both* redistribution and recognition' (1997, p. 12), and continues in a different piece '[j]ustice requires both, as neither is sufficient' (Fraser 1996).

Misrecognition, in the debate on environmental justice, then, has to have a spatial dimension applied to places and people alike (Davoudi and Brooks 2014, p. 2688). This argument materialises in opposition against locally undesired land use, where those places and people have been stigmatised, misrecognised and devalued (Fraser 1997). Important in this realm is the comment by Walker that misrecognitions are not 'just the product of siting decisions, but also underlie the processes through which certain spaces get to be chosen for the development in the first place' (2009a, p. 626). Such underlying processes can be informed by racial discrimination (as well studied in the USA; Bryant 1995), global-local interplays of land grabbing (Zoomers 2010), one-sided spatial planning or capitalist dynamics (Pellow 2004).

Relating to misrecognition, I find it particularly useful to take the critical remark on victimisation of local communities (Lawson 2008, p. 155) by Debbané and Keil into account:

Any notion of 'local' communities victimised by 'global/universal' dynamics will not hold up to critical scrutiny: instead, we have to envision such communities as participant in a narrative and material process of co-production of the world in which they live.

(2004, p. 211)

Following a post-colonial (Williams and Mawdsley 2006; Souza 2008) thought style, local communities in the Global South, including indigenous groups (e.g. Valdivia 2015), as well as indigenous communities in the Global North (e.g. Rosier 2008; Whiteman 2009), are not oppressed per se; the next dimensions of environmental justice have major importance to discursively empower those communities rather than revealing the injustices they suffer (Swyngedouw and Heynen 2003).

Participation

Fraser (1996) sees 'parity of participation' and fair representation and distribution of power as central to her bivalent theory of justice. Once again, the question 'what is fair participation?' is philosophical; it relates back to the different understandings of fairness. From the egalitarian standpoint, procedural fairness means equal representation of every actor, while from a libertarian point of view, those who are more invested should have a greater say; utilitarianists, finally, see the needs of actors as central and want some form of distribution in order to achieve the greatest benefit for the greatest number of people (Hunold and Young 1998, pp. 83–84). This implies that those who have greatest needs or share the greatest environmental burden in a particular conflict situation, for example, should have most rights in participation and the decision-making processes.

Capabilities

Criticising Rawls' (1973) 'primary goods' metric for being too little context-sensitive (Sen 2010; Nussbaum 2013), Amartya Sen and Martha Nussbaum have developed the capabilities approach, going beyond the descriptive measurement of distribution and looking into the effects of the distribution on well-being and functioning of individuals (Sen 1985, 1999a, 1999b; Nussbaum and Sen 1993; Nussbaum 2000, 2006). *Functioning* in this understanding refers to the being (e.g. being healthy) and acting (e.g. eating) of individuals, i.e. something that a person achieves (Ballet *et al.* 2013, p. 29). *Capability* is defined as 'an aspect of freedom, concentrating in particular on substantive opportunities' (Sen 2010, p. 287). The focus of this approach lies on the freedom of capabilities rather than on utility-based individuals' welfare or resource-centred income and wealth. Thus, 'a serious departure from concentrating on the *means* of living to the *actual opportunities* of living' (ibid., p. 233; emphasis in original) is observed. The capabilities approach deals with the opportunities available to individuals to combine functioning according to the best outcome perceived; the capability of choice of options is thus pivotal (Sen 2005, p. 154). Thus, 'the central measure of justice is not just how much we have, but whether we have what is necessary to enable a more fully functioning life, as we chose to live it' (Schlosberg 2009, p. 30).

It lies in the nature of such lists that they spark harsh criticism, particularly focusing on Nussbaum's top-down theorising what a 'good life' should look like or contain (Deneulin 2002). Sen, in his own right, denies the drafting of such lists and highlights the necessity of public participation in order to do so (2005, p. 158). Nussbaum is much closer to Rawlsian ideas of ideal situations in developing universal principles, but Schlosberg (2009, p. 33), for example, considers her claims not as strong as Nussbaum proposes. Such a characteristic deconstructing the very nature of a universal list is that it can change with time, adapting to new contexts and contents. Beyond all criticism, I consider Nussbaum's list to be a good starting point for empirical fieldwork; the list itself can then be altered and modified according to the particular case study.

Considering the capabilities approach in general, it offers the advantage of combining issues of economic inequality and cultural disrespect/misrecognition (Olsen 2001, p. 7). Additionally, redistribution and recognition are as much represented as in Fraser's (2000) bi-/trivalent approach (Robeyns 2003; Schlosberg 2009, p. 34). Referring back to Nussbaum's list of capabilities, three obstacles (and thus sources of unjustified inequality and inequity; Issaoui 2011) to achievements (and therefore functioning) are identified (Ballet *et al.* 2011, p. 1831, 2013, p. 29): (1) personal (e.g. disabilities); (2) social (e.g. exclusion, discrimination); and (3) (bio-)physical (e.g. arid region; cf. Kuklys 2005; Robeyns 2005). They become particularly relevant in the empirical analysis.

In relation to the theoretical standing, the capabilities concept has been drawn up in order 'to broaden the understanding of economics and development' (Ballet *et al.* 2013, p. 28), but does not hold up to being a fully-fledged ethical theory (Martins 2011, p. 2). Nevertheless, with the focus not only on desires and needs (and consequently achievements), but also on the freedom of choice and achievement, the capabilities approach, according to Ballet *et al.* (2013, p. 28), serves as a basis for theory development. In terms of Martins' critical realist ontology, capabilities are considered to be causal powers (Martins 2005, 2007) for well-being. 'Environmental burdens and benefits have a profound impact on people's capabilities' (Davoudi and Brooks 2014, p. 2690); hence, a starting point for elaborating environmental justice based on Martins' reinterpretation is the analysis of the set of capabilities available to the actors focused on in a particular case study. Ballet *et al.* see great potential here to integrate the reinterpreted capabilities approach 'into a concept of justice that includes the environment as mediation between human beings' (2013, p. 28).

Thus, Schlosberg and Carruthers (2010) argue for a frame expansion of the capabilities approach as part of environmental justice: Particularly when dealing with indigenous communities, this expansion of thought style 'can offer an important vehicle for understanding the multifaceted discourse and demands of environmental justice activists and their communities', since 'contemporary movements do not limit themselves to understanding injustice as faced only by individuals; justice for communities is often at the forefront of their interests and prospers' (ibid., p. 17). Hence, they follow Stewart (2005), who sees the 'need to analyse and categorize group capabilities as well as individual' in order to obtain a more holistic view, since the group capabilities are considered more than just the sum of their individual ones, also taking into account that injustices are not experiences of individuals but are 'embedded in community' (Schlosberg and Carruthers 2010, p. 17). They continue: 'for movement groups, environmental injustice takes away the ability of individuals and their communities to function fully, through poor health, destruction of economic and cultural livelihoods, general environmental threats, and political exclusion' (ibid., p. 18).

Groves adds another feature to capabilities in the debate on environmental justice: attachment: 'Attachment is a capability through which intersubjectivity emerges' (2015, p. 3), arguing that:

> Inhabitants of communities affected by land-use decisions more widely also frame their activism in terms of complex links between everyday experiences of socio-environmental degradation and place attachment … that undergirds individual and collective capacities for making sense of and influencing intrinsically-uncertain individual and collective futures.
>
> (Ibid., p. 2)

Attachment, in this sense is considered an active element, bringing together place, identity and agency for resilience. In so doing, attachment as a capability is the link to 'ecological citizenship' (Latta 2007), 'recognizing the embeddedness of political and moral agents in the material, biophysical world' (Groves 2015, p. 3). For Groves (ibid., p. 3), claims-making due to environmental injustices, then, is a matter of non-recognition of this sort of citizenship.

Justice and the environment

David Schlosberg can be considered one of the most influential scholars in the field of environmental justice. In particular, his book *Defining Environmental Justice* (2009) offers a concise overview of the different strands of the concept to hand and, certainly, there are many arguments and elaborations that I would follow and accept. Nevertheless, Schlosberg himself writes, '[b]ut as someone who has studied both the movements and theories, I have found these discussions inadequate and somewhat frustrating – there has always seemed to be something missing in them' (Schlosberg 2009, p. 3). I share this concern. To put it very provocatively: it seems that environmental justice has become – or, for that matter, has always been – a mere shell of vague descriptions trying to discursively construct new arguments for social struggles where everything goes and nothing is thoroughly underpinned by a sound theoretical or conceptual basis. Or, reframing this statement, the concept of environmental justice comes with a baggage of four challenges:

1   *The combination of environmental and human factors*: Environmental justice has the great potential to break up disciplines and linear ways of thinking by bringing together natural as well as social sciences, and in the humanities; lateral thinking is a must. The question, however, is: to what extent are the people dealing with environmental justice willing to go, with regard to such thought style expansions, and deal with bridging of different traditions and – ultimately – world views?
2   *The theoretical context*: Two different approaches towards theories of justice exist. One is top-down, universal and theory-driven and the other is bottom-up, context-based and praxis-nurtured. I do not consider environmental justice to have the potential for a theory but rather justifies a combination of both theory-induced conceptualisation of justice *plus* the environment and the praxis-driven conceptualisation of varying perspectives, ideas and thought styles. Each context brings about variations of environmental justice, making it difficult, if not impossible, to put everything under one global umbrella.
3   *The circulation of the concept among activists, scientists and the community*: Environmental justice has emerged from a specific activist-driven context; it then was taken up by scientists who attempted to create a theoretical basis. Each group has its own agenda and goals; the combination and visualisation of those expectations towards environmental justice remain a huge challenge, as much as the question of how to deal with or how to include the community (if this was even wanted).
4   *The practical branding of content under the roof of 'environmental justice'*: This challenge is closely tied to the previous one. Social-ecological issues are studied under a great variety of concepts, whether social-ecological conflicts, popular epidemiology, environmental racism or environmental inequality. In some regional contexts, environmental justice is left aside, due to changes of meaning when translating the term into other languages.

The role of the environment

In a first attempt to get a grasp of the concept of environmental justice, Schlosberg (2009) describes environmental justice based on four cornerstones: (1) equitable distribution of environmental goods and bads; (2) (both procedurally and substantially fair) participation in decision-making on environmental issues; (3) recognition of local ways of living, local knowledge and cultural diversity; and (4) the capability of both individuals and communities to function and thrive. So far, the only difference between 'justice' and 'environmental justice' lies in the inclusion of the term 'environmental'.

The four pillars of the concept have already appeared in the general discussion on justice.

Generally, the role of the environment is reduced to being a contextual constant of justice, often implicitly defined and considered as a given.[3] One of the major challenges for environmental justice, then, is the combination of environmental and human factors. It has been widely recognised that the link between the quality of the environment and human equality exists (e.g. Agyeman *et al.* 2003). However, activists often face the dilemma of pursuing competing goals from ecological and social justice points of view, weakening their respective position in contested arenas (Newell 2006). One form to even out such internal competition is described by Bloomfield (2014, pp. 263–264), focusing on activists' strategies of market-based shame campaigning in order to directly confront corporations. Tackling the issue from the other side, Davies (2006, p. 708) highlights in her case of anti-incineration campaigning in Ireland that environmental justice campaigners focus on the link between environmental issues and social justice, allowing a better handling of discrimination, poverty and environmental degradation. Even when only focusing on social aspects of (environmental) justice, the very nature of understanding of the relationship between the environment and human beings influences the thought style and subsequent modes of action.

Revealing these conceptions of human-environment relationships, then, facilitates the understanding of the respective positions, lines of argumentation and actions of the actors involved in environmental justice issues. A general classification of the understanding of environment is vital here. Vincent (1998) distinguishes three main categories: (1) anthropocentrism; (2) intermediate axiology; and (3) ecocentric theories (Table 4.1).

Framing of environmental justice

Martínez-Alier (2002) positions environmental justice as an alternative to both preservationism (i.e. attributing a nostalgic touch in the form of a certain 'cult of wilderness') as well as to eco-efficiency (i.e. the linking of environmental management and resource efficiency to the notion of sustainable development) (Figure 4.1).

Based on one's understanding of the environment, it is easier to identify one's conception of environmental justice. Elvers, very pragmatically, characterises environmental justice as 'the smallest common denominator of an anthropocentric and at most decidedly social-ecological approach towards aspects of the interdependence of man and environment' (2011, p. 464; my translation). Elvers *et al.* (2008, pp. 835–836) implicitly deny environmental justice its relevance as a concept (even though it is called as such) by defining it as an 'inherent feature of controversial decision processes, evolving around any kind of regulation perceived to affect the environments of heterogeneous stakeholders'; analytical or normative features are equally neglected as justice in this context is being reduced to trial-and-error schemes of negotiation processes.

Table 4.1 Categorisation of environmental theories

Focus	Sub-focus and definition	
(a) anthropocentrism	(a.1) pliant anthropocentrism • humans are the criterion of value • value of nature is quasi-instrumental: the natural world (including animals) has value for humans	(a.1.1) conservationism • 'wise use' of nature to prevent reckless exploitation (a.1.2) preservationism • stronger sense of interrelation of humanity and nature • wider concern for whole ecosystem • often expressed in religious or aesthetic terms
	(a.2) deep anthropocentrism • nature in general can be destroyed, manipulated or polluted, as long as it serves humans	

(b) intermediate axiology	• no acceptance of anthropocentrism or ecocentrism
	• commitment to environmental axiology
	• most contemporary environmental ethics are found in this category
		(b.1) moral extensionism
		• closer to anthropocentrism
		
		Consequentialist utilitarian ethics of 'sentientism' (Singer, 1981)
		• 'Animals are sentient, therefore animals are of value'
		• non-sentient life does not possess value
		
		(b.2) reluctant holism
		• closer to pliant ecocentrism
		• e.g. Baird Callicott, Holmes Rolston
		
		Deontological rights-based approach
		• value is located beyond humans, sometimes beyond animals
		• life-centred ethics
		  • 'wholes' (like biotic community) have intrinsic value
		  • decentring of animals and humans
		  • systematic interdependence with each other is key
		  • clearly holistic approach

(c) eco-centrism	• locus of value is the whole ecosphere (Gaia) • value is embedded in whole ecosphere • value is not given by humans and therefore not instrumentally usable for human ends • most controversial eco-philosophy • e.g. Leopold (1970)	

Source: Based on Vincent (1998), pp. 125–127.

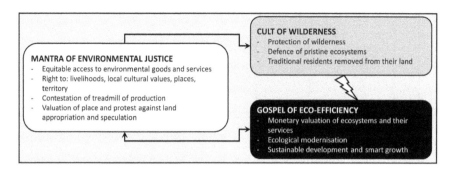

Figure 4.1 Forms of environmentalism and their connections.

Source: Based on Anguelovski and Martínez-Alier (2014, p. 173).

Drummond (2008) criticises most of the environmental justice literature on account of two categories: ideology and methodology. Ideologically, he is 'in favor of more balanced approaches on subjects that are simultaneously politically important to scientists and politically sensitive to citizens and society in general', touching upon the question of the feasibility of combining advocacy and scientific practice (ibid., p. 180). Methodologically, the greatest concern is regarding the discursive positioning of environmental (justice) studies as a bridge between human and nature relations, while in practice he has 'not found a single case designated as being of environmental injustice that is not first and utmost a case of social injustice, political injustice, cultural clash, legal loopholes, or even economic inequality' (ibid., p. 180) and thus he calls – like Clark *et al.* (2007) – for a strengthening of the analysis of natural variables. He offers a two-step analysis: (1) what do humans do with natural variables?; and (2) how are humans then influenced by natural variables? Drummond polemically argues that '[t]he adjectives "just" or "unjust" simply do not apply to natural variables', but then softens his statement and agrees that such categories do have an important role (2008, p. 180). Following a similar train of thought, Holland (2008) argues for more process orientation, particularly when applying the capabilities approach; environmental quality (though not extensively defined; Agyeman 2001) should be more prominently considered. Similarly, Holifield *et al.* (2009) see a scientific gap in the theoretical discussion on the role of non-human environmental subjects/objects that foster environmental inequalities.

Environmental justice, in my understanding, deals with the social relations between human beings, materialised through the use of nature in space and time (Agyeman *et al.* 2003; Wapner and Matthew 2009). This particular aspect has to be seen in relation to theoretical discussions on justice, since nature plays a double role: (1) as a living space for individuals (both from a bio- and anthropocentric point of view; freedom of perspective allows, in the end, a more holistic view on social-ecological conflict situations); and (2) as a neutral mediator 'in relationships between people … [highlighting] the responsibility of one person in his/her relationships with others' and thus feeding back into individual responsibilities of social and environmental justice (Ballet *et al.* 2013, p. 31).

Time, space and content: the development of environmental justice

While the previous sections have focused on the theoretical expansion of justice and its implementation of environmental aspects, in order to contextualise environmental justice in a temporal, spatial and content dimension, the following developmental phases are identified.

Phase 0: non-labelling of environmental justice

> Environmental injustices, it is said, started around the time of Columbus in 1492.
>
> (Agyeman and Evans 2004, p. 156)

Environmental justice activism is nothing new. Records as early as from the 1800s show that people of colour have struggled for improvements in living conditions as slaves, for the opportunity to acquire land, as well as sharecropping rights. Particularly from the 1940s to the 1960s, activism in relation to the environment increased in communities of colour in the USA. Already then, core issues were related to health issues, workers' rights, or pesticide contamination (Taylor 2000, p. 535), all topics still present in today's discussions. Taylor (ibid., p. 535) clearly puts those struggles in the master frame of the civil rights movement, but also highlights the importance of this frame for the sequential development of an environmental justice master frame.

In 1972, Freeman considered environmental risks to be crucial factors in a theory of choice and welfare at the individual level. Cross-referencing census data from 1960 on race, housing tenure and income in six US states with indices of average annual pollution exposure per family, he visualised the link between income and exposure to environmental bads. In a call for action, he suggested tackling the improvement of environmental quality would bring an improvement in wealth distribution. Even though criticised for the poor quality of his analysis (Bowen 2002, p. 4), it is recognised that Freeman's study offered two valuable aspects: (1) the analysis was based on economic theory, allowing substantial embeddedness in an already firm theoretical body; and (2) Freeman called for the avoidance of hurried generalisations (ibid., p. 4).

Another ground-breaking study, *Toxic Wastes and Race in the United States'* by the United Church Commission for Racial Justice (1987), unearthed evidence that the environmental bads due to toxic waste disproportionally often affected communities of colour. The results were confirmed in the years to come (Bullard 1990; Mohai and Bryant 1992; Adeola 1994), leading to

Chavis coining the term 'environmental racism' (Agyeman and Evans 2004, p. 156). Nurtured by those injustices, a 'fully fledged environmental justice movement made up of tenants' associations, religious groups, civil rights groups, farm workers, professional non-for-profits, university centers and academics, and labor units amongst others' was established (ibid., p. 156). This movement was multiracial in its organisation and had its core interests in working against locally undesired land uses (LULU) (Pulido 1996b).

Phase 1: introduction of 'environmental justice': distribution and methodological challenges

The first wave of environmental justice research centred around social problems and social movements with an intrinsic desire to influence public policy (Sze and London 2008, p. 1333). It was characterised by individual case studies, predominantly describing the uneven distribution of environmental bads, in relation to environmental racism (Williams 1999, pp. 60–61). Examples of such studies are those of Bryant and Mohai (1992), Bullard (1983), or Pollock and Vittas (1995). The central concern was pollution and risk related to the siting of potentially harmful treatment/storage/disposal facilities (TSDF). From a theoretical-conceptual perspective, the main objective was to establish frameworks to define, operationalise and measure environmental justice (Phillips and Sexton 1999; Holifield *et al.* 2009, p. 596).

Conventional environmentalism has been challenged by the combination of environmental and health issues (Shrader-Frechette 2002). Most of the 'first generation' environmental justice literature[4] has had this particular focus of distribution, the emergence of socio-spatial patterns (Hurley 1995), as well as the place-based outcome of environmental justice claims (Walker 2009a, p. 616). Early work on environmental justice faced fundamental methodological problems and flaws (Boerner and Lambert 1995):

1   *Definition of 'community'*: The definition of a minority community in the USA was based on the higher percentage of non-white members within the community in relation to the overall country, leading to often ridiculous results.
2   *Ignoring population density*: This led to the outcome that the actual number of people affected by environmental bads were not accounted for in the studies; only the spatial distance and distribution were analysed, leading to the geographical area analysed being too broad or simply not studied adequately (i.e. working with political community boundaries).
3   *Risks of TSDFs were ex ante implied, without looking at the context and factual basis.*

Additionally, problems of comparability arise: how can sources of environmental racism be classified, analysed and compared? What are the characteristics of the physical sites in order to fit into the framework of analysis? Still in the context of TSDF, the comparability of the cases has been questioned (Cutter 1995, pp. 114–115; Williams 1999, p. 61), also due to issues of scales of aggregation. Depending on the case study, the composition and distribution of the population affected (crucial for the argumentation in environmental racism and the highlighting of economically poor communities) did not follow concise standards.[5] Thus, it goes without saying that results differed widely, based on the sources being based on the community, city, county, state or regional level, leading to the point that the actual correlation between certain characteristics of a population and affectedness of environmental bads was itself questioned per se (Anderton *et al.* 1994). This aspect led to the second phase of environmental justice discussions focusing on underlying processes of change.

Phase 2: environmental justice beyond distribution: unearthing the underlying processes

In part of a meta-analysis on environmental inequality, Harper and Rajan (2007, p. 328) compile three types of reasons why marginalised communities are often more prone to pollution and environmental degradation:

1   *Siting*: Here, the already often disenfranchised ethnic minority has been living in a certain place for a time; later, environmental hazards and pollutions are installed there (Bullard 1994).
2   *Moving in*: Due to the market dynamics of lower property prices, socio-economically disfavoured groups move to environmentally degraded areas.
3   *Vulnerability*: Due to higher risks of malnutrition, bad health care, or insurance, among others, Harper and Rajan (2007) argue that socio-economically disadvantaged groups have higher levels of vulnerability (Leatherman 2005).

Two major distinctions of analysis in relation to the existence of a certain environmental justice can be made (Szasz and Meuser 1997). The connection between the siting of TSDF and demographic aspects is one major point of analytical distinction. If, as the first point, demographic features have played a visible role in the decision of construction, the next question deals with the actual form of influence. If this sort of influence includes prejudged decision-making as well as active discrimination, the analysis focuses on the term 'environmental racism' (Bullard 1993, 2000). If the first point does not apply, then a second set of analysis is carried out, mainly focused on the underlying processes of siting and its local/regional effects. Here the chronological starting point of research lies after the respective TSDF site has been built. Continuing with demographic aspects, it is asked what kinds of influence does the site under question have on demographic development in the region (e.g. decrease in property prices leading to migration, both from and to the area under discussion, leading to the establishment of what is later called an 'environmental justice population'; Commonwealth of Massachusetts 2002, p. 5). Its definition includes

> those segments of the population that EOEA has determined to be most at risk of being unaware of or unable to participate in environmental decision-making or to gain access to state environmental resources. They are defined as neighborhoods (U.S. Census Bureau census block groups) that meet one or more of the following criteria:
>
> - The median annual household income is at or below 65 percent of the statewide median income for Massachusetts; or
> - 25 percent of the residents are minority; or
> - 25 percent of the residents are foreign born, or
> - 25 percent of the residents are lacking English language proficiency.
>
> (Ibid., p. 5)

Even though underlying causes are increasingly considered, the dominance of distribution, however, has not yet been questioned. Faber (1998), following the trend of the 1990s debate on environmental justice, focuses on distributional justice. In so doing, he makes a clear distinction between reactive and proactive environmental justice: '[T]he struggle for environmental justice is not just about distributing risks equally but about preventing them from being produced in the first place' (ibid., p. 14). This definition is also reflected in the Environmental Justice Policy by the Commonwealth of Massachusetts (2002), stating that environmental justice is

> based on the principle that all people have a right to be protected from environmental pollution and to live in and enjoy a clean and healthful environment. Environmental Justice is the equal protection and meaningful involvement of all people with respect to the development, implementation and enforcement of environmental laws, regulations and policies and the equitable distribution of environmental benefits.
>
> (Ibid., p. 2)

This definition offers three dimensions (cf. Agyeman and Evans 2004, p. 156):

1   It includes procedural fairness ('meaningful involvement of all people').
2   It makes reference to substantial fairness ('right to … live in and enjoy a clean and healthful environment').
3   It highlights proactive rather than reactive attributes of environmental justice, demanding the 'equitable distribution of environmental benefits'.

Phase 3: broadening of the geographical area and differentiation of environmental justice analyses

The main trends in this phase are twofold: 'new populations and problems, and new places and sites of analysis – specifically the relationship between the local and the global' (Sze and London 2008, p. 1336). This phase is characterised by a 'fast conceptual transfer from a mostly American history and use of the concept to other parts of the word' (Debbané and Keil 2004, p. 210).[6] It is highly influenced by the attempts to frame the environmental justice discussion in terms of claims making (cf. Čapek 1993). Moving beyond siting conflicts of TSDF, topics such as distribution of climate change effects (Harris 2000; Kamminga 2008; Okereke 2008), outdoor recreation sites (Tarrant and Cordell 1999), urban decision-making in China (Xie 2011), or struggles due to electronic waste disposal (Iles 2004), but also environmentally just technology (Ottinger 2011) are covered.

Another trend seen is the combination of the environmental justice approach with other concepts, such as sustainability (Dobson 1998; Agyeman *et al.* 2002; Agyeman and Evans 2004; Gottlieb 2009), climate change (Adger 2006; Beckman and Page 2008; Wilson *et al.* 2010; Davoudi 2012), the capabilities approach (Ballet *et al.* 2011), ecosystem services (Pham *et al.* 2012; Ernstson 2013), and the scope and form of embedding environmental justice in curriculums and learning (Nussbaum 2013, 2014).

This new development opens the space for the combination of justice debate and geography. Issues of justice 'intertwine with the question of how to understand foundational geographical concepts' (Harvey 1996, p. 5); 'spatialities of different forms, of different things, and working at different scales need to be integral in our understanding of the multiplicity of contemporary environmental justice concerns and claims' (Walker 2009a, p. 615). The social constructionist perspectives of the likes of Čapek (1993) or Taylor (2000) are thus explicitly enhanced by a physical component and vice versa. It is made clear that the connection between space and distribution cannot be reduced to a geographical analysis of proximity and spatial patterns of an environmental justice conflict, since other distributional inequalities may fuel such conflicts and have to be laid bare in order to obtain a holistic picture of the case at hand. Or as Walker highlights, 'overreliance on simple and unidimensional geography in environmental justice analysis may serve to obscure inequalities that are constituted and spatialized in different ways' (2009a, p. 622). Additionally, context is once again highlighted, influencing the perception and nature of justice claims, which goes hand in hand with Harvey's view, arguing that 'different socio-ecological circumstances imply quite different approaches to the question of what is or is not just' (1996, p. 6). Or to put it in the words of Agyeman, 'an international, "one size fits all" version of environmental justice is neither possible nor desirable' (2002, p. 49). As Schroeder *et al.* highlight, 'the geography of burdens/benefits can often be quite complex' (2008, p. 551). In this context the metaphor of 'landscapes of privilege' (Duncan and Duncan 2004) can be helpful to systematise conflict situations beyond the analysis of American suburbs and beyond the distinction of class and ethnicity (as in the case of Leichenko and Solecki 2008).

Environmental justice going global

Environmental justice here is understood as highly context-based and thus offers the burden as well as the benefit of multiplicity of understanding and meaning. Seen as a challenge to be dealt with, Agyeman (2014, p. 236) observes significant changes in the concept itself, driven by the increased spatial circulation of environmental injustices driven by globalisation processes, further fostering a 'global brand of environmental justice'. Flitner (2003, p. 156), however, highly doubts the feasibility of global environmental justice; he argues that levels of abstraction and generalisation from a clear-cut local case to global issues are problematic, a standpoint supported by Debbané and Keil (2004, p. 210): '[Environmental justice] as a concept and practice is locally grounded.' Nevertheless, particularly beginning in the second half of the 2000s, evidence (Harper and Rajan 2007; Carruthers 2008; Schroeder 2008; Sze and London 2008; Schlosberg 2009; Martin 2013; Sikor and Newell 2014) shows that environmental justice activism has gone global 'as a dynamic frame for activism, research and policy that has international as well as local manifestations and agenda' (Walker 2009b, p. 356).

Walker then follows a simple strategy to categorise those new developments according to horizontal (among similar actors in different cultural, national, thematic contexts) and vertical (i.e. on cross-border issues involving two or more countries) extensions of the environmental justice concept, reviewing literature by mid-2008 according to the case studies and the exact use of the term 'environmental justice'. Walker himself sees this list of countries as incomplete due to differences between the use of environmental justice frames and the actual naming of such, as well as due to different interpretations between academics and activists. Going beyond Walker's list, examples from around the world are observed in South Africa (London 2003), Australia (Hillman 2006), New Zealand (Pearce *et al.* 2006), the UK (Agyeman and Evans 2004), Sweden (in relation to age; Chaix *et al.* 2006), Israel (Omer and Or 2005), Taiwan (Fan 2012), Brazil (Porto and Milanez 2009; Acselrad 2010; Coy 2013; Kaufmann 2014), but also non-state-based at the global level (Adeola 2000; Sikor and Newell 2014). Without a doubt, from an activist perspective, transnationalisation of environmental justice movements (in the form of 'globalization from below'; Brecher *et al.* 2000) has gained pace in recent years. New cooperations, alliances, networks and coalitions are, to give some examples, the Environmental and Economic Justice Project in Los Angeles supporting international networking and grassroots activities (Faber 2005), the Coalition for Environmental Justice promoting an environmental justice frame in Central and Eastern European Countries (Walker 2009b, pp. 361–362), the Transatlantic Initiative on

Environmental Justice, and the Environmental Justice Organisations, Liabilities and Trade, a FP7 project supported by the European Commission (EJOLT 2015). Particularly for Latin America, a number of transnational initiatives (such as Corporación Observatorio Latinoamericano de Conflictos Ambientales, OCLA) have been set up (Roberts and Thanos 2003; Carruthers 2008), but also in Africa (Kalan and Peek 2005). Other forms and networks have a clear focus on particular areas of interest, such as 'anti-toxic' issues (Pellow 2007).

Especially in the Global South, more systematic approaches to analysing environmental justice have turned up in the 2000s (Peluso and Watts 2001; McDonald 2002; Agyeman *et al.* 2003; Anand 2003; Walker and Bulkeley 2006). According to Schroeder *et al.* (2008), this is particularly due to the increasing transnationalisation of environmental bads. Harper and Rajan (2007, p. 329) categorise environmental inequality among countries in a Global North (beneficiary)–Global South (non-beneficiary) context according to (1) source, in the form of provision of raw materials (Hafner *et al.* 2016), going along with globalised financialisation of agrarian structures and frontier expansions (Coy 2013); (2) sink, through disposal opportunity of hazardous waste and pollution (Clapp 2010); and (3) wilderness through 'coercive conservation', through which ecosystems are being protected through the prohibition of access and use by local communities.

Fundamental in this phase is the replacement of the focus of socio-spatial (mal-)distribution (Dobson 1998) by increasingly multi-dimensional understandings of environmental justice beyond conflict description and claims-making (Schlosberg 2004, 2009; Walker 2009a, pp. 614–615). Additionally, not only environmental bads are taken into account, but also environmental benefits and resources (Laird *et al.* 2000; Mutz *et al.* 2002; Schroeder 2008).

Concepts of environmental justice

Over the last few years, it has become commonly accepted that environmental justice research has developed into a 'plurality of environmental (in)justice experiences', including 'the focus on recognition, participation, and, more recently, on basic needs, capabilities, and functioning – has spread across the growing literature' (Schlosberg 2013, p. 40). As Holifield *et al.* so empathetically write, this form of 'investigation of environmental justice as a contested, complex discursive frame has just begun – and needs to continue' (2010, p. 17). This chapter presents examples of analytical environmental justice concepts.

With the sole focus on actors

In the Argentine context, Carlos Reboratti (2012) has a very strong focus on the actors involved in environmental justice conflicts (or what in Argentina they call socio-ecological conflicts). In so doing, he elaborates a pentagon of actors (national government, provincial government, environmentalism, private companies and local movements). While his focus is on the actors, the actual relational links among them remain vague. Additionally, unlike other concepts of environmental justice, Reboratti (2012) does not refer to any theoretical considerations, or highlight backlinks to greater theoretical discussions. Additionally, while interesting to see which types of actors he considers relevant, the concept lacks – probably due to the focus on one particular example of an investment project – depth, embeddedness and the inclusion of core actors, such as the local population.

With a focus on claims making

Social movement-inspired claims making

Čapek (1993), drawing on the interpretative frame of Snow *et al.* (1986), develops an environmental justice frame around claims making of environmental justice groups. In so doing, she understands environmental justice – in the spirit of social constructionism – 'as a conceptual construction … fashioned simultaneously from the bottom up (local grass-roots groups discovering a pattern to their grievance) and from the top down (national organizations conveying the term to local groups)' (Čapek 1993, p. 5). Simultaneous to and as a causality for framing, she criticises the broad use of the term environmental justice in actual claims making of activist groups, diluting their respective cause; a specific set of analytical dimensions has to be developed (ibid., pp. 6–9). Her frame analysis focuses on structural obstacles due to lower socio-economic status or being a member of a minority (among other characteristics), ultimately leading to more limited access to resources in the legal, scientific and political realms. While those structural difficulties may apply for a geographically broader discussion, Čapek's dimensions of environmental justice are closely connected 'by a strong emphasis on citizenship rights, democratic process, and respect for "grass-roots" knowledge (i.e. the experiential reality of those most directly affected by problems' and concludes that '[t]hey are firmly grounded in existing beliefs about fairness in the United States' (ibid., p. 8). Claims-making is central to an environmental justice frame. Čapek follows Spector and Kitsuse in their definition of claims as 'a form of interaction: a demand made by one party to another that something be done about some putative conditions' (Spector and Kitsuse 1987, p. 78). Thus, it is made clear that – taking social justice movements as a model – parties involved in environmental justice issues have to take an active and equal role within the process. As a result, bringing together structural obstacles and subsequent claims about it, Čapek talks of four dimensions of environmental justice (1993, pp. 12–20): (1) the right to information about a particular situation one is involved in; (2) the right to a hearing in case of claims related to contamination; (3) democratic participation and social solidarity; and (4) the right to compensation from the originators of pollution.

Pluralistic framework for the analysis of environmental claims making

Davoudi and Brooks (2014) set up a pluralistic framework to analyse environmental justice claims. They do not claim to have developed a universal set of principles, but predominantly try to illustrate one form of approaching claims-making. In so doing, they have developed guiding questions in relation to justice dimensions of distribution, recognition, participation, responsibility and capabilities.

They are well aware of the fact that – conceptually – this framework does not take into account how injustices come into existence, nor does it reveal underlying socio-ecological structures, questions of scale or time (ibid., p. 2699). In order to make this framework work properly, the layout has to be established as top-down from the bottom. While the top-down approach is considered to break up 'tendencies to habituate to restrictive and unjust conditions' (ibid., p. 2699) and thus caters to the requirements of becoming part of a concept, the bottom-up conceptual link allows clear contextualisation through narratives and people's perception, meaning and valorisation of their environment. Davoudi and Brooks (ibid., p. 2699) also see great potential for the connection of the different dimensions of justice, something they have not yet achieved. As seen later, one of my aims is to approach this gap via the application of an environmental justice incommensurabilities framework.

With a focus on environmental inequity formation

David Pellow (2000) presents his analysis and theory development on nascent environmental inequities as the basis for further environmental justice analyses. Szasz and Meuser (1997) or Weinberg (1998) have previously highlighted that the analytical focus on environmental inequities had been based on the status quo rather than the (emergence of) underlying mechanisms. Pellow (2000) – well aware that those mechanisms have been studied – agrees, but he is missing a more theoretically grounded and conceptually based approach.

Thus, he develops a process-oriented environmental inequity formation perspective, linking three concerns: (1) time-focused process: environmental inequity has to be seen as a socio-historical process instead of an enclosed event (Pulido 1996a, 1996b; Szasz and Meuser 1997); (2) actor-based understanding: the complexity of actors' needs and interests is to be visualised in order to avoid the simplified 'pepetrator-victim scenarios' (Pellow 2000, p. 588); and (3) multi-locational understanding, through a life-cycle analysis of the ecology of hazardous production and consumption (Mol 1995).

Thus, the core question for Pellow's (2000) environmental inequity formation model circulates around how environmental inequities are produced. Three areas are identified: (1) negotiation (among stakeholders); (2) problem identification (subdivided between environmental racism and environmental inequity); as well as (3) solution (i.e. the ideal situation of environmental justice) (Sze and London 2008, p. 1333). To find answers, ethnographic and historical approaches are particularly helpful here.

With a focus on a robust process

Elvers *et al.* (2008) – much like Flitner (2003, 2007) or Agyeman (2002) – work with environmental justice in a European environment. They develop a pluralistic framework concept of environmental justice as a robust process (cf. Carlson and Doyle 2002). In this framework, Elvers *et al.* see environmental justice as fluid, not yet fully 'designed, controlled, or predicted, but as result of process which is affected by the properties and activities of several dimensions' (2008, p. 842). Thus, they elaborate on eight different dimensions in their process model:

1   *Impact level*: Here, proof of impacts on the individual from the natural and social environment should be discovered and visualised.
2   *Effect level*: The effects of the impacts are analysed according to elements of (physical and psychological) health, quality of life and subjective well-being.
3   *Uncertainties*: Relating to future events, Elvers *et al.* (ibid.) argue that the consequences of (even one's own) actions cannot be fully predicted (cf. Luhmann 2003 [1991], p. 21), thus calling for risk assessment and conceptual inclusion of elements of surprise and precaution.
4   *Objectivity*: Individual and scientific perceptions of effects should be taken into account. The authors remain very vague on how this dimension can be operationalised, they only refer to the methodological shortcomings of early-stage environmental justice research (see Anderton *et al.* 1994; Williams 1996; Bowen 2002).
5   *Morality*: Inequality is not seen as injustice per se, a clear distinction is made here. Additionally, implicit links to procedural justice and participation are made, referring to consensual decision-making and deliberative democracy (e.g. Fishkin 1991; Habermas 1992). Equality is considered, but lacking a clear definition on how far equality is considered beyond the procedural.
6   *Disproportion*: Proof of disproportionate burdens is to be collected in a three-step approach, first, detecting environmental injustice through the screening of spatial units for environmental bads. Second, perceptions on quality of life and well-being are investigated, followed by a third step of verifying the correlation between environmental burdens and already deprived social groups (e.g. in the form of income, education, religion, ethnic origin, age, etc.).
7   *Policy fields*: Here, a call (directed towards policy-makers rather than researchers on environmental justice issues) for cross-referencing of

environmental and social policy is being made, in order to avoid environmental protection laws actually promoting social injustice, for example.

8   *Information*: Information should be actively transmitted to all parties involved, and bottom-up input by the people affected should be considered in order to obtain satisfying levels of policy ownership by the people affected.

Elvers *et al.* (2008, p. 848) establish a hybrid framework in which the analysis of potential environmental injustice (dimensions of impact level and effect level) are evaluated according to future change (i.e. transformation: dimensions of uncertainty and 'objectivity') and interpreted[7] (dimensions of morality and disproportion). For the last step (implementation: dimensions of policy field and information), a clear shift of focus and transfer of conceptual responsibility to policy-makers is observed. One core characteristic of their model is the non-definition of a start or end-point for the analysis.

With a focus on policy development

Fredericks (2011) focuses on the development of indicators for environmental justice policies and highlights the need for activists not just to focus on policy change but also to take the subsequent step of monitoring and evaluation more seriously and critically. In so doing, he proposes a three-step model (ibid., p. 64):

1   Analysis of the relevance of the monitoring progress.
2   Evaluation of trends in environmental justice indicators and context-based relevance.
3   Based on an integrative framework for sustainability indexes, a set of multi-temporal and multi-spatial environmental justice indexes is the outcome.

Even though Fredericks mentions that participatory justice is vital, he states the common problem when predominantly quantitative methods are being used: GIS analyses are the most common ones, allowing relatively fast and procedurally fair visualisation of proximity effects of environmental bads; but local knowledge of local ecosystems, however, is – due to the difficulty of not being able to quantify it – hardly ever taken into account (ibid., pp. 64–66). Nevertheless, some scholars (e.g. Schroeder *et al.* 2008) still rely on quantitative distributive research and a universal environmental justice definition to avoid a broadening and watering down of the concept itself. Well aware of the pitfalls of quantitative methods in the field of environmental justice, Collins *et al.* (2015) compile a fine-scale – and thus downscaled – analysis at the household level and thus try to avoid incoherently generalised data interpretation. According to them, this type of approach as only been exercised twice before (Mohai *et al.* 2009; Crowder and Downey 2010), but unlike Collins *et al.* (2015) only using secondary literature for their analysis.

With a focus on scales, underlying processes and justice

Michael Flitner sees environmental justice as an analytical framework with great potential to fill gaps in political and human ecology, particularly in highly conflictive and thus well-articulated conflict situations (Flitner 2007, p. 35). Flitner's (2003, 2007) basic idea is to find a workable approach – connecting scales and social science debates on justice – to the question of how social science can approach the physical-material world; the concept of environmental justice is one such a workable form. Central in his debate on environmental justice is the relationship and positioning of certain conflicts in terms of scale. Starting from locally-based conflicts, nurtured by locally undesired land use (LULU) and subsequent locally-based grassroots activism against this land use, Flitner points out that the local level is too short-sighted to be able to fully understand the dimensions of conflict. Implicitly taking up Taylor's (2000) rhetoric of claims-making, Flitner reveals the critically cited and highly ego-centric NIMBYism ('not in my backyard'; see Walsh *et al.* 1993), goes beyond this line of thought and then finds new, more ideology-based rhetoric of NIABYism ('not in anybody's backyard'; Flitner 2007, p. 42), BANANA ('build absolutely nothing anywhere near anything'), or NOPE ('not on planet earth') (Boerner and Lambert 1995, p. 69). Origins and effects of conflicts, hence, have to be considered with a trans-scalar perspective; actor-oriented *scalar politics* are put in the foreground, analysing the outcomes of actors' behaviour and their subsequent success in achieving their goals at different levels (Flitner 2007, p. 43); or as Towers puts it: '[T]hey put geographic scale to their political advantage' (2000, p. 24). The main goal of Williams (1999), for example, is to highlight the nonsense of fixed scalar frames on a sub-national level, an aspect supported by Flitner in principle, but then criticised for the non-consequential continuation of fluidisation of scales on and beyond the national level (Flitner 2007, p. 43).

For the development of Flitner's environmental justice matrix, he draws on George Towers (2000) for approaches to the application of scale in political geography analyses. Towers, well aware of his social-constructionist understanding of scale – and thus referring back to the likes of Smith (2008) or Lefebvre (1991) – differentiates between 'scales of regulation' and 'scales of meaning' (Towers 2000, p. 26). Those two categories emerge since 'social production of space invests the landscape with meaning and regulation'; the intersection between the (as I understand it, physical) geographical and the political thus creates 'analytical complexity and productivity' (ibid., p. 26). Flitner has initially – due to the multiple meanings of the German word *Maßstab* (i.e. scale) – preferred the term 'sphere' to 'scale' (Flitner 2003), but ultimately decided for the latter (Flitner 2007). His 'scale of regulation' focuses on administratively delineated 'landscapes' (which is once again a reference to Towers 2000, p. 26) of organised and institutionalised influence (e.g. by political institutions or bureaucracies, but also unions, etc.); 'scales of meaning', then, are considered products for – as the name already indicates – adding meaning and perspective to the aforementioned 'landscapes' rather than focusing on formal allocations of competences and responsibilities (Flitner 2007, p. 44). In its own right, if 'scales of regulation' are put under the label of a concept, 'scales of meaning', then they share more characteristics with the category of a conception. Here, it is interesting to see that framing (Soyez 2000, p. 10; Taylor 2000; Kurtz 2003) once again is used to conceptionalise perspectivist and normative aspects of particular cases.

Flitner argues that the focus on the two scales (i.e. the formal-regulatory concept and the interpretative conception of the first) would be too limited. Hence, the two dimensions of distribution and recognition – in the 1990s very rarely discovered in the field of environmental justice (examples are Harvey 1996; Dobson 1998; Shue 1999) but in some debates on justice they were already applied (Fraser 1996, 1997; Young 2011a) – complete the outline of his environmental justice matrix.

Filling the dimensions of Flitner's matrix with the respective types of justice, he starts out with the first field scales of regulation/distributive justice and calls it material justice: Distribution, much like in most discussions on environmental justice, lies at the beginning of the analysis. Here, Flitner mixes – in the sense of Towers (2000) – structure and action, institutions and processes as the result of distributive effects. Thus, the starting point of analysis is not the questioning of distribution in itself, but the consequences resulting thereof. The second analytical cell (scale of meaning/distributive justice) he calls 'symbolic justice' and deals with the framing of meaning of grid one; a differentiated analysis of the 'social sense' that is created by different actors (independent from factual or formal relationships) is the objective (Flitner 2007, p. 49). The third cell (scales of regulation/recognition justice) covers the relationships of recognition of the institutions and processes involved. Core features for Flitner are issues of access to information and participation in decision-making, including the protection of minorities. The last cell (scales of meaning/recognition justice) deals with underlying factors implicitly influencing maldistribution, that do not necessarily have a direct relationship to the conflict at hand but have high impact through (often long-term) inequalities and injustices. Examples of such can be hegemonic, patriarchal or discriminatory societal structures as well as struggles for recognition of (indigenous) rights often materialised in fights for preserving biodiversity (Bryant 2002; Flitner and Heins 2002). While Flitner considers cultural justice as the cornerstone upon which the (physical as well as social) territory is being developed, he also sees a major challenge in pinpointing analytical indicators and approaches to satisfactorily analyse this field (Flitner 2007, p. 50).

Concerning practical applicability, Flitner (2003) – critically observing environmental justice – considers an environmental justice analysis only useful when clearly manifested conflict situations with visible actors are present and organised. Furthermore, he highlights the limitations of the concept, taking into account issues of data availability and credibility of statistics as well as context-based socio-cultural differences of interpretation, which he considers can more easily be overcome in the urban Global North with higher potential for 'produced nature' rather than in the Global South (ibid., pp. 156–157). Thus, it remains unclear if Flitner then – i.e. in cases outside the USA and rural areas – prefers a stricter definition of environmental justice, stating that the groups analysed suffering from environmental bads should also be disadvantaged as well as suffering the concrete conflict (Getches and Pellow 2002, pp. 24–25). Nevertheless, Flitner's environmental justice matrix is by its design less normative or ideology-driven, since different perspectives can be explored without lessening the matrix.

Comparison of conceptual focuses

Figure 4.2 visualises the seven different concepts of environmental justice and their analytical focuses. Here, it is obvious that all approaches have – to some

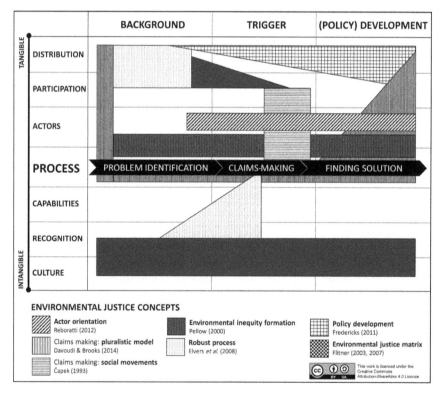

Figure 4.2 Comparison of environmental justice concepts.
Source: Hafner (2016).

degree – the aspect of claims making in their analytical structure; the articulation of environmental injustice (or for that matter inequity, inequality, maldistribution, etc.) is considered one universal cornerstone for environmental justice.

Popular concepts related to environmental justice

Much like Walker (2009a), Barnett (2011, p. 248) highlights the fact that the concepts of equality and justice do not derive from within academia but rather emerge from certain contested arenas in real life, investigated by researchers. As a consequence, a great variety of environmental justice contexts and their subsequent translations can be observed (e.g. Dikec 2007; Wright 2009; Parnell and Pieterse 2010), which is highly influenced by what Barnett calls the '"direction of fit" between normative concepts like justice and social practices' (2011, p. 248).

Environmental justice activism, particularly in the USA, has been widely described, discussed and criticised (Bullard 1993, 2000; Čapek 1993; Gottlieb 1993, 2001; Pulido 1993, 1996a, 2000; Goldman 1996; Pulido *et al.* 2013). The great majority of research on environmental justice organisations is based on case studies of grass-roots organisations (Bullard 2000; McGurty 2000; Wilkes 2006; Marshall 2010; Stretesky *et al.* 2012, p. 343). Christopher Foreman (1998) suggests that a major aspect of differentiation between environmentalists and environmental justice activists lies in the fact that the former are more fond of 'rational' processes of interaction, based on objective scientific research on risks and hazards, while the latter favour the 'theatrics' of bottom-up, participative story-telling about community and individual experiences (Pastor 2007, p. 354).

From the perspective of environmental justice activism, there has always been a broader conception beyond questions of distribution (Wenz 1988), exploring issues of procedural justice inclusion in decision-making and access to information (Hunold and Young 1998; Hampton 1999; Dunion 2003; Petts 2005). '[E]nvironmental justice activism is about racial, geographic and local identity, as much at the same time as it is about a specific facility, issue or campaign' (Sze, cited in Walker 2009a, p. 626). The improvement of involvement in decision-making processes is one central proposal (and common ground) of environmental justice movements (Marshall 2010). Thus, it comes naturally that environmental justice activists – rather than clearly defining and delimiting what environmental justice actually is – pragmatically mix elements of distribution, recognition, responsibility and participation (among other aspects) in order to adapt to specific case- and place-based settings (Holifield *et al.* 2009, p. 596; Schlosberg 2009). Thus, 'strategic fitting' and 'strategic selection' (Benford and Snow 2000), on an action-based level, are much more freely and commonly used in the activist scene than in research on environmental justice. This phenomenon often leads to the creation and/or hybridisation of concepts that fit the particular case of activist groups. Following this line of thought, Martínez-Alier *et al.* (2014) have undertaken the task of listing concepts of political ecology with origins outside the academic realm. Focusing on the production of a 'political ecology from the bottom up', they argue that the time delay from non-scientific emergence to mainstream research area and representation in academic literature takes about five to ten years (ibid., p. 21).

Popular epidemiology

Popular epidemiology can be characterised as the active inclusion of locals in research when, for example, statistics are not available or lack validity. In the example of pollution, it implies that '"lay" knowledge of illnesses from pollution is more valid than the (sometimes non-existent) official knowledge' (ibid., pp. 22–23). It can be categorised as a post-normal science approach, which has been particularly influential in ecological economics (Funtowicz and Ravetz 1993). The core idea is the de-objectification of normal science, since this objectivity is criticised for focusing on hard facts while values, perceptions, uncertainties or locally-based knowledge or hidden hegemonic interests are hidden (Martínez-Alier *et al.* 2014, p. 23). This critique is also found among environmental justice followers (Porto 2012); thus, the application of popular epidemiology, or 'street science' (Corburn 2005), and environmental justice are very useful in community-based participatory action research with a focus on 'more-than-normal science-making'. Another advantage of this thought style lies in the ability to go beyond pre-set structures of creating knowledge (which often afterwards is confirmed by 'traditional' scientific studies; Martínez-Alier *et al.* 2014, p. 23) and thus makes previously invisible actors and their concerns visible (Porto and Finamore 2012).

Environmentalism of the poor

Environmentalism of the poor has been used by environmental justice organisations since the late 1980s, focusing on 'activist interventions by poor and/ or indigenous peoples in many struggles to defend their livelihoods against resource extraction' (Martínez-Alier *et al.* 2014, p. 24). The term is not uniformly accepted, some prefer to speak of *ecologismo popular*, i.e. environmental populism (Martínez-Alier 1994).

In general terms, environmentalism of the poor (initially both studied in India and Latin America; Guha and Martínez-Alier 1997; Martínez-Alier 2002; Nixon 2011) is considered to be fighting against what Harvey (2004) has called 'accumulation by dispossession' – this time developed in a university seminar and then adopted by environmental justice movements and organisations.

This concept highlights the close proximity to environmental justice, even though '[t]he thesis of the "environmentalism of the poor" does not assert that as a rule poor people feel, think and behave as environmentalists' but often 'have an abusive relationship with the environment and their struggles are sometimes projected against conservation programs' (Anguelovski and Martínez-Alier 2014, p. 169). Another shared aspect is the wide recognition that both in the environmentalism of the poor and in environmental justice movements, women play an important role in the movements. Today, environmental justice movements have taken up environmentalism of the poor, a concept not recognised in the 1980s and 1990s (ibid., p. 174).

Defence of the commons

Another concept gaining importance among environmental justice movements is *the commons*, understood 'as a crucial sector of the economy that must be defended to preserve de-commodified access to food, water, housing, forests, clean air (and also public goods, like the internet)' (Martínez-Alier *et al.* 2014, p. 34).

Activists working with the defence of the commons take inspiration from Massimo de Angelis (e.g. 2007) and Antonio Negri (2004), but are – interestingly enough – criticised by environmental justice scholars (Adger 2006) for their lack of clarification of their understanding of an environment discourse, the disconnection from global environmental justice movements and the non-discussion of 'social metabolism', i.e. the 'manner in which human societies organize their growing exchange of energy and materials with the environment' (Martínez-Alier *et al.* 2014, p. 34).

Notes

1 Exceptions, of course, can be made. On no account, would I argue for universal(ist) understandings of theories, concepts, or conceptions, since the context (both temporally, spatially but also subjectively) forms and re-forms the aforementioned constructions.
2 Similar arguments are made by Borges (2016) who, by focusing on environmental displacement, calls it Rawls' 'General Conception' of Justice.
3 For example, Lawson defines environmental justice as 'the fair treatment and meaningful involvement of all people regardless of race, color, national origin, culture, education, or income with respect to the development, implementation, and enforcement of environmental laws, regulations, and policies' (2008, p. 155).
4 In the German-speaking scientific community, the German term for environmental justice (i.e. *Umweltgerechtigkeit*) was only introduced in the 2000s, predominantly used for questions of distribution, and has not attracted too much attention so far; see Maschewsky (2001); Flitner (2003); Bolte and Mielck (2004); or Kloepfer (2000, 2006).
5 As Kedron (2016) highlights, methodological problems related to the selection of case study areas continue to be found in the current literature on environmental justice.
6 Reed and George (2011), however, have taken up this statement and carried out a literature-based analysis on publications (with a special focus on geography) about environmental justice from 2000 to 2009 and came to the conclusion that the core

of research is still being conducted in the USA and in relation to its original topics of landfill sites, toxic waste and air pollution. The only major difference is based on improved GIS methods (Higgs and Langford 2009) as well as community information systems (Lloyd-Smith 2009).
7 This phase, however, is subject to major critique due to the lack of definition of what is interpreted by whom and why.

References

Acselrad, H., 2010. Ambientalização das lutas sociais – o caso do movimento por justiça ambiental. *Estudos Avançados*, 24 (68), 103–119.

Adeola, F.O., 1994. Environmental hazards, health, and racial inequity in hazardous waste distribution. *Environment and Behavior*, 26 (1), 99–126.

Adeola, F.O., 2000. Cross-national environmental injustice and human rights issues: a review of evidence in the developing world. *American Behavioral Scientist*, 43 (4), 686–706.

Adger, W.N., 2006. *Fairness in Adaptation to Climate Change*. Cambridge, MA: MIT Press.

Agyeman, J., 2001. Ethnic minorities in Britain: short change, systematic indifference and sustainable development. *Journal of Environmental Policy and Planning*, 3 (1), 15–30.

Agyeman, J., 2002. Constructing environmental (in)justice: transatlantic tales. *Environmental Politics*, 11 (3), 31–53.

Agyeman, J., 2014. Global environmental justice or Le droit au monde? *Geoforum*, 54, 236–238.

Agyeman, J., Bullard, R.D. and Evans, B., 2002. Exploring the nexus: bringing together sustainability, environmental justice and equity. *Space and Polity*, 6 (1), 77–90.

Agyeman, J., Bullard, R.D. and Evans, B., eds., 2003. *Just Sustainabilities: Development in an Unequal World*. London: Earthscan.

Agyeman, J. and Evans, B., 2004. 'Just sustainability': the emerging discourse of environmental justice in Britain? *The Geographical Journal*, 170 (2), 155–164.

Anand, R., 2003. *International Environmental Justice: A North-South Dimension*. Burlington, VT: Ashgate.

Anderton, D.L., *et al.*, 1994. Environmental equity: the demographics of dumping. *Demography*, 31 (2), 229–248.

Anguelovski, I. and Martínez-Alier, J., 2014. The 'environmentalism of the poor' revisited: territory and place in disconnected glocal struggles. *Ecological Economics*, 102, 167–176.

Ballet, J., Bazin, D., Dubois, J.-L. and Mahieu, F.-R. 2011. A note on sustainability economics and the capability approach. *Ecological Economics*, 70 (11), 1831–1834.

Ballet, J., Koffi, J.-M. and Pelenc, J., 2013. Environment, justice and the capability approach. *Ecological Economics*, 85, 28–34.

Barnett, C., 2011. Geography and ethics: justice unbound. *Progress in Human Geography*, 35 (2), 246–255.

Barry, B., 1999. Sustainability and intergenerational justice. In: A. Dobson, ed. *Fairness and Futurity*: Oxford: Oxford University Press, pp. 93–117.

Barry, B., 2005. *Why Social Justice Matters*. Cambridge: Polity.

Beckman, L. and Page, E.A., 2008. Perspectives on justice, democracy and global climate change. *Environmental Politics*, 17 (4), 527–535.

Benford, R.D. and Snow, D.A., 2000. Framing processes and social movements: an overview and assessment. *Annual Review of Sociology*, 26 (1), 611–639.

Blaikie, P. and Muldavin, J., 2014. Environmental justice? The story of two projects. *Geoforum*, 54, 226–229.

Bloomfield, M.J., 2014. Shame campaigns and environmental justice: corporate shaming as activist strategy. *Environmental Politics*, 23 (2), 263–281.

Boerner, C. and Lambert, T., 1995. Environmental injustice. *The Public Interest*, 118, 61–82.

Bolte, G. and Mielck, A., 2004. *Umweltgerechtigkeit: Die soziale Verteilung von Umweltbelastungen*. Weinheim: Juventa.

Borges, I.M., 2016. Environmental displacement and John Rawls' 'General Conception' of Justice. *Environmental Justice*, 9 (3), 77–84.

Bowen, W., 2002. An analytical review of environmental justice research: what do we really know? *Environmental Management*, 29 (1), 3–15.

Brecher, J., Costello, T. and Smith, B., 2000. *Globalization from Below: The Power of Solidarity*. Cambridge, MA: South End Press.

Bryant, B.I., 1995. *Environmental Justice: Issues, Policies, and Solutions*. Washington, DC: Island Press.

Bryant, B.I. and Mohai, P., eds., 1992. *Race and the Incidence of Environmental Hazards: A Time for Discourse*. Boulder, CO: Westview Press.

Bryant, R.L., 2002. Non-governmental organizations and governmentality: 'consuming' biodiversity and indigenous people in the Philippines. *Political Studies*, 50 (2), 268–292.

Bullard, R.D., 1983. Solid waste sites and the Black Houston community. *Sociological Inquiry*, 53 (2–3), 273–288.

Bullard, R.D., 1990. *Dumping in Dixie: Race, Class, and Environmental Quality*. Boulder, CO: Westview Press.

Bullard, R.D., ed., 1993. *Confronting Environmental Racism: Voices from the Grassroots*. Boston: South End Press.

Bullard, R.D., 1994. *Unequal Protection: Environmental Justice and Communities of Color*. San Francisco: Sierra Club Books.

Bullard, R.D., 2000. *Dumping in Dixie: Race, Class, and Environmental Quality*. 3rd edn. Boulder, CO: Westview Press.

Čapek, S.M., 1993. The 'environmental justice' frame: a conceptual discussion and an application. *Social Problems* [online], 40 (1), 5–24. Available at: www.jstor.org/stable/3097023

Carlson, J.M. and Doyle, J., 2002. Complexity and robustness. *Proceedings of the National Academy of Sciences of the United States of America*, 99 (Suppl. 1), 2538–2545.

Carruthers, D., 2008. The globalization of environmental justice: lessons from the U.S.-Mexico border. *Society & Natural Resources*, 21 (7), 556–568.

Chaix, B., *et al.*, 2006. Children's exposure to nitrogen dioxide in Sweden: investigating environmental injustice in an egalitarian country. *Journal of Epidemiology and Community Health*, 60 (3), 234–241.

Clapp, J., 2010. *Toxic Exports: The Transfer of Hazardous Wastes from Rich to Poor Countries*. Ithaca, NY: Cornell University Press.

Clark, W.C., Kates, R.W., Richards, J.F., *et al.*, 2007. Relationships of environmental justice to ecological theory. *Bulletin of the Ecological Society of America*, 88, 166–170.

Cohen, G.A., 2009. *Why Not Socialism?* Princeton, NJ: Princeton University Press.

Collins, T.W., *et al.*, 2015. Downscaling environmental justice analysis: determinants of household-level hazardous air pollutant exposure in greater Houston. *Annals of the Association of American Geographers*, 105 (4), 684–703.

Commonwealth of Massachusetts, 2002. *Environmental Justice Policy*. Boston: State House. Available at: www.mass.gov/eea/docs/eea/ej/ej-policy-english.pdf

Corburn, J., 2005. *Street Science: Community Knowledge and Environmental Health Justice*. Cambridge, MA: MIT Press.

Coy, M., 2013. Environmental Justice? Sozialökologische Konfliktkonstellationen in Amazonien. In: H.-J. Burchardt, K. Dietz and R. Öhlschläger, eds. *Umwelt und Entwicklung im 21. Jahrhundert: Impulse und Analysen aus Lateinamerika*. Baden-Baden: Nomos, pp. 121–132.

Crowder, K. and Downey, L., 2010. Inter-neighborhood migration, race, and environmental hazards: modeling micro-level processes of environmental inequality. *AJS, American Journal of Sociology* [online], 115 (4), 1110–1149. Available at: www.ncbi.nlm.nih.gov/pmc/articles/PMC2908425/ (accessed 23 July 2015).

Cutter, S.L., 1995. Race, class and environmental justice. *Progress in Human Geography*, 19 (1), 111–122.

Davies, A.R., 2006. Environmental justice as subtext or omission: examining discourses of anti-incineration campaigning in Ireland. *Geoforum*, 37 (5), 708–724.

Davoudi, S., 2012. Climate risk and security: new meanings of 'the environment' in the English planning system. *European Planning Studies*, 20 (1), 49–69.

Davoudi, S. and Brooks, E., 2014. When does unequal become unfair? Judging claims of environmental injustice. *Environment and Planning A*, 46 (11), 2686–2702.

de Angelis, M., 2007. *The Beginning of History: Value Struggles and Global Capital*. London: Pluto Press.

Debbané, A. and Keil, R., 2004. Multiple disconnections: environmental justice and urban water in Canada and South Africa. *Space and Polity*, 8 (2), 209–225.

Deneulin, S., 2002. Perfectionism, paternalism and liberalism in Sen and Nussbaum's capability approach. *Review of Political Economy*, 14 (4), 497–518.

Dikec, M., 2007. *Badlands of the Republic: Space, Politics and Urban Policy*. Oxford: Blackwell.

Dobson, A., 1998. *Justice and the Environment: Conceptions of Environmental Sustainability and Dimensions of Social Justice*. Oxford: Oxford University Press.

Drummond, J., 2008. What I would like to see published in *Environmental Justice*. *Environmental Justice*, 1 (4), 179–182.

Duncan, J.S. and Duncan, N., 2004. *Landscapes of Privilege: Aesthetics and Affluence in an American Suburb*. New York: Routledge.

Dunion, K., 2003. *Trouble Makers. The Struggle for Environmental Justice in Scotland*. Edinburgh: Edinburgh University Press.

EJOLT, 2015. Project [online], EJOLT. Available at: www.ejolt.org/project/ (accessed 20 July 2015).

Elvers, H.-D., 2011. Umweltgerechtigkeit. In: M. Groß, ed. *Handbuch Umweltsoziologie*. Wiesbaden: VS Verlag für Sozialwissenschaften, pp. 464–484.

Elvers, H.-D., Gross, M. and Heinrichs, H., 2008. The diversity of environmental justice. *European Societies*, 10 (5), 835–856.

Ernstson, H., 2013. The social production of ecosystem services: a framework for studying environmental justice and ecological complexity in urbanized landscapes. *Landscape and Urban Planning*, 109 (1), 7–17.

Faber, D.R., 1998. *The Struggle for Ecological Democracy: Environmental Justice Movements in the United States.* New York: Guilford Press.

Faber, D.R., 2005. Building a transnational environmental justice movement: obstacles and opportunities in the age of globalization. In: J. Bandy and J. Smith, eds. *Coalitions across Borders: Transnational Protest and the Neoliberal Order.* Lanham, MD: Rowman & Littlefield, pp. 43–68.

Fan, M.-F., 2012. Justice, community knowledge, and waste facility siting in Taiwan. *Public Understanding of Science*, 21 (4), 418–431.

Fishkin, J.S., 1991. *Democracy and Deliberation: New Directions for Democratic Reform.* New Haven, CT: Yale University Press.

Flitner, M., 2003. Umweltgerechtigkeit. Ein neuer Ansatz der sozialwissenschaftlichen Umweltforschung. In: P. Meusburger and T. Schwan, eds. *Humanökologie: Ansätze zur Überwindung der Natur-Kultur-Dichotomie.* Stuttgart: F. Steiner Verlag, pp. 139–160.

Flitner, M., 2007. *Lärm an der Grenze: Fluglärm und Umweltgerechtigkeit am Beispiel des binationalen Flughafens Basel-Mulhouse.* Stuttgart: Steiner.

Flitner, M. and Heins, V., 2002. Modernity and life politics: conceptualizing the biodiversity crisis. *Political Geography*, 21, 319–340.

Foreman, C.H., 1998. *The Promise and Peril of Environmental Justice.* Washington, DC: Brookings Institution.

Fraser, N., 1996. *Social Justice in the Age of Identity Politics: Redistribution, Recognition, and Participation.* The Tanner Lectures on Human Values. Stanford, CA: Stanford University.

Fraser, N., 1997. *Justice Interruptus: Critical Reflections on the 'Postsocialist' Condition.* New York: Routledge.

Fraser, N., 2000. Rethinking recognition. *New Left Review* [online], 3 (May–June), 107–120. Available at: http://newleftreview.org/II/3/nancy-fraser-rethinking-recognition (accessed 9 July 2015).

Fraser, N., 2009. *Scales of Justice: Reimagining Political Space in a Globalizing World.* New York: Columbia University Press.

Fredericks, S.E., 2011. Monitoring environmental justice. *Environmental Justice*, 4 (1), 63–69.

Freeman, A.M., 1972. Distribution of environmental quality. In: A.V. Kneese and B.T. Bower, eds. *Environmental Quality Analysis: Theory and Method in the Social Sciences.* Baltimore, MD: Johns Hopkins University Press, pp. 243–278.

Funtowicz, S.O. and Ravetz, J.R., 1993. Science for the post-normal age. *Futures*, 25 (7), 739–755.

Getches, D.H. and Pellow, D.N., 2002. Beyond 'traditional' environmental justice. In: K.M. Mutz, G.C. Bryner and D.S. Kenney, eds. *Justice and Natural Resources: Concepts, Strategies, and Applications.* Washington, DC: Island Press, pp. 3–30.

Goldman, B.A., 1996. What is the future of environmental justice? *Antipode*, 28 (2), 122–141.

Gottlieb, R., 1993. *Forcing the Spring: The Transformation of the American Environmental Movement.* Washington, DC: Island Press.

Gottlieb, R., 2001. Linking environmental justice and pollution prevention: livable communities and cleaner production. *Pollution Prevention Review* [online], Winter 2001, 15–28. Available at: http://scholar.oxy.edu/uep_faculty/306/

Gottlieb, R., 2009. Where we live, work, play … and eat: expanding the environmental justice agenda. *Environmental Justice*, 2 (1), 7–8.

Groves, C., 2015. The bomb in my backyard, the serpent in my house: environmental justice, risk, and the colonisation of attachment. *Environmental Politics*, 25 (6), 1–21.

Guha, R. and Martínez-Alier, J., 1997. *Varieties in Environmentalism: Essays North and South*. London: Earthscan.

Habermas, J., 1992. Drei normative Modelle der Demokratie: Zum Begriff deliberativer Demokratie. In: I. Fetscher and H. Münkler, eds. *Die Chancen der Freiheit: Grundprobleme der Demokratie*. München: Piper, pp. 11–24.

Hafner, R., 2016. Figures [online]. Available at: http://roberthafner.at/figures (accessed 7 November 2017).

Hafner, R., Rainer, G. Ruiz Peyré, F. and Coy, M., 2016. Ressourcenboom in Südamerika: Alte Praktiken – Neue Diskurse? *Zeitschrift für Wirtschaftsgeographie*, 60 (1–2), 25–39.

Hampton, G., 1999. Environmental equity and public participation. *Policy Sciences*, 32 (2), 163–174.

Harper, K. and Rajan, R., 2007. International environmental justice: building the natural assets of the world's poor. In: E.A. Stanton, J.K. Boyce and S. Narain, eds. *Reclaiming Nature: Environmental Justice and Ecological Restoration*. London: Anthem Press, pp. 327–350.

Harris, P.G., 2000. Defining international distributive justice: environmental considerations. *International Relations*, 15 (2), 51–66.

Harvey, D., 1996. *Justice, Nature, and the Geography of Difference*. Malden, MA: Blackwell.

Harvey, D., 2004. The 'new' imperialism: accumulation by dispossession. *Socialist Register* [online], 40, 63–87. Available at: http://socialistregister.com/index.php/srv/article/view/5811/2707#.VbOjdvnGBMF (accessed 25 July 2015).

Higgs, G. and Langford, M., 2009. GIScience, environmental justice, and estimating populations at risk: the case of landfills in Wales. *Applied Geography*, 29 (1), 63–76.

Hillman, M., 2006. Situated justice in environmental decision-making: lessons from river management in Southeastern Australia. *Geoforum*, 37 (5), 695–707.

Holifield, R., Porter, M. and Walker, G., 2009. Introduction to spaces of environmental justice: frameworks for critical engagement. *Antipode*, 41 (4), 591–612.

Holifield, R.B., Porter, M. and Walker, G.P., 2010. *Spaces of Environmental Justice*. Chichester: Wiley-Blackwell.

Holland, B., 2008. Justice and the environment in Nussbaum's 'capabilities approach': why sustainable ecological capacity is a meta-capability. *Political Research Quarterly*, 61 (2), 319–332.

Honneth, A., 1996. *The Struggle for Recognition: The Moral Grammar of Social Conflicts*. Cambridge, MA: MIT Press.

Honneth, A., 2001. Recognition or redistribution?: Changing perspectives on the moral Order of Society. *Theory, Culture & Society*, 18 (2–3), 43–55.

Hunold, C. and Young, I.M., 1998. Justice, democracy, and hazardous siting. *Political Studies*, 46 (1), 82–95.

Hurley, A., 1995. *Environmental Inequalities: Class, Race, and Industrial Pollution in Gary, Indiana, 1945–1980*. Chapel Hill, NC: University of North Carolina Press.

Iles, A.T., 2004. Mapping environmental justice in technology flows: computer waste impacts in Asia. *Global Environmental Politics*, 4 (4), 76–107.

Issaoui, F., 2011. Amartya Sen: relecture de l'Etat de la justice. *African Sociological Review/Revue Africaine de Sociologie*, 15 (1), 72–87.

Kalan, H. and Peek, B., 2005. South African perspectives on transnational environmental justice networks. In: D.N. Pellow and R.J. Brulle, eds. *Power, Justice, and the Environment: A Critical Appraisal of the Environmental Justice Movement*. Cambridge, MA: MIT Press, pp. 253–263.

Kamminga, M.R., 2008. The ethics of climate politics: four modes of moral discourse. *Environmental Politics*, 17 (4), 673–692.

Kaufmann, G.F., 2014. Seeking environmental injustice with help of Q Methodology on APA Algodoal-Maiandeua. *Environmental Justice*, 7 (3), 61–69.

Kedron, P., 2016. Identifying the geographic extent of environmental inequalities: a comparison of pattern detection methods. *The Canadian Geographer/Le Géographe canadien*, 60 (4), 479–492.

Kloepfer, M., 2000. Environmental Justice und geographische Umweltgerechtigkeit. *Deutsches Verwaltungsblatt*, 11, 750–754.

Kloepfer, M., 2006. *Umweltgerechtigkeit: Environmental Justice in der deutschen Rechtsordnung*. Berlin: Duncker and Humblot.

Kuklys, W., 2005. *Amartya Sen's Capability Approach: Theoretical Insights and Empirical Applications*. Berlin: Springer.

Kurtz, H.E., 2003. Scale frames and counter-scale frames: constructing the problem of environmental injustice. *Political Geography*, 22 (8), 887–916.

Laird, S., Cunningham, A.B. and Lisinge, E., 2000. One in ten thousand? The Cameroon case of Ancistrocladus korupensis. In: C. Zerner, ed. *People, Plants, and Justice: The Politics of Nature Conservation*. New York: Columbia University Press, pp. 345–373.

Latta, P.A., 2007. Locating democratic politics in ecological citizenship. *Environmental Politics*, 16 (3), 377–393.

Lawson, B.E., 2008. The value of environmental justice. *Environmental Justice*, 1 (3), 155–158.

Leatherman, T., 2005. A space of vulnerability in poverty and health: political-ecology and biocultural analysis. *Ethos*, 33 (1), 46–70.

Lefebvre, H., 1991. *The Production of Space*. Oxford: Blackwell.

Leichenko, R.M. and Solecki, W.D., 2008. Consumption, inequity, and environmental justice: the making of new metropolitan landscapes in developing countries. *Society & Natural Resources*, 21 (7), 611–624.

Leopold, A., 1970. *A Sand County Almanac: With Essays on Conservation from Round River*. New York: Ballantine Books.

Lloyd-Smith, M., 2009. Information, power and environmental justice in botany: the role of community information systems. *Journal of Environmental Management*, 90 (4), 1628–1635.

London, L., 2003. Human rights, environmental justice, and the health of farm workers in South Africa. *International Journal of Occupational and Environmental Health*, 9 (1), 59–68.

Luhmann, N., 2003 [1991]. *Soziologie des Risikos*. Berlin: De Gruyter.

Marshall, A.-M., 2010. Environmental justice and grassroots legal action. *Environmental Justice*, 3 (4), 147–151.

Martin, A., 2013. Global environmental in/justice, in practice: introduction. *The Geographical Journal*, 179 (2), 98–104.

Martínez-Alier, J., 1994. *De la economía ecológica al ecologismo popular*. 2nd edn. Barcelona: Icaria.

Martínez-Alier, J., 2002. *The Environmentalism of the Poor: A Study of Ecological Conflicts and Valuation*. Northhampton, MA: Edward Elgar.

Martínez-Alier, J., Anguelovski, I.; Bond, P., et al., 2014. Between activism and science: grassroots concepts for sustainability coined by environmental justice organizations. *Journal of Political Ecology* [online], 21, 19–60. Available at: http://jpe.library.arizona.edu/volume_21/Martinez-Alier.pdf (accessed 29 September 2014).

Martins, N., 2005. Capabilities as causal powers. *Cambridge Journal of Economics*, 30 (5), 671–685.

Martins, N., 2007. Ethics, ontology and capabilities. *Review of Political Economy*, 19 (1), 37–53.

Martins, N., 2011. Sustainability economics, ontology and the capability approach. *Ecological Economics*, 72, 1–4.

Maschewsky, W., 2001. *Umweltgerechtigkeit, Public Health und soziale Stadt*. Frankfurt: VAS.

McDonald, D.A., 2002. *Environmental Justice in South Africa*. Cape Town: University of Cape Town Press.

McGurty, E.M., 2000. Warren County, NC, and the emergence of the environmental justice movement: unlikely coalitions and shared meanings in local collective action. *Society & Natural Resources*, 13 (4), 373–387.

Mohai, P., Lantz, P.M., Morenoff, J., House, J.S. and Mero, R.P. 2009. Racial and socioeconomic disparities in residential proximity to polluting industrial facilities: evidence from the Americans' Changing Lives Study. *American Journal of Public Health*, 99 (Suppl. 3), 56.

Mohai, P. and Bryant, B.I., 1992. Environmental racism: reviewing the evidence. In: B.I. Bryant and P. Mohai, eds. *Race and the Incidence of Environmental Hazards: A Time for Discourse*. Boulder, CO: Westview Press, pp. 161–176.

Mol, A.P.J., 1995. *The Refinement of Production: Ecological Modernization Theory and the Chemical Industry*. Utrecht: Van Arkel.

Mutz, K.M., Bryner, G.C. and Kenney, D.S., eds., 2002. *Justice and Natural Resources: Concepts, Strategies, and Applications*. Washington, DC: Island Press.

Negri, A., 2004. *Time for Revolution*. New York: Continuum.

Newell, P., 2006. Environmental justice movements: taking stock, moving forward. *Environmental Politics*, 15 (4), 656–660.

Nixon, R., 2011. *Slow Violence and the Environmentalism of the Poor*. Cambridge, MA: Harvard University Press.

Nussbaum, M.C., 2000. *Women and Human Development: The Capabilities Approach*. Cambridge: Cambridge University Press.

Nussbaum, M.C., 2006. *Frontiers of Justice: Disability, Nationality, Species Membership*. Cambridge, MA: Harvard University Press.

Nussbaum, M.M., 2013. Embedding issues of environmental justice in the mainstream curriculum. *Environmental Justice*, 6 (1), 34–40.

Nussbaum, M.M., 2014. Environmental justice in the college and university curriculum: a survey of the literature. *Environmental Justice*, 7 (4), 95–101.

Nussbaum, M. and Sen, A., eds., 1993. *The Quality of Life*: Oxford: Oxford University Press.

Okereke, C., 2008. *Global Justice and Neoliberal Environment Governance: Ethics, Sustainable Development and the International Co-Operation*. London: Routledge.

Olsen, K., 2001. Distributive justice and the politics of difference. *Critical Horizons*, 2 (1), 5–32.

Omer, I. and Or, U.D., 2005. Distributive environmental justice in the city: differential access in two mixed Israeli cities. *Tijdschrift voor Economische en Sociale Geografie*, 96 (4), 433–443.

Ottinger, G., 2011. Environmentally just technology. *Environmental Justice*, 4 (1), 81–85.

Owens, S., 2004. Siting, sustainable development and social priorities. *Journal of Risk Research*, 7 (2), 101–114.

Oxford English Dictionary, 2015. Justice. Available at: www.oxforddictionaries.com/definition/english/justice (accessed 1 July 2015).

Parnell, S. and Pieterse, E., 2010. The 'right to the city': institutional imperatives of a developmental state. *International Journal of Urban and Regional Research*, 34 (1), 146–162.

Pastor, M., 2007. Environmental justice: reflections from the United States. In: E.A. Stanton, J.K. Boyce and S. Narain, eds. *Reclaiming Nature: Environmental Justice and Ecological Restoration*. London: Anthem Press, pp. 351–378.

Pearce, J., Kingham, S. and Zawar-Reza, P., 2006. Every breath you take?: Environmental justice and air pollution in Christchurch, New Zealand. *Environment and Planning A*, 38 (5), 919–938.

Pellow, D.N., 2000. Environmental inequality formation: toward a theory of environmental injustice. *American Behavioral Scientist*, 43 (4), 581–601.

Pellow, D.N., 2004. *Garbage Wars: The Struggle for Environmental Justice in Chicago*. Cambridge, MA: MIT Press.

Pellow, D.N., 2007. *Resisting Global Toxics: Transnational Movements for Environmental Justice*. Cambridge, MA: MIT Press.

Peluso, N.L. and Watts, M., 2001. *Violent Environments*. Ithaca, NY: Cornell University Press.

Petts, J., 2005. Enhancing environmental equity through decision-making: learning from waste management. *Local Environment*, 10 (4), 397–409.

Pham, T.-T.-H, Apparicio, P., Séguin, A.-M., Landry, S. and Gagnon, M., 2012. Spatial distribution of vegetation in Montreal: an uneven distribution or environmental inequity? *Landscape and Urban Planning*, 107 (3), 214–224.

Phillips, C.V. and Sexton, K.E.N., 1999. Science and policy implications of defining environmental justice. *Journal of Exposure Analysis and Environmental Epidemiology*, 9 (1), 9–17.

Pollock, P.H. and Vittas, M.E., 1995. Who bears the burdens of environmental pollution? Race, ethnicity, and environmental equity in Florida. *Social Science Quarterly*, 76 (2), 294–310.

Porto, M., 2012. Complexity, vulnerability processes and environmental justice: an essay in political epistemology. *RCCS Annual Review* [online], 4 (4). Available at: http://rccsar.revues.org/420 (accessed 25 February 2015).

Porto, M.F. and Finamore, R., 2012. Riscos, saúde e justiça ambiental: o protagonismo das populações atingidas na produção de conhecimento. *Ciência & Saúde Coletiva*, 17 (6), 1493–1501.

Porto, M.F. and Milanez, B., 2009. Eixos de desenvolvimento econômico e geração de conflitos socioambientais no Brasil: desafios para a sustentabilidade e a justiça ambiental. *Ciência & Saúde Coletiva*, 14 (6), 1983–1994.

Pulido, L., 1993. Sustainable development at Ganados del Valle. In: R.D. Bullard, ed. *Confronting Environmental Racism: Voices from the Grassroots*. Boston: South End Press, pp. 123–139.

Pulido, L., 1996a. A critical review of the methodology of environmental racism research. *Antipode*, 28 (2), 142–159.

Pulido, L., 1996b. *Environmentalism and Economic Justice: Two Chicano Struggles in the Southwest*. Tucson, AZ: University of Arizona Press.

Pulido, L., 2000. Rethinking environmental racism: white privilege and urban development in Southern California. *Annals of the Association of American Geographers*, 90 (1), 12–40.

Pulido, L., Sidawi, S. and Vos, R.O., 2013. An archaeology of environmental racism in Los Angeles. *Urban Geography*, 17 (5), 419–439.

Rawls, J., 1973. *A Theory of Justice*. Oxford: Oxford University Press.

Rawls, J., 1993. *Political Liberalism*. New York: Columbia University Press.

Rawls, J., 2001. *Justice as Fairness: A Restatement*. Cambridge, MA: Harvard University Press.

Reboratti, C., 2012. Socio-environmental conflict in Argentina. *Journal of Latin American Geography*, 11 (2), 3–20.

Reed, M.G. and George, C., 2011. Where in the world is environmental justice? *Progress in Human Geography*, 35 (6), 835–842.

Roberts, J.T. and Thanos, N.D., 2003. *Trouble in Paradise: Globalization And Environmental Crises in Latin America*. New York: Routledge.

Robeyns, I., 2003. Is Nancy Fraser's critique of theories of distributive justice justified? *Constellations*, 10 (4), 538–554.

Robeyns, I., 2005. The capability approach: a theoretical survey. *Journal of Human Development*, 6 (1), 93–117.

Rosier, P.C., 2008. 'We, the Indian people, must set an example for the rest of the nation': environmental justice from a Native American perspective. *Environmental Justice*, 1 (3), 127–130.

Schlosberg, D., 2004. Reconceiving environmental justice: global movements and political theories. *Environmental Politics*, 13 (3), 517–540.

Schlosberg, D., 2009. *Defining Environmental Justice: Theories, Movements and Nature*. Oxford: Oxford University Press.

Schlosberg, D., 2013. Theorising environmental justice: the expanding sphere of a discourse. *Environmental Politics*, 22 (1), 37–55.

Schlosberg, D. and Carruthers, D., 2010. Indigenous struggles, environmental justice, and community capabilities. *Global Environmental Politics*, 10 (4), 12–35.

Schofield, P., 2006. *Utility and Democracy: The Political Thought of Jeremy Bentham*. Oxford: Oxford University Press.

Schroeder, R., 2008. Environmental justice and the market: the politics of sharing wildlife revenues in Tanzania. *Society & Natural Resources*, 21 (7), 583–596.

Schroeder, R. Martin, K. S., Wilson, B. and Sen, D. 2008. Third World environmental justice. *Society & Natural Resources*, 21 (7), 547–555.

Sen, A., 1985. Well-being, agency and freedom: the Dewey Lectures 1984. *The Journal of Philosophy*, 82 (4), 169–221.

Sen, A., 1999a. *Commodities and Capabilities*. New York: Oxford University Press.

Sen, A., 1999b. *Development as Freedom*. New York: Knopf.

Sen, A., 2005. Human rights and capabilities. *Journal of Human Development*, 6 (2), 151–166.

Sen, A., 2010. *The Idea of Justice*. London: Penguin.

Shrader-Frechette, K.S., 2002. *Environmental Justice: Creating Equality, Reclaiming Democracy*. Oxford: Oxford University Press.

Shue, H., 1999. Global environment and international inequality. *International Affairs*, 75 (3), 531–545.

Sikor, T. and Newell, P., 2014. Globalizing environmental justice? *Geoforum*, 54, 151–157.

Simpson, E., 1980. The subject of justice. *Ethics*, 90, 490–501.

Smith, N., 2008. *Uneven Development: Nature, Capital, and the Production of Space*. 3rd edn. Athens, GA: University of Georgia Press.

Snow, D., Burke Rochford, Jr E., Worden, S.K. and Benford, R.D., 1986. Frame alignment processes, micromobilization, and movement participation. *American Sociological Review*, 51 (4).

Souza, A., 2008. The gathering momentum for environmental justice in Brazil. *Environmental Justice*, 1 (4), 183–188.

Soyez, D., 2000. Anchored locally – linked globally. Transnational social movement organizations in a (seemingly) borderless world. *GeoJournal*, 52 (1), 7–16.

Spector, M. and Kitsuse, J.I., 1987. *Constructing Social Problems*. Hawthorne, NY: Aldine de Gruyter.

Stanley, A., 2009. Just space or spatial justice?: Difference, discourse, and environmental justice. *Local Environment*, 14 (10), 999–1014.

Stewart, F., 2005. Groups and capabilities. *Journal of Human Development*, 6 (2), 185–204.

Stretesky, P.B., Huss, S. and Lynch, M.J., 2012. Density dependence and environmental justice organizations, 1970–2008. *The Social Science Journal*, 49 (3), 343–351.

Swyngedouw, E. and Heynen, N.C., 2003. Urban political ecology, justice and the politics of scale. *Antipode*, 35 (5), 898–918.

Szasz, A. and Meuser, M., 1997. Environmental inequalities: literature review and proposals for new directions in research and theory. *Current Sociology*, 45 (3), 99–120.

Sze, J. and London, J.K., 2008. Environmental justice at the crossroads. *Sociology Compass*, 2 (4), 1331–1354.

Tarrant, M.A. and Cordell, H.K., 1999. Environmental justice and the spatial distribution of outdoor recreation sites: an application of geographic information systems. *Journal of Leisure Research*, 31 (1), 18–34.

Taylor, C., 1994. Multiculturalism. In: A. Gutmann, ed. *Multiculturalism: Examining the Politics of Recognition*. Princeton, NJ: Princeton University Press.

Taylor, D.E., 2000. The rise of the environmental justice paradigm: injustice framing and the social construction of environmental discourses. *American Behavioral Scientist*, 43 (4), 508–580.

Towers, G., 2000. Applying the political geography of scale: grassroots strategies and environmental justice. *The Professional Geographer*, 52 (1), 23–36.

United Church Commission for Racial Justice, 1987. *Toxic Wastes and Race in the United States*. New York: United Church Commission for Racial Justice.

Valdivia, G., 2005. On indigeneity, change, and representation in the northeastern Ecuadorian Amazon. *Environment and Planning A*, 37 (2), 285–303.

Vincent, A., 1998. Is environmental justice a misnomer? In: D. Boucher and P.J. Kelly, eds. *Social Justice: From Hume to Walzer*. New York: Taylor & Francis, pp. 123–145.

Walker, G., 2009a. Beyond distribution and proximity: exploring the multiple spatialities of environmental justice. *Antipode*, 41 (4), 614–636.

Walker, G., 2009b. Globalizing environmental justice: the geography and politics of frame contextualization and evolution. *Global Social Policy*, 9 (3), 355–382.

Walker, G. and Bulkeley, H., 2006. Geographies of environmental justice. *Geoforum*, 37 (5), 655–659.

Walsh, E., Warland, R.H. and Smith, D.C., 1993. Backyards, NIMBYs, and incinerator sitings: implications for social movement theory. *Social Problems* [online], 40 (1), 25–38. Available at: www.jstor.org/stable/3097024 (accessed 22 July 2015).

Walzer, M., 1983. *Spheres of Justice: A Defense of Pluralism and Equality*. New York: Basic Books.

Wapner, P. and Matthew, R.A., 2009. The humanity of global environmental ethics. *The Journal of Environment & Development*, 18 (2), 203–222.

Weidner, H., 2005. *Global Equity Versus Public Interest? The Case of Climate Change Policy in Germany*. Berlin: Wissenschaftszentrum Berlin für Sozialforschung.

Weinberg, A.S., 1998. The environmental justice debate: a commentary on methodological issues and practical concerns. *Sociological Forum*, 13 (1), 25–32.

Wenz, P.S., 1988. *Environmental Justice*. Albany, NY: State University of New York Press.

Whiteman, G., 2009. All my relations: understanding perceptions of justice and conflict between companies and indigenous peoples. *Organization Studies*, 30 (1), 101–120.

Wilkes, R., 2006. The protest actions of indigenous peoples: a Canadian-U.S. comparison of social movement emergence. *American Behavioral Scientist*, 50 (4), 510–525.

Williams, C., 1996. Environmental victimization and violence. *Aggression and Violent Behavior*, 1 (3), 191–204.

Williams, G. and Mawdsley, E., 2006. Postcolonial environmental justice: government and governance in India. *Geoforum*, 37 (5), 660–670.

Williams, R.W., 1999. Environmental injustice in America and its politics of scale. *Political Geography*, 18 (1), 49–73.

Wilson, S.M., et al., 2010. Climate change, environmental justice, and vulnerability: an exploratory spatial analysis. *Environmental Justice*, 3 (1), 13–19.

Wright, M.W., 2009. Justice and the geographies of moral protest: reflections from Mexico. *Environment and Planning D: Society and Space*, 27 (2), 216–233.

Xie, L., 2011. Environmental justice in China's urban decision-making. *Taiwan in Comparative Perspective*, 3, 160–179.

Young, I.M., 2011a. *Justice and the Politics of Difference*. Princeton, NJ: Princeton University Press.

Young, I.M., 2011b. *Responsibility for Justice*. Oxford: Oxford University Press.

Zoomers, A., 2010. Globalisation and the foreignisation of space: seven processes driving the current global land grab. *Journal of Peasant Studies*, 37 (2), 429–447.

5 Argentina and soy agribusiness

Environmental justice analyses, both from a scientific as well as an activist perspective (and all kinds in between), share the characteristic of focusing on empirical cases as an anchor of analysis and action. In this sense, this book will not be of any different. The main focus here lies on the soy agribusiness in North-west Argentina and its effects on the local community of Las Lajitas. Since one of my main – and quite simple – arguments is 'context matters', it goes without saying that a thorough embedding of the empirical case will take place. In so doing, the following sub-headings deal with the thematic context of soy production, particularly with genetically modified (GM) crops and the application of pesticides and herbicides, the temporal context (i.e. the unique evolution of soy production in Argentina), as well as the spatial context that ultimately explains why the North-west of Argentina makes an excellent case study for environmental justice research.

Thematic context

While soy is considered a super-crop, rich in proteins and nutrients, the application of the genetically modified organisms (GMO) scheme to soy production is a hot topic of debate. In particular, the large-scale use of the broad-band herbicide glyphosate is at the centre of the debate.

To put this into context, the creation of a scientific fact has to be borne in mind. Thus, retracing the steps from approved crops to the initial research is helpful here (Cuhra 2015). Policy-makers generally rely on scientific advice from (international) authorities such as the World Health Organization (WHO), the Organisation for Economic Cooperation and Development (OECD), the US Food and Drug Administration (US FDA), the US Environmental Protection Agency (US EPA), the European Food Safety Authority (EFSA) or for the particular case of Argentina, the SENASA (*Servicio Nacional de Sanidad y Calidad Agroalimentaria*, i.e. the National Service for Health and Quality of Agrifoods). Those institutions rely on the collection, aggregation as well as the selection of a large and complex body of different research. It goes without saying that different projects may have different outcomes depending on the thought styles of the researchers involved and the contextual basis, including the methodological approaches and forms of inter-pretation of data retrieved, an aspect that Knorr-Cetina (1999) has elaborated on. Additionally, economic interests or visceral elements of personal rivalries and conflicts also play a role in the making of conclusions (Cuhra 2015, p. 89). Bearing this context in mind, the case of glyphosate's (non-)toxicity starts in 1978 when a group of researchers at the Analytical BioChemistry (ABC) laboratories in Columbia, Missouri, were contracted to test negative side effects of the new herbicide. Using the then standards, the results showed that it 'would place technical glyphosate into the category of practically non-toxic' (McAllister and Forbis, cited in Cuhra 2015, p. 90). This result and subsequent other studies marked the basis for US EPA and Monsanto's risk assessment studies. They were backed up by scientific facts created by other commercial laboratories working for Monsanto, some of which have later been discovered to have produced false data (for a detailed analysis, see ibid.). In the end, Cuhra concludes:

> [R]esearch performed at ABC strongly indicates that unsuitable method-ologies have been employed, evidenced as flaws in the experimental setup, misinterpretation of the data and miscalculation of endpoints. Fur-thermore, the regulatory importance of these documents has been exag-gerated and scientific conclusions have been changed in subsequent revisions. Also, the documentation indicates that US EPA staff assisted in such manipulation of conclusions.
>
> (Ibid., p. 93)

Bearing in mind the high international relevance of institutions like the US EPA, it goes without saying that the creation of scientific facts has major impacts on the thought styles of policy-makers and a direct influence on national regulations. This brings us to the root of the problem of the per-ceived axiomatic nature of scientific facts (Fleck 1980):

> To say that something is a scientific fact is to bring in epistemology and show awareness of the epistemic brittleness of common sense. Advertisers often do it. Many products are sold (sometimes correctly and sometimes wrongly) in the name of science. As consumers, we are often told that products have been scientifically tested, and that the promised effects have been scientifically proven to be there.
>
> (Johansson and Lynøe 2008, pp. 43–44)

As a result, it is not surprising that a number of research projects have come to the conclusion that glyphosate has harmful effects. Richard *et al.* (2005), for example, discovered placental human cells' sensitivity to Roundup, high-lighting that it kills high numbers of placental cells at even lower dosage than used in agricultural production. This feature is considered a key reason for the high miscarriage rates of rural workers in the USA. Similar results are observed in glyphosate studies carried out by Benachour and Séralini (2009). Even though the WHO re-evaluated the toxicological classification of glyphosate in 2009, new results have not been taken into account. This means that the non-causality between glyphosate and certain illnesses is confirmed (WHO 2010; Arancibia 2013, p. 83). In 2011, the Argentine SENASA followed in the steps of the WHO's classification. However, as Arancibia (2013, p. 83) highlights, those 'official "truths" regarding the effects of glyphosate on human health' are increasingly being contested by experts (e.g. Paganelli *et al.* 2010) and lay people alike. Thus, Cuhra *et al.* raise the question whether the application of glyphosate can be 'too much of a good thing' (2016, p. 28). This thought is also considered by Lapegna (2016), who studied how local peasant movements understand GM soy-related social-environmental problems.

To put it more concretely, three different Argentinian GM soy thought styles are observed:

1 Soy is for human consumption.
2 The right dosage of glyphosate is not harmful.
3 Soy is the source of Argentinian well-being.

Soy is for human consumption

PEA², the official Argentine Agricultural Strategic Plan 2010–2020, is a clear example of the discursive elements used to highlight the thought style that soy production should be increased (through technological innovation) in order to provide food. Presenting the unique capabilities of Argentina as the global provider of food, the country is listed as 'first-ranked worldwide exporter of honey, concentrated lemon juice, peanut oil, soy oil, and soy meal' (Ministerio de Agricultura, Ganadería y Pesca 2011, p. 52; my translation). However, as Leguizamón clearly states, this 'narrative ... hits the wall when faced with the fact that GM soy in Argentina is produced not for human consumption but ... entirely for export, as livestock feedstuff' and continues that 'Argentina, historically the Breadbasket of the World and still today a net-crop exporter, has lost its food sovereignty' (Leguizamón 2014, pp. 156–157).

The right dosage of glyphosate is not harmful

Skill and Grinberg (2013, pp. 96–98), in their chapter on risk production related to GM crops, identify a pragmatic position of the dominant actors related to soy issues. The quintessence can be summarised as the use of glyphosate is not harmful to humans or the environment if applied in the right dosage. The main driving actors behind this thought style are identified as some public organisms, large transnational companies and NGOs related to the industry. The ultimate facilitator is then the public body in the form of the SENASA, issuing permits for agrochemicals to be introduced. An interesting approach here is that taken by CONICET (National Commission of Scientific and Technical Research), which states: 'in Argentina no sufficient data about the effects of glyphosate on human health exist, therefore it is important to promote the realisation of such studies' (CONICET 2009, p. 132, my translation). Considering the fact that this statement is made by the CONICET, a public scientific entity, the pragmatic (if not to say uncritical) approach to the biotechnological development is remarkable. In this train of thought, Skill and Grinberg (2013, pp. 101–103) talk about the ambivalent position held by some scientists, doctors or social NGOs. Particularly interesting in this context is the fact that this group talks about '*agrotóxicos*' ('agrotoxics') rather than '*agroquímicos*' ('agrochemicals'), reflecting their negative stance towards biochemical substances in agribusiness (ibid., p. 103).

Soy is the source of Argentinian well-being

Particularly in the thought style of capitalist producers, as Naharro *et al.* (2010, p. 145) put it, the land for soy is used as a resource, valued for its productivity potential. The concept of 'region' then is considered a symbol of success, development and well-being. This also holds true for the general thought style held by the rural worker and *campesino*: the one who works the land should possess it (Naharro *et al.* 2010, p. 146).

After the lock-out in 2009 (explained below), President Kirchner signed a decree to establish the *Fondo Solidario de Soja* (Solidary Soy Fund) (Ministerio de Economía y Finanzas Públicas 2009) to research the direct effect soy production had on the whole of society. The purpose of the fund is to distribute the income from soy export taxation from the federal level to the provinces and town governments (i.e. 'co-participation'; Leguizamón 2014, p. 158). This measure has also led to high local dependencies on this new form of income, manifested in the high percentage of soy-related financial means of particular local budgets (in the form of social infrastructure investment, subsidies for social programmes, etc.). In the words of Leguizamón:

> [S]oy revenue is used to pave dirt roads, bring clean water, build sewers, and to maintain or renovate the main plaza, schools, and hospitals; as well as to directly sustain a part of the population, by handing out monthly payments – as part of cash transfer programs – or new homes – as part of housing projects (programas de vivienda social).
>
> (Ibid., p. 158)

The temporal context

Influenced by the thematic context, this chapter focuses on the five phases of soy cultivation in Argentina. The result is a timeline of soy production in Argentina with indications of the changing thought styles of soy agribusiness actors:

1   Experimental phase.
2   Phase of consolidation of research and technical studies.
3   The INDO phase: bringing together technical and entrepreneurial expertise.
4   Phase of entry into the world market.
5   Phase of political-economic conflict: devaluation and *retenciones*.

Experimental phase

Soy cultivation is not a new business in Argentina. Even though Brazil was the first country in Latin America to cultivate this legume in 1882 at the Agricultural School of Bahía (D'Utra 1882), followed by French Guyana (1893), Guyana (1905) and Suriname (1905), initial experiments in Argentina had already been undertaken at the Córdoba Experimental Station in 1908 (Shurtleff and Aoyagi 2009, p. 7). Tonnelier (1912) pointed out that the experiments with soy have proved to be successful due to its high-level acclimatisation; he concluded that positive effects of the legume are expected not only for farmers or landowners, but would go as far as large-scale industrial benefits. Experiments on the crop continue without major growth until 1924, when the Ministry of Agriculture starts distributing – free of charge – 15 tonnes of 15 varieties of soybeans from the US seed company T. Wood and Sons (of Richmond, Virginia) to agricultural schools, experimental stations and 8,000 farmers willing to participate in trials (Faura 1933, p. 10). That year is a milestone in Argentine soy production, since it is the first time that soy was cultivated outside experimental facilities. Over the next decade, the seed distribution spread over the country and large quantities of data on varieties adopted in different regions could be drawn upon. Faura (1933) then pinpoints that 1932 marks another stepping stone towards the third sub-phase of soy cultivation. In the province of Córdoba, the oil mill Río Segundo – with the landowner Adolof Coscia in particular – conducted further promotion to regional 'colonisers' (Martínez Dougnac 2013, p. 4) of the legume for the production of edible oil with the – self-proclaimed – success of having 6,000 hectares of soy outsourced to be produced in Córdoba, Santa Fe and the province of Buenos Aires. While this initial attempt of Río Segundo proved to be a failure at first, this project still reached the amount of 1,500 tonnes of processed soy targeted at the internal oil market for human consumption. In the end, the project was abandoned in the 1940s due to the inability of soy to combat weeds and pests and the subsequent increase in manual labour.

The 1930s were marked by the financial crisis, and the looming Second World War offered new potential for the production of soy and its derivatives. Until then, traditionally, the demand for comestible oil had been met by importing olive oil from Spain or Italy; but due to ever more complicated international trade, the Argentine internal market was considered to have major theoretical growth potential. Underlying this statement, during the season of 1941/1942, soy became a relevant commodity as it was officially decided to statistically survey its cultivation and production on a five-year basis until 1960.

However, during the 1940s, the soy market did not take off, since it was considered 'absurd' to replace commodities like sunflower seeds or peanuts with soy, since soy was thought to have lower levels of oil content. The focus on the vegetable oil obtained from soy as the only form of commercial soy product rather than protein meal persisted until the early 1960s (Freire de Sousa *et al.* 2008, p. 235). The only market possible for soy would be external, i.e. Europe, which had high discrepancies between supply and demand (Martínez Dougnac 2013, p. 6). The 1950s did not bring major changes to the way soy was produced. The agricultural engineer, Ramón Agrasar, one of the great drivers for the soy expansion, sums up his frustration at the Argentine situation by saying 'here … it continued to be a curiosity' (my translation, based on Reca 2010b, p. 18).

Another failed project, this time in the mid-1950s, is Agrosoja SRL, set up to spread soy cultivation in the Province of Santa Fe. The founder, Ramón Agrasar (at one time, general manager of the seed company Dekalb in Argentina, now part of the Monsanto Company), was still positively seen as a utopian dreamer, considering soy the solution to world hunger. They established a laboratory with products mainly deriving from the USA and gained the support of the Dirección de Investigaciones Agrícolas (now INTA). Even though the laboratory generated vital information on the crop in different areas of Argentina, the project failed for five reasons (Reca 2010b, p. 19; SAB11): (1) There was no internal market for soy products; the oil industry in particular lacked any interest in soy. (2) The external market was difficult to penetrate due to the lack of Argentinian gatekeepers to open the door to the European market. Internationally, in addition, major competition came from Asia in general and Manchuria in particular (Martínez Dougnac 2013, p. 6). (3) The problem of weed control had not yet been successfully solved, significantly increasing the production costs . (4) The Ministry of Agriculture was too slow to see the potential of soy production which had already been observed in the USA (Reca 2010b, p. 19). And, finally, (5) Agrosoja SRL exported soy as a primary good 'like beans', i.e. as raw material without refinement, creating high opportunity costs (SAB11).

This era is defined by individual and isolated projects related to soy investigation. An interesting detail here is that the centres are located in the provinces of Santa Fe, Córdoba and relatively remotely in Misiones in the north-east of the country. The latter province benefitted from Japanese colonists bringing their own soy seeds and using soy to support subsistence farming (Hougen 1957). The statistical data on soy production, discussed above, have so far predominantly taken into account the production in Misiones and filed them under the category of 'industrial crop'. Nevertheless, the core area for development was considered to be Santa Fe and the adjacent provinces as well as western Chaco.

Summing up, the multiplicity of factors influencing soy production can be summarised as, even though the political framework starts to support the cultivation of this legume, at a macro-level, this trend has not yet been fully accepted. This aspect is particularly relevant for external marketing strategies and the facilitation of the market entry on a global scale. Another issue here is the internal market, where even though the supply was increasing, the demand had not yet caught up. And, finally, human-environmental aspects on a predominantly technical basis were not developed enough to foster the Argentine soy economy.

Phase of consolidation of research and technical studies

In this phase, programmes of technical exchange and training with and in the USA, as well as farm monitoring in Argentina are mentioned (Hougen 1957). In parallel to on-site training – however, it is unclear whether cooperation was carried out or not – an agrometeorological study shows the potential for soy cultivation in Argentina. This project carried out at the Agronomic Faculty of the University of Buenos Aires sparks increasing interest, since different varieties of soy plants are tested for their reaction in different areas of Argentina to determine their specific agro-climatic aptitudes (Pascale 1969; Remussi and Pascale 1977; see Reca 2010b, p. 19).

Economically, 1962 marks a milestone with the first exports of Argentine soy: 6,000 tonnes are exported to Hamburg (Martínez Dougnac 2013, p. 8).[1] This event, preceded by a tenfold increase in Argentine soy production, leads Coscia to identify the second stage of soy production (Coscia 1972, p. 7). This growing interest is also highlighted in the 1964 foundation of the *Red Nacional de Soja* (i.e. the National Soy Network) comprising various official institutions such as the agronomic faculties of national universities, INTA, as well as stakeholders from the breeding as well as the seeds industry. The main aim is to instigate a plan of further investigation and field-testing of soy crops. One of the most interesting details about this soy network is the predominant focus on technical issues rather than economic ones. The potential is seen, but the support and creation of demand are still ignored most of the time.

One particularly interesting piece of information is that the regions outside of the Pampas region (especially Tucumán and Misiones) are strongly represented in the development of soy. Farmers in Misiones in particular are early adopters as they see the risk diversification of traditional products like yerba mate and tea (Reca 2010b, p. 10) The production itself occurs on very small entities and rarely includes the mechanisation of work. Additionally, the actors involved in soy cultivation are characterised by their physical and mental proximity to the soil.

The INDO phase: bringing together technical and entrepreneurial expertise

So far, the cultivation of soy has been dominated by technicians, researchers and individual enthusiasts/utopians. The technical groundwork on the supply side has been completed. However, as the previous examples have shown, the aspect of commercialisation and customer relations has been – for the most part – ignored. One emblematic example of the parallel-isolated thought styles and the thought style expansion/combination is the remodelling of the vegetable oil company INDO, located in Puerto San Martín, in the province of Santa Fe. INDO had been refining traditional products such as flax, peanuts, or sunflower seeds. In the bleak economic downturn, in 1968 the company was bought over by La Plata Cereal SA, then a subsidiary company of the Switzerland-based André Company, one of the big five cereal companies worldwide at that time.

This scenario in Box 5.1 clearly shows the gap between the technical and entrepreneurial thought styles in relation to soy production. INDO, without a doubt one of the major players at that time, is taken as an example of the dynamics in the 1970s to understand the thought style expansions towards new business ventures.

Additionally, on a global scale, US president Richard Nixon's decision to restrict soy exports from the USA in 1973 led to the global decrease in supply, allowing Latin American countries (and Brazil in particular, due to new co-operation agreements with Japan and the Japanese Long Term Credit Bank) to increase their market share (Freire de Sousa *et al.* 2008, p. 236). The effects for Argentina are especially observed in the following phase.

Phase of entry into the world market

> When the saturation of the internal market was reached, right at that time the sky opened towards the world.
>
> (José Luis Porzio, SAB11; my translation)

The next milestone for soy production is coupled with macroeconomic and political changes. With the overthrow of Isabel Perón in the 1976 *coup d'état* and the installation of the military junta, a new economic ideology, headed by the economic minister José Alfredo Martínez de Hoz (1976–81), was introduced: '*Programa de recuperación, saneamiento y expansión de la economía argentina*' [Programme of recuperation, stabilisation and expansion of the Argentine economy]. The cornerstones affecting soy production are the liberalisation of fixed prices, the devaluation of the Argentinian peso in relation to the US$ in order to eliminate the currency exchange black market.[2] The main underlying rationale is based on the assumption that agriculture and mining are the backbones of the Argentinean economy and thus have to be liberated from export taxation and currency restrictions.

Box 5.1 Oral business history: the connection of agro-knowledge and the business mind

One of the key actors in the merger of thought styles is José Luis Porzio (SAB11), a public accountant working at La Plata Cereal SA. Having bought INDO, Porzio was put in charge as the general manager of the newly acquired vegetable oil plant. Having studied the financial situation of the plant, Porzio arranged a meeting with the head of La Plata Cereal SA and claimed: 'I need money' – but the reply was: 'No, no, there is no money. Fix it yourself!'

At that time, as Porzio tells it, he had – together with three colleagues from La Plata Cereal SA – invested in 575 hectares of arable land in General San Martín, approximately 150 km north-west of Resistencia, in the Chaco Province. An agrarian engineer compiled a report on the land and, says Porzio, 'He writes things that are incomprehensible to me as an accountant.' In an interview in 2014, Porzio recalls what happened next (my translation):

ENGINEER: The land has a good suitability for agriculture, to rotate legumes.
SAB11: What are legumes?
ENGINEER: Soy.
SAB11: What is soy?
ENGINEER: Caupí. ['Only the old engineers knew what Caupí was'; SAB11.]
SAB11: Where is soy being sown?
ENGINEER: It is sown a lot in the USA.
SAB11: And where else?
ENGINEER: In Brazil.
SAB11: And where else, in Argentina?
ENGINEER: No, very little.

Not wanting to believe that soy is produced in countries like the USA and Brazil but not in Argentina, Porzio looks for reasons and inquires at La Plata Cereal SA, and the common result is distilled in the phrase: 'You don't mess with soy – soy does not work in Argentina.' The main reasoning behind this statement is that an affiliate had tried to cultivate soy in Montevideo, in Uruguay, but had failed dramatically.

Porzio, however, continues investigating and concludes that once refined, soy has two major sub-products: (1) oil for human consumption; and (2) the remainder of the oil production. At that time there is no market for the latter, since nobody in Argentina knows what to use it for; exports are not considered due to unfavourable Argentinian peso–US$ exchange rates (particularly due to the difference between the official and the black market US$ rates) as well as high *retenciones* (i.e. taxes on goods exported).

In conclusion, soy production at that time could only be economically successful if it could cater for the national market, provided a demand is created. Context becomes key for the thought style expansion. At the end of the 1960s, a new branch is growing: the production of concentrated feed. Two main companies divide the market share: Cargill and Ganave. The latter company uses fish meal from Peru as a source of proteins. However, due to over-fishing,

> as well as later the effects of bad weather from El Niño in 1972, making the fish disappear, and considering the currency issues mentioned above, Ganave was looking for fish meal substitutes and found a partner in INDO, who had just started promoting soy derivatives as part of concentrated feed. At a later stage, Cargill would follow Ganave by using soy as an ingredient for concentrated feed, strengthening the position of INDO.

Additionally, new machinery can be imported, leading to increased foreign direct investment and growth in the soy economy (Martínez Dougnac 2013, p. 14; SAB11).

Phase of technical innovation

The 1990s mark significant changes in Argentina. After a major economic crisis in 1989, structural reforms and trade liberalisation, alongside massive privatisation processes were established. Argentina becomes the '"poster child" for the implementation of the so-called Washington Consensus' (Chudnovski 2007, p. 85, see Hafner *et al.* 2016) In this vein, the organisational structure of the soy agribusiness sector becomes more dynamic. One game-changing factor is observed: the introduction and legalisation of GM crops. This step is an intrinsic part of what the Biomass Research and Development Board has called the 'bioeconomy', a revolutionary way to return to sustainability through new forms of economic development (Biomass Research and Development Board 2001; Pavone 2012, p. 4). The current use of this term is coined by the OECD, defined as 'the aggregate set of economic operations in a society that use the latent value incumbent in biological products and processes to capture new growth and welfare benefits for citizens and nations' (OECD 2009). These definitions already reflect the global master narrative of the connection between biotechnology and society (Latour 2003).

In relation to soy production, this type of genetic engineering, particularly a higher tolerance of herbicides, permits better economic performance. Argentina is the second country in the world, after the USA, to legalise those crops and holds the record for the world's fastest adoption of GM soy.[3] Particularly in Argentina, neoliberalism and the introduction of the GM crop go hand in hand (Otero 2008). I agree with other studies that this 'success story' has a lot to do with context (Glover 2010; Schnurr 2012; Leguizamón 2014) as the reasons for this development are based on a variety of factors:

* The general notion of agricultural innovation in Argentina in the 1990s is marked by a positive image. Opposition to GMOs is considered weak, also due to Argentina's traditional dependence on agriculture, low participation of consumers' associations and the high level of GMO promotion by scientists, the public, producers and the media (Delvenne *et al.*

2013, p. 156). During the presidency of Carlos Menem, five GM seeds were approved.

• Non-tillage farming is almost simultaneously introduced with GM soy, having a greater positive impact on system changes.

• The patent for the broadband herbicide glyphosate runs out in 1991. This fact is particularly important in the Latin American context: The price of one litre of glyphosate was about US$40 in the 1980s in Argentina and thus significantly higher than in countries like the USA (Albin and Paz 2000). Due to the patent-free situation, the number of glyphosate-producing companies rose to 14 in 1996 and to 22 in 2001, leading to price drops to US$10 and US$3 respectively (Delvenne *et al.* 2013, p. 156).

• Non-patenting of the new technology. The Argentine system of protection of intellectual property rights is weak (Pengue 2005; Qaim and Traxler 2005; Teubal 2006; Chudnovski 2007). Monsanto is best known for its core product Roundup Ready (RR), a broadband herbicide including the above-mentioned glyphosate. At first, it is surprising that RR has not been patented. This is due to some particular factors and relationships before the official legalisation of GM crops in Argentina. At the beginning of the 1990s, Asgrow International, belonging to UpJohn, signed an agreement with Monsanto to be able to incorporate the glyphosate-tolerant gene in their soy product. UpJohn's Latin American subsidiaries of Asgrow International were sold shortly after; the multinational Nidera bought the Argentine branch and asked for regulatory approval of the introduction of RR soy in Argentina, since it then had access to all the technological innovations of Asgrow International. When Monsanto tried to patent RR-tolerant soy in Argentina, the product had already been 'liberated' (Delvenne *et al.* 2013, p. 156) Additionally, due to the fact that Argentina follows the 1978 edition of the International Union for the Protection of New Varieties of Plants (UPOV), this allowed farmers to save seeds for personal re-use, registering a spike in black market sales of the so-called *bolsa blanca* soybean seed. By 2009, it is estimated that those seeds made up to between 70 and more than 80 per cent of the overall production. Thus, the 1990s are particularly relevant for the investment in technological innovation, since the ARS–US$ parity (i.e. artificial overvaluation of the ARS) allowed the cheap import of new machinery and an update in modes of production (Newell 2009, p. 45).

Nowadays, as Delvenne *et al.* (2013, p. 154) highlight, GM crops 'have turned into a central axis of the national economy'. Soy is particularly relevant for export, since almost all of the crop production is sold to foreign customers. Here, we note that soy is technically not a mere commodity (even though this is the common impression); value is added in the form of processing (e.g. crushing, extraction of oil, etc.) before its export (Delvenne *et al.* 2013, p. 155). Thus. by 1997, Argentina's local seed market is worth over

US$850 million (and soy is the most important element in this market), has become one of the largest worldwide and the second largest in Latin America (Chudnovski 2007, pp. 89–90).

Phase of political-economic conflict: devaluation and retenciones

The Argentine financial crisis in 2001 left a major mark on the economic and social landscape of Argentina; the era of Carlos Menem's openly neoliberal ideology comes to a halt. For the soy agribusiness, two important changes are observed:

- *Devaluation of the ARS:* Viewed from a macroeconomic perspective, the devaluation of the national currency has the advantage that the products exported (i.e. soy and its derivatives) become cheaper. Continuing this train of thought, the post-2001 situation presents a perfect situation for the farmers: contracts are predominantly in US$, while employees are paid in ARS. Additionally, the greatest investments have already been made in the 1990s when the currency rates were still lucrative.
- *(Re-)introduction of the retenciones:* Export taxation is not a new item in Argentina; there were export taxes at the end of the nineteenth century as well as starting in 1955 with the Decreto 2002/1955 (see Colomé 2008, p. 125), implementing *retenciones* of 20 per cent on the agricultural production to be exported (Reca 2010a, p. 438). During the second half of 1989, at the beginning of the first presidency of Carlos Menem, a rapid process of the elimination of the *retenciones* was started; the 1990s are known as the longest period in the second half of the twentieth century without any or with very low export taxation. Even though the agricultural sector has never approved of the *retenciones* as a form of just and adequate taxation, the greatest frictions with the government occur during the presidencies of Néstor Kirchner and Cristina Fernández de Kirchner (2002–2015), culminating in the *lock-out*, initiated by the Sociedad Rural Argentina [Argentinian Rural Society], CONINAGRO (Confederación Intercooperativa Agropecuaria Limitada), Confederaciones Rurales Argentinas [the Argentinian Rural Confederations], as well as the Federación Agraria Argentina [the Argentinian Agrarian Federation]. The driving force for the large-scale strike in the agrarian sector was the Resolution 125/2008 (Ministerio de Economía y Producción 2008), proposing a flexibilisation of the *retenciones*. Table 5.1 gives an overview of the evolution of the *retenciones* in the last 20 years.

Even though the official political discourse of the Kirchner presidencies was full of conflict and predominantly against large-scale farmers, it is interesting to observe that during Cristina Fernández de Kirchner' tenure, the highest number of GM soy seeds (24) were approved for cultivation, totalling 35 varieties suitable for production in Argentina (Longoni 2016).

Table 5.1 Retenciones for soy and its derivatives based on FOB prices (%)

	Period				
	Pre-Kirchner	Kirchner			Post-Kirchner
	1993–2001	2002–2007	1/2007–11/2007	11/2007–12/2015	12/2015–
Soy	4	24	28	35	30
Soy oil	–	20	24	32	27
Soy meal	–	20	24	32	27

Source: Author's calculations based on Reca (2010a, p. 440) and Ministerio de Agroindustria (2015).

Panopticon perspective: the Argentinian soy industry

Figure 5.1 highlights and contextualises the five stages of the development of the soy agribusiness in Argentina. The aim here is to present the core characteristics of the agribusiness thought style combined with the effects of changing ways of thinking represented by the five different phases. Consequently, Figure 5.1 presents four panopticon-esque statements of the soy expansion:

- *The global demand* for soy is constantly increasing, so is the Argentinian supply. The latter is achieved through an improvement in yields per hectare (cf. the opening gap between cultivation and production in Figure 5.1), as well as significant spatial expansions of soy fields and the opening up of new frontiers.
- *The role of actors*: The role of economic actors increases from non-representation to the dominant factor in soy production. Here, capital centralisation, concentration as well as transnationalisation occur. This holds particularly true for the Pampas region, the heart of production. Actors and their thought styles play a fundamental role here. From the soy industry's perspective, three main types of actors are relevant: the technical, the economic and the political. The first are the foundation for crop production and innovation, i.e. the executive branch implementing the demands from the – second – economic actors to be able to produce commodities that satisfy the needs of (potential) customers. The – third – political actors have different roles to fulfil: Particularly at the beginning of soy expansion, the political side acts as an enabler, creating and (partially) financing platforms for research and development at the beginning and then opening up the national market to the international business stage. Another prominent feature here is labelled 'actors' interest in soy production', visualising the stages upon which soy and soy-related issues are on the agenda of the respective actors. Generally speaking, (besides the last period of conflict), whenever soy is on the agenda, a positive connotation by the actors is observed.

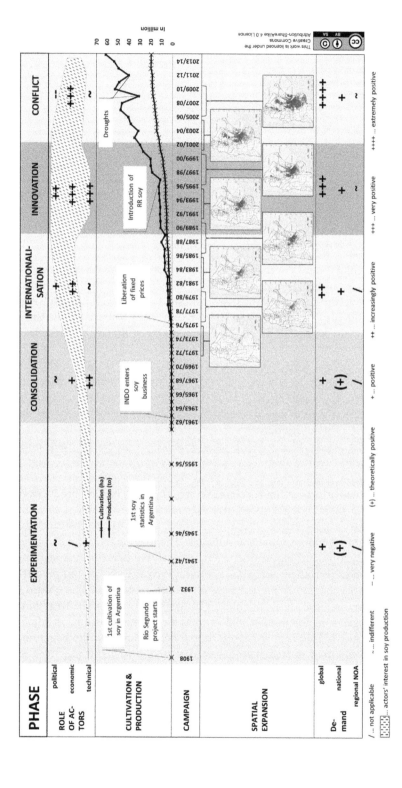

Figure 5.1 Overview of the phases of soy expansion, supply and demand from the perspective of soy agribusiness.

Source: Hafner (2016), based on: Bolsa de Cereales; Ministerio de Agricultura y Ganadería; Martínez Dougnac (2013, p. 9); SIIA (2016), PROATLAS (2016).

- Major production losses are predominantly due to weather conditions, particularly droughts. This holds especially true for the harvesting season of 2008–2009 and 2011–2012. Despite major financial losses, representatives of the agribusiness confirm that they are 'part of the game' (SAB11) and have to be accounted for.
- Of more concern for the agribusiness, however, is considered the role and unpredictability of the Kirchner governments. However, the conflictive role of the national governments is over-estimated. It has been shown that the national governments acted as facilitators during the early phases of soy production. Even though the liberation of the fixed prices during the internationalisation phase or the abolishment of the *retenciones* in the 1990s are significant factors in the development of soy, the major driver for soy expansion has to be seen as based on the world demand. Major potentials for conflict arise particularly during the Néstor and Cristina Fernández de Kirchner governments. Despite the strong discursive friction, the governments have always followed an action-oriented pragmatism (Hafner *et al.* 2016), allowing the soy industry to thrive and capturing parts of the sector's revenues (in the form of *retenciones*) to finance the 60+ social subsidy plans in Argentina.

Spatial context

Agriculture is intrinsically linked to physical space. Argentina is no exception here. As already seen in Chapter 3, the spatial expansion of agriculture is connected to physical space, i.e. the longer soy production is carried out in Argentina, the further it has spread to the peripheral areas, creating new frontiers of cultivation. This will be the main focus to follow.

Agriculture has always played a vital role in Argentina. Traditionally, two main categories were established: the Pampas Region (i.e. in the provinces of Santa Fe, Córdoba, Entre Ríos, La Pampa or Buenos Aires) is the core agricultural production region. It focuses on the production of grain and meat and has a long-standing tradition of doing so. Due to the proximity to waterways, naval transport and export of those commodities are relatively easy to manage. The transformation of the previous grassland to productive land had already started in the first half of the sixteenth century by European settlers (Báez 1944; Baldi *et al.* 2006, p. 197). The second category deals with the regions outside the Pampas. Here, the products is a much more varied, perennial cultivation traditionally targeted at the national market. Examples of such are the yerba mate in the north-east, wool in Patagonia, vines and olives in the Cuyo (the provinces of Mendoza and San Juan), rice in Mesopotamia (Corrientes and Entre Ríos), as well as sugar cane in the north-west of Argentina (Parellada 2010, p. 83).

The last three decades have seen huge increases in the cultivation of agricultural products in the Extra-Pampean Regions. One talks about the 'Pampeanisation', a term used to describe the 'tendency to introduce agro-industrial crops such as soy in other provinces than the ones usually corresponding to such activities, for instance, in the north of the country (like the province of Salta)' (Delvenne *et al.* 2013, p. 159). Parellada (2010, p. 83) gives three reasons responsible for those frontier expansions:

1   *Technological innovation*, put forward by both the private and the public sector.
2   *Macroeconomic politics*: During the 1990s, generally marked by neoliberal trends, price levels stabilised, the economy opened internationally and the state was reduced to its basic functions. This led to the increase in capital and access to materials and supplies with high productive potential. There was parity between the ARS and the US$ and thus the overvalued Argentine currency had not yet had a high negative influence on the Argentinian export of cereals and legumes. Starting in 1998 until 2000, the aforementioned negative effects entered, particularly due to the mix of the increasing over-valuation of the ARS and a drop in international prices. Starting in December 2001, the under-valuation of the currency had the opposite effect, leading to competitive advantages of Argentinian agrarian products.
3   *Opening of the Argentine economy to the international market*: This issue has two opposing effects; on the one hand, high foreign capital investments were made in specific fields of business, such as viticulture; on the other hand, other production branches, such as nuts from La Rioja or cotton from Santiago del Estero and the Chaco suffered greatly from international competition.

Goldfarb and Zoomers (2013, p. 78) identify another reason for the expansion particularly relevant for soy production:

4   *Availability of land*: Until the 1990s, and particularly at the beginning of the 1990s, interest in farming had decreased, leaving significant areas of non- or under-used *haciendas*. This phenomenon goes hand in hand with the Washington Consensus and the loss of interest is additionally highlighted by the dissolution (Ministerio de Economía y Producción 1991) of the *Junta Nacional de Granos* [National Grain Board]. Hence, during the appearance of non-tillage farming and GM soy, land (even in the Pampas region) was readily available for (also extra-sectoral) financial investment.

The so-called *pooles de siembra* (sowing pools) are a direct reason for this development. Those pools include

> family-owned firms and corporations in diverse contractual agreements with various levels of integration throughout the supply chain.... [They] are innovative arrangements to combine land, capital and human

resources ... [including] leasing or providing property in trust, contracting machines and services, using technology packages based on modern machinery, heavy utilising biotechnology or agrochemicals and incorporating digital systems and individuals who specialise in field selection, production, management and marketing.

(Murmis and Murmis 2012, p. 491)

Unlike the popular belief, '[l]arge-scale farming is not a necessary characteristic' of *pooles de siembra* (ibid., p. 492). This has been observed particularly in the Chaco Salteño, where small-scale and medium-scale farmers build cooperations to outsource and/or provide services to other actors in the field (SAB12).

Soy expansion to the North-west

According to Viglizzo *et al.* (2011, p. 12), there are two core regions of production (both in the Pampas) and four advancing soy frontiers in Argentina (Figure 5.2): the northernmost frontier 1 in the Umbral al Chaco covering parts of Tucumán, north-western Santiago del Estero, western Chaco and the Salta lowlands; frontier 2, advancing in the south-east of Santiago del Estero, northern Santa Fe and south-western Chaco; frontier 3, spanning over the north of Córdoba and central Santa Fe; and frontier 4 in Entre Ríos, which is relatively close to the core of production around the major soy ports in Rosario (Jasanoff 2006; Paolasso and Krapovickas 2013).

Figure 5.2 visually underpins the previous argument that due to increased soy production, the area of soy expansion goes beyond the Pampean core, where the soy fronts are either static or as in the case of frontier 6, retreating. Furthermore, the areas for frontier potentials are predominantly located in the Gran Argentine Chao area, particularly in the ecoregion of the Chaco *semiárido* (half-dry Chaco). Both frontiers 1, 2, as well as 3, show expansion directions towards the core of this region since it is the most suitable area for soy production besides the Pampas.

It goes without saying that the greatest soy expansion has occurred in the Pampas region. Significant changes in the surfaces used for soy production can be seen from the 1990s onwards in the extra-Pampean regions ('"soyization" of the Pampas'; Goldfarb and Zoomers 2013, p. 80), whereby the greatest growth rates are observed in the North-west ('"agriculturalization"[4] of the Chaco Region'; Goldfarb and Zoomers 2013, p. 80).[5] Goldfarb and Zoomers (ibid., p. 78) argue that by the end of the 1990s, the shift of investment patterns from the Pampas region to the NOA is due to the increased demand manifested by international soy prices and the saturation of the core area.

In NOA, Santiago del Estero is clearly the province with the highest number of areas under soy cultivation. However, one has to take into account, that this province hosts two advancing frontiers, one in the north-west and the other one in the central to eastern part.

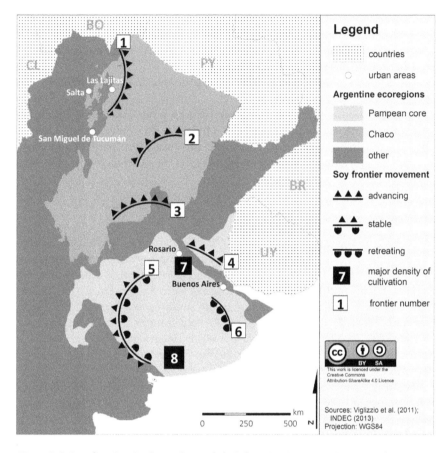

Figure 5.2 Soy frontiers in Argentina and their location in respective ecoregions.
Source: Hafner (2016).

The greatest dynamics, as observed, are now in the Salta province. More precisely, all soy cultivation takes place in the so-called Chaco Salteño. This analysis also correlates with the general notion of Salta being the most affected province of this frontier, implying the highest levels of conflict. This is one of the reasons for the choice of the case studies in this region. Further reasons are presented in Chapter 5.

Five factors for the increased interest in the soy agribusiness in the Chaco Salteño

This book is based on the assumption that social-ecological change is occurring in the research area. In this sense, land use change is a central characteristic and selection criterion. Five factors influencing land use change are identified (Geist *et al.* 2006; Verburg *et al.* 2006; Volante and Gavier-Pizarro 2016, p. 154; particularly for South America, see Kirby *et al.* 2006; Müller *et al.* 2011, p. 11): (1) biophysical aspects: such as slope, elevation, soil composition and drainage conditions, climate; (2) technological factors: machinery applied, type of seeds, organisation; (3) economic features: supply and demand, pricing, access to resources and infrastructure; taxation and subsidies; (4) socio-cultural factors: demographic features, migration patterns, lifestyle, path dependencies; and (5) political actions: related to infrastructure and defence as well as natural conservation.

Biophysical aspects

The Chaco Salteño lies completely within the semi-arid Chaco ecoregion (Cabrera 1976), with a rainy season in summer (November to March) and a dry winter (Bravo 2010; Amdan *et al.* 2013, p. 2). Precipitation is a central feature for agriculture; even though the overall rainfall is significantly lower in the Chaco Salteño compared to the Pampas region, it is considered enough for soy cultivation. Due to the relatively young agricultural frontier and 'virgin' soils, nutritional values are considered still very high; soil degradation is not a problem (yet) (SAB2).

Depending on the understanding and classification of 'biophysical change', one or two major factors are identified: deforestation and change in precipitation. While the former represents a clear anthropogenic activity, the correlation and causality of anthropogenic influences on the latter are disputed. Taking the perspective from agro-actors in the region, the most mentioned feature is the change in precipitation:

Crop production depends on climatic conditions. It goes without saying that changes in those conditions (e.g. increased temperatures, changing CO_2 concentration or changing precipitation levels) have a direct influence on the agricultural outcome (Rosenzweig and Parry 1994; Magrin *et al.* 2005; p. 230). NOA has particularly benefitted from such climatic changes (Murgida *et al.* 2014, p. 1387), or as Paolasso *et al.* (2010, p. 3) term it, had a 'positive climate jump'.

The department of Anta (the centre of the Chaco Salteño), having a 'semi-arid climate with just enough moisture for agriculture', shows an increase in rainfall, which also contributes to the regional transformation from '"marginal" areas into an "agricultural frontier" that competes with the more humid Pampas to the southeast' (Murgida *et al.* 2014, p. 1387). Precipitation trends in the Chaco show an increase, as several studies have confirmed (Liebmann *et al.* 2004; Barros *et al.* 2008; González *et al.* 2011). This feature is presented in Figure 5.3. Here, Volante *et al.* (2015), studying the period from 2000/2001–2010/2011, come to the same conclusion that precipitation is increasing in the research area. It is shown that in the core areas of production an increase in rainfall is observed by 2–3 mm/year, particularly favouring soy production.

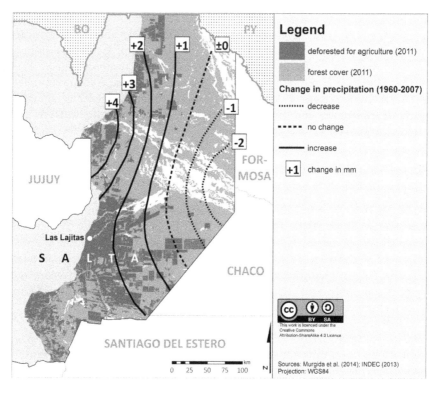

Figure 5.3 Change in precipitation in the Chaco Salteño 1960–2007.
Source: Hafner (2016).

Those increases in precipitation are not on a major scale. However, Murgida *et al.* (2014, p. 1392) argue, based on results from Lee and Berbery (2012), Collini *et al.* (2008), and Lee (2010), negative effects of deforestation and agricultural expansion are likely to lead to a decrease in precipitation. This in turn makes the region less susceptible for agribusiness activity (unless changes in crop properties suited to less rainfall are successfully implemented). The last argument in particular highlights the non-linearity of correlation and causality of environmental change.

Technological factors

Much like in the Pampas Region, soy production in the Chaco Salteño was very influenced by technological changes in the 1990s. Non-tillage farming as well as the introduction of GM crops have facilitated land use change. Two major forms of soy production area expansion are observed: deforestation or land use change of already cleared land (Slutzky 2007). As a result, when zooming into the Chaco Salteño, three main hubs of soy expansion are identified:

1 *Southern Chaco Salteño (Rosario de la Frontera and Metán):* The southern-most departments of Salta have a – for the region – highly developed agricultural tradition and a great variety of crops are cultivated there. This region has traditionally been the area with most cultivated land until the end of the 1980s. Land use change is originally based on the rotation of the crops cultivated; this is also reflected in the reduced variety; the latest statistics show that only five different cultures are grown.

2 *Central Chaco Salteño (Anta):* This is the current nucleus of production and accounts for major land use changes, particularly due to deforestation. The steepest increase in number of arable hectares is observed by the beginning of the millennium, almost coinciding with the decoupling of the ARS from the US$ and subsequent drop in the land prices for international investors. The department of Anta can be further subcategorised into four zones (van Dam 2003, p. 142):

   (a) The soy nucleus of modern agriculture around the town of Las Lajitas: van Dam describes it as 'the agrarian area *par excellence*' (2003, p. 142; my translation and emphasis).
   (b) The area around the town of Apolinario Sarávia: The main characteristic of this production region is the high number of small-scale horticultures predominantly run by Bolivians.
   (c) Joaquín V. González and its surroundings around the River Río Juramento is known for low levels of precipitation and a mix of small-scale and medium-scale farmers (often of Spanish descent), as well as large companies such as LIAG or Agropecuaria Río Juramento.
   (d) The last area is the eastern part of Anta, the driest area, most prone to deforestation but still important for extensive cattle farming and forest exploitation.

3 *Northern Chaco Salteño:* Rivadavia, San Martín and Orán experience similar trends observed in Anta in relation to the increase in cultivated land, which are the youngest parts of the frontier and experience high level of irregularities. This is partially due to the high density of the indigenous population and unresolved land tenure issues, incurring the effect of activist resistance (Venencia *et al.* 2012). To summarise, this region is also considered to experience the most pronounced changes, in terms of advancement of the agricultural frontier, but also due to the replacement of traditional products like cotton (Paolasso *et al.* 2010, p. 4).

Economic aspects

The region benefits from the increasing global demand for soy and soy derivatives; soy expansion in the Chaco Salteño is clearly an extra-regional and demand-driven operation. Economically speaking, the region offers low land prices, 'availability of land' either for lease or purchase (including long-term contracts for official land at very low cost) ranging from already prepared areas or yet to be deforested lots.

The economic prospects of the research area can be imagined and sold by many international brokers and consultancies. One prominent example is a publication by Knight Frank, a worldwide operating consultancy with a focus on residential as well as commercial property markets around the globe. The Knight Frank international farmland index 2011 (Knight Frank 2011, p. 37) shows the valuation of the northern provinces of Argentina as a positive investment. Land prices are clearly depicted lower than in the Pampas region, while land prices have increased by 10 per cent from 2010 to 2011 – a clear indicator of increasing demand for land. Additionally, while economic and political land value risks are considered (predominantly due to the then Kirchner government and their unpredictability of action related to economic activities), climatic issues are not considered a threat to investment in land (Hafner and Rainer 2017).

Socio-cultural factors

This category is closely connected to economic activities carried out in the region. Stepping back and applying an environmental historical perspective, van Dam (2003, p. 138) distinguishes four periods of development:

- *'Ganaderización' of the Chaco*: This period, also called the 'occupation phase', starts in the eighteenth century and lays the foundation for large-scale cattle-breeding *haciendas*. Until then, the research area has been lightly populated, with predominantly members of the indigenous groups of the Wichí or Toba (Qom). Going hand in hand with cattle breeding, the strongly hierarchical patron–peon system between large landowners and workers has culturally been introduced.
- *Forest exploitation*: Even though it started in the nineteenth century, the Chaco forest had been used for the production of fence posts, railroad-related construction and operation as well as for extensive cattle grazing; the height of forest exploitation was reached between 1920 and 1930. Train tracks were finally constructed and trains reached the remote area of the Chaco Salteño. Anta becomes part of the railway track from Metán to Resistencia. The relevance of cattle breeding diminishes in favour of the production of railway sleepers and coal to be able to reach further into the Chaco biome.
- *The first agrarian expansion of the 1970s*: The expansion is facilitated by major deforestation within the region in order to cultivate beans. The main incentive to buy and cultivate land in Anta is the very high return on investment, based on low land prices and deforestation as well as high levels of soy fertility.

- *'Pampeanisation'* (Delvenne *et al.* 2013, p. 159): The second agrarian expansion from the 1990s onwards, focusing on soy production, non-tillage farming and the application of GM seeds. The soy frontier extends towards previously marginal or cattle-breeding areas.

From the business perspective, the population of the Chaco Salteño is considered predominantly reactive and still embedded in the patron–peon system (ASC9). One particularly interesting feature of Anta is that the migratory balance for the periods 2001–2010 compared to 1991–2001 shows an increase in emigration by 100 per cent and the demographic growth decreasing by more than 20 per cent (Barbarán *et al.* 2015, p. 28). Considering the fact that the first decade of the twenty-first century was the period of massive soy expansion in the region, the indirect proportional correlation between the perceived future of locals and new business opportunities becomes obvious.

Political actions

In order to counteract deforestation in Argentina, the *Ley 26.331 de Presupuestos Mínimos de Protección Ambiental de los Bosques Nativos* [Law 26.331 of the Minimal Requirements of Environmental Protection of Native Forests; Ley de Bosque, i.e. the Forest Law for short] was passed in 2007. The aim is to classify Argentina's native forest according to three categories:

- red = sectors with very high conservational character;
- yellow = sectors with high and intermediary conservational value where it is theoretically not allowed to deforest – other forms of usage are permitted;
- green = sectors that can be partly or entirely transformed, with the prerequisite of an environmental impact plan).

Figure 5.4 shows the classification for the Chaco Salteño. The zonification processes on the provincial level are vividly discussed from a political as well as a technical standpoint (Seghezzo *et al.* 2011; REDAF 2012; García Collazo *et al.* 2013, p. 98; Vallejos *et al.* 2015).

In theory, the passing of the Forest Law is considered a major step towards environmental protection. However, as seen in particular in the department of Anta, the classification leans positively towards agricultural activities. Setting aside that most of the area has already been deforested, the immediate expansion areas– with few exceptions – are classified as productive use potential and thus very likely to be transformed in the near future (provided the global push factors for soy expansion remain positive). This also means that the few remaining *puesteros* will experience major challenges in maintaining their cattle-breeding and small-scale farming lifestyle in the forests; further migration from the rural surroundings to the nearest towns will occur (Krapovickas *et al.* 2016).

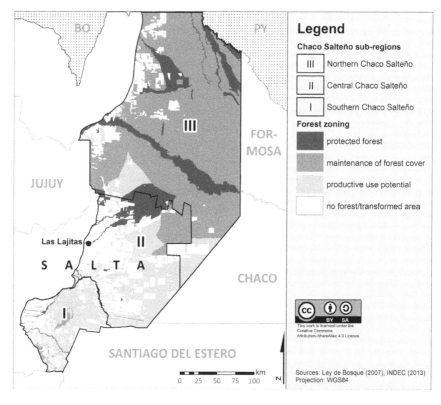

Figure 5.4 Forest Law Zoning of the Chaco Salteño.

Source: Hafner (2016).

Besides deforestation regulations and national political influences, personal connections to the political sphere (both provincial as well as regional/local) are to be considered. Positive effects for entrepreneurs are observed, for example, in the case of Salta Forestal, where politics and business were de facto unipersonal or at least within family ties.

Notes

1 It is interesting to note that the year before, in 1961, wheat was the crop most produced in Argentina (31.4 per cent of the total area harvested), followed by corn (19.5 per cent) (Campos Mesquita and Lemos Alves 2013, p. 17).

2 The devaluation of the ARS was carried out based on 'La Tablita', a table showing the planned exchange rates ARS–US$ for the following eight months.

3 In this context, the phenomenon of *soja Maradonna*, the illegal transfer of GM seeds from Argentina to Brazil and Paraguay, is particularly interesting. This de facto introduction of GMOs in those countries added further pressure on the national governments to liberate GM soy (Newell 2009, p. 42).

4 For a more detailed discussion on 'agriculturalisation', see Paruelo *et al.* (2006).
5 At this point,, note that soy production is not the only 'new' phenomenon in the NOA. Particularly cattle breeding (*bajo monte*, i.e. under semi-deforested *monte*, which is increasingly via feed lots) has gained importance, also due to the fact that this branch of business has been for the most part displaced from the Pampas region in favour of soy production. Goldfarb and Zoomers (2013, p. 80) talk about the combination of push and pull processes of cattle breeding.

References

Albin, E. and Paz, S., 2000. *Productos transgénicos y exportaciones agrícolas: Reflexiones en torno de un dilema argentino*. Buenos Aires: Cancillería Argentina.

Amdan, M.L., Aragon, R., Jobbagy, E.G., Volante, J.N. and Paruelo, M., 2013. Onset of deep drainage and salt mobilization following forest clearing and cultivation in the Chaco plains (Argentina). *Water Resources Research*, 49, 1–12.

Arancibia, F., 2013. Challenging the bioeconomy: the dynamics of collective action in Argentina. *Technology in Society*, 35 (2), 79–92.

Báez, J.R., 1944. La primera colonia agro-hispana en el Río de la Plata. Sancti Spiritu, cuna de la agricultura platense. *Revista Argentina de Agronomía*, 11, 186–278.

Baldi, G., Guerschman, J.P. and Paruelo, J.M., 2006. Characterizing fragmentation in temperate South America grasslands. *Agriculture, Ecosystems & Environment*, 116 (3–4), 197–208.

Barbarán, F., Rojas, L. and Arias, H., 2015. Sostenibilidad institucional y social de la expansión de la frontera agropecuaria. Boom sojero, políticas redistributivas y pago por servicios ambientales en el norte de Salta, Argentina. *Revista Iberoamericana de Economía Ecológica* [online], 24 (21–37). Available at: www.redibec.org/IVO/rev24_02.pdf

Barros, V.R., Doyle, M.E. and Camilloni, I.A., 2008. Precipitation trends in southeastern South America: relationship with ENSO phases and with low-level circulation. *Theoretical and Applied Climatology*, 93 (1–2), 19–33.

Benachour, N. and Séralini, G.-E., 2009. Glyphosate formulations induce apoptosis and necrosis in human umbilical, embryonic, and placental cells. *Chemical Research in Toxicology*, 22 (1), 97–105.

Biomass Research and Development Board, 2001. *Fostering the Bioeconomic Revolution in Biobased Products and Bioenergy: An Environmental Approach*. Golden, CO: Biomass Research and Development Board.

Bravo, A.L., 2010. *Los señores de la soja: La agricultura transgénica en América Latina*. Ciudad de Buenos Aires: CLACSO; Ediciones CICCUS.

Cabrera, A.L., 1976. Regiones fitogeográficas de la República Argentina. In: *Enciclopedia de Agricultura, Jardinería y Fruticultura*. 2nd edn. Buenos Aires: ACME S.A. C. I., pp. 1–85.

Campos Mesquita, F. and Lemos Alves, V.E., 2013. Globalización y transformación del paisaje agrícola en América Latina: las nuevas regiones de expansión de la soja en Brasil y la Argentina. *Revista Universitaria de Geografía*, 22 (1–2), 11–42.

Chudnovsky, D., 2007. Argentina: Adopting RR soy, economic liberalization, global markets and socio-economic consequences. In: S. Fukuda-Parr, ed. *The Gene Revolution: GM Crops and Unequal Development*. London: Earthscan, pp. 85–103.

Clarín, 2016. La Argentina aprobó 35 transgénicos, pero la mayoría no se siembra. *Clarín* [online], 28 Mar. Available at: www.ieco.clarin.com/Argentina-aprobo-transgenicos-mayoria-siembran_0_1548445314.html (accessed 30 March 2016).

Collini, E.A., Berbery, E., Barros, V. and Pyle, M., 2008. How does soil moisture influence the early stages of the South American monsoon? *Journal of Climate*, 21 (2), 195–213.

Colomé, R.A., 2008. Sobre política agraria Argentina en el período 1933–2007. *Revista de Economía y Estadística*, XLVI (1), 109–133.

CONICET, 2009. *Evaluación de la información científica vinculada al glifosato en su incidenica sobre la salud humana y el ambiente*. Buenos Aires: CONICET.

Coscia, A., 1972. *Soja. Sus perspectivas económicas en la Argentina*. Informe técnico 112. Pergamino.

Cuhra, M., 2015. Glyphosate nontoxicity: the genesis of a scientific fact. *Journal of Biological Physics and Chemistry*, 15 (3), 89–96.

Cuhra, M., Bøhn, T. and Cuhra, P., 2016. Glyphosate: too much of a good thing? *Frontiers in Environmental Science*, 4, 17.

Delvenne, P., Vasen, F. and Vara, A.M., 2013. The 'soy-ization' of Argentina: The dynamics of the 'globalized' privatization regime in a peripheral context. *Technology in Society*, 35 (2), 153–162.

D'Utra, G., 1882. Soya. *Jornal do Agricultor*, 4 (7), 185–188.

Faura, R.E., 1933. La soja: su historia, cultivo composición del grano y de la planta estudio de la materia grasa, conclusiones. *Boletin Mensual del Ministerio de Agricultura de la Nacion*. 33 (1), 9–22.

Fleck, L., 1980. *Entstehung und Entwicklung einer wissenschaftlichen Tatsache: Einführung in der Lehre von Denkstil und Denkkollektiv*. Frankfurt am Main: Suhrkamp.

Freire de Sousa, I. S. and Cássia Milagres Teixeira Viera, R. de, 2008. Soybeans and soyfoods in Brazil, with notes on Argentina: sketch of an expanding world commodity. In: C.M. Du Bois, C.-B. Tan and S.W. Mintz, eds. *The World of Soy*. Urbana, IL: University of Illinois Press, pp. 234–256.

García Collazo, M.A., Panizza, A. and Paruelo, J.M., 2013. Ordenamiento territorial de bosques nativos: Resultados de la zonificación realizada por provincias del Norte argentino. *Ecología Austral*, 23, 97–107.

Geist, H., McConnell, W., Lambin, E.F., *et al.*, 2006. Causes and trajectories of land-use/cover change. In: E.F. Lambin and H. Geist, eds. *Land-Use and Land-Cover Change: Local Processes and Global Impacts*. Berlin: Springer-Verlag, pp. 41–70.

Glover, D., 2010. Exploring the resilience of Bt Cotton's 'pro-poor success story'. *Development and Change*, 41 (6), 955–981.

Goldfarb, L. and Zoomers, A., 2013. The drivers behind the rapid expansion of genetically modified soya production into the Chaco region of Argentina. In: Z. Fang, ed. *Biofuels – Economy, Environment and Sustainability*. Rijeka, Croatia: InTech.

González, M.H., Dominguez, D. and Nuñez, M.N., 2011. Long term and interannual rainfall variability in Argentinean Chaco Plain region. In: O.E. Martín and T.M. Roberts, eds. *Rainfall: Behavior, Forecasting and Distribution*. Hauppauge, NY: Nova Science Publishers, pp. 69–89.

Hafner, R., 2016. Figures [online]. Available at: http://roberthafner.at/figures/ (accessed 7 November 2017).

Hafner, R., Rainer, G., Ruiz Peyré, F. and Coy, M., 2016. Ressourcenboom in Südamerika: Alte Praktiken – Neue Diskurse? *Zeitschrift für Wirtschaftsgeographie*, 60 (1–2), 25–39.

Hafner, R. and Rainer, G., 2017. Resourcing salta: viticulture, soy farming and the contested commodification of land. *Die Erde*, 148 (2–3), 121–133.

Hougen, V.H., 1957. The Argentine soybean venture. *Foreign Agriculture*, 21 (9), 13–14.

Jasanoff, S., 2006. Biotechnology and empire: the global power of seeds and science. *OSIRIS*, 21, 273–292.

Johansson, I. and Lynøe, N., 2008. *Medicine and Philosophy: A Twenty-First Century Introduction*. Frankfurt: Ontos Verlag.

Kirby, K.R., Larrance, W.F., Albernaz, A., *et al.*, 2006. The future of deforestation in the Brazilian Amazon. *Futures*, 38 (4), 432–453.

Knight Frank, 2011. *The Wealth Report. A Global Perspective on Prime Property and Wealth 2011*. London: Knight Frank.

Knorr-Cetina, K., 1999. *Epistemic Cultures: How the Sciences Make Knowledge*. Cambridge, MA: Harvard University Press.

Krapovickas, J., Sacci, L. and Hafner, R., 2016. Firewood supply and consumption in the context of agrarian change: the North Argentine Chaco from 1990 to 2010. *International Journal of the Commons*, 10 (1), 220–243. Available at: www.thecommonsjournal.org/articles/10.18352/ijc.609/

Lapegna, P., 2016. Genetically modified soybeans, agrochemical exposure, and everyday forms of peasant collaboration in Argentina. *The Journal of Peasant Studies*, 43 (2), 517–536.

Latour, B., 2003. Is re-modernization occurring – and if so, how to prove it?: A commentary on Ulrich Beck. *Theory, Culture & Society*, 20 (2), 35–48.

Lee, S.-J., 2010. Impacts of land surface vegetation change over the La Plata Basin on the regional climatic environment: a study using conventional land-cover/land-use and newly developed ecosystem functional types. PhD thesis. University of Maryland.

Lee, S.-J. and Berbery, E.H., 2012. Land cover change effects on the climate of the La Plata Basin. *Journal of Hydrometeorology*, 13 (1), 84–102.

Leguizamón, A., 2014. Modifying Argentina: GM soy and socio-environmental change. *Geoforum*, 53, 149–160.

Liebmann, B., Vera, C.S., Carvalho, L.M.V., *et al.*, 2004. An observed trend in Central South American precipitation. *Journal of Climate*, 17 (22), 4357–4367.

Longoni, P. 2016. La Argentina aprobó 35 transgénicos, pero la mayoría no se siembra. *Clarín* [online], 28 Mar. Available at: www.ieco.clarin.com/Argentina-aprobo-transgenicos-mayoria-siembran_0_1548445314.html (accessed 30 March 2016).

Magrin, G.O., Travasso, M.I. and Rodríguez, G.R., 2005. Changes in climate and crop production during the 20th century in Argentina. *Climatic Change*, 72 (1–2), 229–249.

Martínez Dougnac, G., 2013. De los márgenes al boom. Apuntes para una historia de la sojización. In: G. Martínez Dougnac, ed. *De especie exótica a monocultivo: Estudios sobre la expansión de la soja en Argentina*. Buenos Aires: Imago Mundi, 1–38.

Ministerio de Agricultura, Ganadería y Pesca, 2011. *Plan Estratégico agroalimentario y agroindustrial participativo y federal 2010–2020*. Buenos Aires: Ministerio de Agricultura, Ganadería y Pesca.

Müller, R., Müller, D., Schierhorn, F. and Gerold, G., 2011. Spatiotemporal modeling of the expansion of mechanized agriculture in the Bolivian lowland forests. *Applied Geography*, 31 (2), 631–640.

Murgida, A.M., González, M.H. and Tiessen, H., 2014. Rainfall trends, land use change and adaptation in the Chaco salteño region of Argentina. *Regional Environmental Change*, 14 (4), 1387–1394.

Murmis, M. and Murmis, M.R., 2012. Land concentration and foreign land owner-ship in Argentina in the context of global land grabbing. *Canadian Journal of Development Studies/Revue canadienne d'études du développement*, 33 (4), 490–508.

Naharro, N., Álvarez, M.A. and Klarik, M.F., 2010. Territorios en disputa: reflexiones acerca de los discursos que legitiman la propiedad de la tierra en el Chaco salteño. In: C.P. Medina, M. Zubillaga, M. de las and M.Á. Taboada, eds. *Suelos, producción agropecuariay cambio climáticoAvances en la Argentina*. Buenos Aires, pp. 133–154.

Newell, P., 2009. Bio-hegemony: the political economy of agricultural biotechnology in Argentina. *Journal of Latin American Studies*, 41 (1), 27.

OECD, 2009. *The Bioeconomy to 2030: Designing a Policy Agenda*. Paris: Organization for Economic Co-operation and Development.

Otero, G., ed., 2008. *Food for the Few: Neoliberal Globalism and Biotechnology in Latin America*. Austin, TX: University of Texas Press.

Paganelli, A., Gnazzo, V., Acosta, H., *et al.*, 2010. Glyphosate-based herbicides produce teratogenic effects on vertebrates by impairing retinoic acid signaling. *Chemical Research in Toxicology*, 23 (10), 1586–1595.

Paolasso, P. Ferrero, M.E., Gasparri, I. and Krapovickas, J.2010. *The Farming Transformation in the Dry Chaco of Argentina and the Climatic Jump*. Göttingen: ReCALL.

Paolasso, P. and Krapovickas, J., 2013. Avance de la frontera agropecuaria y trans-formaciones demográficas en el Chaco Seco argentino durante la primera década del siglo XXI. In: N. Formiga and E. Garriz, eds. *XII Jornadas Argentinas de Estudios de Población*. Bahía Blanca: Ediuns, pp. 1366–1399.

Parellada, G.H., 2010. La transformación de la agricultura no pampeana. In: L.G. Reca, D. Lema and C. Flood, eds. *El Crecimiento de la Agricultura Argentina: Medio siglo de logros y desafíos*. Buenos Aires: Universidad de Buenos Aires, pp. 83–116.

Paruelo, J.M., Guerschman, J.P.; Piñero, G., *et al.*, 2006. Cambios en el uso de la tierra en Argentina y Uruguay: marcos conceptuales para su análisis. *Agrociencias*, X (2), 47–61.

Pascale, A.J., 1969. Tipos agroclimáticos para el cultivo de la soja en la Argentina. *Revista Facultad de Agronomía y Veterinaria*, 17 (31–48).

Pavone, V., 2012. Ciencia, neoliberalismo y bioeconomia. *Revista Iberoamericana de Ciencia, Tecnología y Sociedad – CTS* [online], 7 (20), 1–15. Available at: www.redalyc.org/pdf/924/92424169013.pdf

Pengue, W.A., 2005. Transgenic crops in Argentina: the ecological and social debt. *Bulletin of Science, Technology & Society*, 25 (4), 314–322.

Qaim, M. and Traxler, G., 2005. Roundup ready soybeans in Argentina: farm level and aggregate welfare effects. *Agricultural Economics*, 32 (1), 73–86.

Reca, L.G., 2010a. Retenciones a las exportaciones agropecuarias: medio siglo de conflictos y una crisis. In: L.G. Reca, D. Lema and C. Flood, eds. *El Crecimiento de la Agricultura Argentina: Medio siglo de logros y desafíos*. Buenos Aires: Universidad de Buenos Aires, pp. 435–454.

Reca, L.G., 2010b. Una agricultura renovada: la producción de cereales y oleaginosas. In: L.G. Reca, D. Lema and C. Flood, eds. *El Crecimiento de la Agricultura Argentina: Medio siglo de logros y desafíos*. Buenos Aires: Universidad de Buenos Aires, pp. 1–28.

REDAF, 2012. *Monitoreo de Deforestación de los Bosques Nativos en la Región Chaqueña Argentina: Informe Nº 1: Ley de Bosques, análisis de deforestación y situación del Bosque chaqueño en la provincia de Salta*. Reconquista.

Remussi, C. and Pascale, A.J., 1977. *La soja. Cultivo, mejoramiento, comercialización y usos*. 2nd edn. Buenos Aires: ACME S.A.C.I.

Richard, S., Moslemi, S., Sipahutar, H., *et al.*, 2005. Differential effects of glyphosate and Roundup on human placental cells and aromatase. *Environmental Health Perspectives*, 113 (6), 716–720.

Rosenzweig, C. and Parry, M.L., 1994. Potential impact of climate change on world food supply. *Nature*, 367 (6459), 133–138.

Schnurr, M.A., 2012. Inventing Makhathini: creating a prototype for the dissemination of genetically modified crops into Africa. *Geoforum*, 43 (4), 784–792.

Seghezzo, L.,Volante, J.N., Paruelo, M., *et al.*, 2011. Native forests and agriculture in Salta (Argentina): conflicting visions of development. *The Journal of Environment & Development*, 20 (3), 251–277

Shurtleff, W. and Aoyagi, A., 2009. *History of Soybeans and Soyfoods in South America (1882–2009): Extensively Annotated Bibliography and Sourcebook*. Lafayette, CA: Soyinfo Center.

Skill, K. and Grinberg, E., 2013. Controversias sociotécnicas en torno a las fumigacionescon glifosato en Argentina. Una mirada desde la construcción social del riesgo. In: M.G. Merlinsky, ed. *Cartografías del conflicto ambiental en Argentina*. Ciudad Autónoma de Buenos Aires: Ediciones CICCUS, pp. 91–118.

Slutzky, D., 2007. *Situaciones problemáticas de tenencia de la tierra en Argentina. Estudios e investigaciones 14*. Buenos Aires: Secretaría de Agricultura, Ganadería, Pesca y Alimentos.

Teubal, M., 2006. Expansión del modelo sojero en Argentina. *Realidad Económica*, 220, 71–96.

Tonnelier, A.C., 1912. Soja híspida, Moench: Métodos industriales de elaboración de sus diversos derivados. *Revista Industrial y Agrícola de Tucumán*, 3 (6), 236–239.

Vallejos, M., Volante, J.N., Mosciaro, J. and Paruelo, M., 2015. Transformation dynamics of the natural cover in the Dry Chaco ecoregion: a plot level geodatabase from 1976 to 2012. *Journal of Arid Environments*, 123, 3–11.

van Dam, C., 2003. Cambio tecnológico, concentración de la propiedad y desarrollo sostenible. Los efectos de la introducción del paquete soja-siembra directa en el umbral al Chaco. *Debate Agrario*, 35, 133–181.

Venencia, C.D., Correa, J.J.; Del Val, V.; Buliubasich, C.; Seghezzo, L 2012. Conflictos de tenencia de la tierra y sustentabilidad del uso del territorio del Chaco Salteño. *Avances en Energías Renovables y Medio Ambiente*, 16, 105–112.

Verburg, P.H., Kok, K., Pontius Jr, R.G. and Veldkamp, A., 2006. Modeling landuse and land-cover change. In: E.F. Lambin and H. Geist, eds. *Land-Use and Land-Cover Change: Local Processes and Global Impacts*. Berlin: Springer-Verlag, pp. 117–135.

Viglizzo, E.F., Pereyra, H., Ricard, F. and Pincén, D. 2011. Dinámica de la frontera agropecuaria y cambio tecnológico. In: E. Viglizzo and E.G. Jobbágy, eds. *Expansión de la frontera agropecuaria en Argentina y su impacto ecológico ambiental*. Buenos Aires: Ediciones Instituto Nacional de Tecnología Agropecuaria, 9–16.

Volante, J.N., Mosciaro, M. J., Morales Poclava, M., *et al.*, 2015. Expansión agrícola en Argentina, Bolivia, Paraguay, Uruguay y Chile entre 2000–2010: Caracterización espacial mediante series temporales de índices de vegetación. *Revista de Investigaciones Agropecuarias* [online]. Available at: http://ria.inta.gov.ar/?p=7365

Volante, J.N. and Gavier-Pizarro, G., 2016. Agricultural expansion in the Semiarid Chaco: poorly selective contagious advance. *Land Use Policy*, 55, 154–165.

WHO, 2010. *WHO Recommended Classification of Pesticides by Hazard and Guidelines to Classification 2009*. Geneva: World Health Organization.

Part III
Re-contextualisation

6 Latin America and environmental justice

The great majority of the environmental justice concepts presented in Chapter 4 have been developed within the regional frame of the Global North, particularly the United States of America. As already seen, context-based adaptations are not only central to environmental justice activism but also necessary in order to take into account regional particularities. Especially Brazil, but de facto all Latin American countries, are advocates of the 'capitalist model of development' (Porto 2012), leading to the necessity of a reframing of environmental justice claims according to the region's role in global-local interplays and appropriation of natural resources (Berger 2014). Urkidi and Walter (2011, p. 685) define the elements of the analysis of the emergence of environmental justice movements in Latin America: (1) the novelty of formation; (2) the context-based redefinition of environmental justice; and (3) the close discursive connection to human rights and social justice activism.

Thus, in the Latin American context, a set of explanatory factors for differentiation of the understanding and handling of environmental justice are revealed (Carruthers 2008b):

- *The language barrier.* Literature generated about Northern environmental justice is rarely translated into Spanish or Portuguese. Until the late 2000s, Latin American scholars had seldom published their work on environmental justice in semantics familiar to the Anglophone ear (Leff 2001; OCLA 2005). This is also due to the fact that, according to Reed and George, they 'view and express environmental justice differently from those who adopt western principles and theories, and they are less likely to publish in highly ranked, widely read, peer-reviewed international journal and books' (2011, p. 840).
- *Different contextual background*: US environmental justice emerged out of the civil rights movement in relation to environmental health (Camacho 1998), particularly in terms of resistance to racial discrimination, poverty and the siting decisions of hazardous facilities. 'However, clear correlations between race or poverty and environmental risk do not typically appear in Latin American cities' (Carruthers 2008a, p. 5). Aspects of

articulated environmental racism are thus more likely to surface in the USA; explicit references to environmental racism in Latin America is rarely made – examples of such are more likely to appear in Brazil (Souza 2008; Paes e Silva 2012) or the Caribbean Basin.

- Civil rights vs. *campesino* movements: In the USA, the civil rights movement (and the members' identity thereof; Faber 2005) have had a major impact in shaping the debate and action on environmental justice. The *campesino* and peasant identity have been cornerstones for participation in Latin American rural areas. Through – though implicit – 'strategic fitting' (Benford and Snow 2000, p. 627), these identities offer a socially constructed platform for exchange and resistance for new topics related to environmental justice. Such examples are pesticide spraying (Porto and Milanez 2009; Harrison 2014), poisoned watersheds, massive interference with the environment leading to negative effects for locals and their natural surroundings, but also commodification and financialisation of land and other resources (Tudela *et al.* 1997; Wright 2005; Borras *et al.* 2012).

- *Scope of working legal frameworks*: Challenges of democratic participation as well as legal protection are major differences between the Global North and Latin American countries. Even though in recent years Latin American countries have adopted impressive rules and regulations in relation to social-environmental issues, their implementation (including access to and participation in decision-making processes) is still an important hurdle for locals/environmental justice movements (Carruthers 2001; Alfie Cohen 2003).

- *Environmental or social justice*: In Latin American contexts, social justice activism is of much higher concern than environmental justice in the USA (Faber 1993; Roberts and Thanos 2003; Martínez-Alier 2008), due to the often direct connection to people's lives and livelihoods.

Environmental justice movements: Latin America with a focus on Argentina

Brazil was the first country in Latin America where a formal environmental justice network was established, in 2001, with possibly the first time of the explicit use of the term 'environmental justice' in this region. The framing of the concept had already begun previously through networking activities with US environmental justice movement networks, leading to the strategic fitting of the concept to the regional context, particularly in the field of social groups (e.g. indigenous, peasants, the urban poor), resource access and empowerment of new models, but also recognition of alternative development models (Acselrad 2008). Following Brazil, Chile founded the second environmental justice network in 2006, where one year before, the Citizen Action Network for Environmental Rights (Red de Acción por los Derechos Ambientales, RADA) was established in Temuco, dealing with Mapuche rights and territories.

In Argentina, the first – and small – environmental movements formed during the dictatorship in the 1970s and began to increase in number and size after 1984 with the first national environmental conference of environmental groups in Argentina (Urkidi and Walter 2011, p. 685). However, no explicit network on environmental justice has so far been established, even though Reboratti (2008) talks of an 'informal' environmental justice framework based on the fact that scholars in Argentina prefer to use the term 'social-ecological conflicts', putting more emphasis on the manifestation of social equity, environmental problems and human rights. Some researchers in Argentina limit environmental justice themes to the urban middle class (Maiwaring *et al.* 1985; Reboratti 2008, 2012),[1] even though several case studies have shown the opposite (Urkidi and Walter 2011, p. 686).

Literature dealing with environmental governance and political ecology (e.g. Lemos and Agrawal 2006; Bridge and Perreault 2009; Bebbington 2013) highlights that particularly for extractive and agroindustrial activities the reduction of environmental pressures through institutional change is hard to achieve (Kirsch 2013; Ospina Peralta *et al.* 2015, p. 42). Additionally, as Arellano-Yanguas (2013) shows for the case of mining in Peru, those institutional changes do not necessarily get rid of conflicts arising from industrial activities. In terms of land issues, 'the notion of land is much more polysemic than before: new agrarian and peasant social movements are emerging, the landless are mobilizing, and old and new variants of *indigenismo* can be found throughout the continent' (Teubal 2009, p. 10). In this context, the 1990s struggles for land are of particular importance for Argentina:

> [T]he land entails a polysemic sense: It has diverse meanings to different social actors. For the indigenous Mapuche or Kollas, for example, the land is an essential aspect of their cosmos visions. The Mapuche and the Kolla feel a belonging to the land, and they basically ask for a historical reparation through the laws of recuperation of ancestral land. For the campesinos … the land forms a part of their basic working tools, and they fight for access. Meanwhile, the Fighting Agrarian Mothers, who accessed the land through inheritance from their fathers or grandfathers, generally European colonials, see the land as their family heritage and fight not to lose it. We could add to this polysemy that for the landowner the land is a good much like any other.
>
> (Giarracca 2003; my translation)

Combining the polysemic understanding of land with the transformation of land based on soy frontier expansion involves:

> ecological distribution conflicts which pit multinational corporations and governments who promote the genetically modified industrial of agriculture, against peasant movements which seek to change the

political-economic forces determining what is produced, when and for whom, while trying to protect national resources and subsistence-based agro-ecological farming.

(García-López and Arizpe 2010, p. 197)

García-López and Arizpe (ibid., p. 197) see in this development a representation of Martínez-Alier's (2002) 'environmentalism of the poor'.

Argentina

Collado (2015, p. 125) discusses three kinds of social conflicts in post-crisis Argentina: (1) dealing with the effects of land concentration; (2) the environmental bads in relation to mining; and (3) social conflicts over labour and union organisation. The first type of conflict is particularly relevant to this book. In the Argentine case, several authors are working on the interrelatedness of soy production, environmental costs and social conflict in relation to agribusiness land concentration (van Dam 2003; Morello *et al.* 2008; Manzanal and Villarreal 2010; Barbarán *et al.* 2015).

One of the most pronounced and felt conflicts in the daily lives of Argentinians was the conflict between the Kirchner government and the agribusiness in 2008, culminating in the lock-out described above (Chapter 5). However, one particular conflict is hardly ever highlighted: *campesino* economies, indigenous communities and the producers for the domestic food market. They have not yet been targeted in terms of rural development or far-reaching agricultural policies (Goldfarb and Zoomers 2013, p. 85). The advance of GM soy has led – according to MNCI-Vía Campesina (the National *Campesino*-Indigenous Movement) – to about 200,000 rural families' displacement. REDAF talks about 950,000 affected indigenous and *campesinos* due to soy expansion (ibid., p. 89).

> In other words, the consensus that GM soya expansion had success in the core region seems to be contested at least in Chaco provinces. Here, tensions related to rights, social organization, judicial and political strategies to defend them, and claims for the institutionalization of this defence, have become a new space for land governance that might challenge dominant discourses legitimizing processes of the commoditization of land and privatization of nature.
>
> (Ibid., p. 89)

To put it differently, Leguizamón classifies the Argentine soy model as 'deemed successful within the confines of neoliberalism' but its success 'less certain … particularly [in terms of] socio-environmental considerations such as the protection of livelihoods, social equity, and ecological integrity' (2014, p. 160). Similar analyses of GM soy expansion are drawn by other authors (Daly 1996; Agyeman *et al.* 2003). Furthermore, Arancibia (2013, pp. 83–84) focuses on the role of scientists in conflict situations. She classifies activism against 'science based regulations for agrochemical commercialization and use' based on interventions from

- 'outside' by social movements of lay people;
- 'outside' and 'inside': collaboration between lay people and scientists becomes a central aspect here;
- 'inside' by scientists and experts focusing on the thought style expansion and adaptation of rules of knowledge within scientific institutions.

Madres de Ituzaingó: popular epidemiology

The case of the Madres de Ituzaingó is one of the first public events by mothers in a suburban neighbourhood next to soy fields in the province of Córdoba. Since the introduction of GM seeds and the new processes of bio-economy (particularly the application of agrochemicals), the mothers had noted an increase in illnesses that had further been confirmed by methods of popular epidemiology. Implicitly, they applied a pragmatic and auto-organisational approach of citizen mobilisation (Dewey 1954). To put it simply, the mothers identified certain contaminating patterns by focusing on the bodily scheme – and visceral feelings – of pain (see Weiss 1999; Berger and Ortega 2010, p. 129). The result was a visualisation and geotagging of ill-nesses, leading to the demand for further investigation by the Provincial Ministry of Health. More mothers participated in demonstrations. After significant media coverage, an interdisciplinary environmental study was carried out. The process was highly criticised by the Madres de Ituzaingó, since the investigation did not cover all the cases presented.

The aim of the movement was to ban the use of agrochemicals from the proximity of urban areas, a claim that was achieved in 2004 by officially establishing a 500-metre glyphosate-free buffer around populated areas. The enforcement of this regulation was supposed to be backed up by 24-hour police surveillance, but this failed to be correctly executed.

The next step for this movement was to further investigate illnesses with the help of local doctors. The results presented in 2005 showed approximately 200 cancer cases among 5,000 inhabitants (Arancibia 2013, p. 85). Subsequently, similar results were obtained in a study carried out by doctors sent by the Ministry of Health. However, the Ministry argued that there was no correlation between cancer and the application of agrochemicals (ibid., p. 85).

At this point it is important to note that this movement can be analysed on the basis of three elements: (1) the body; (2) learning; and (3) narrative (Berger and Ortega 2010). Simply put, the bodily experience and its visceral fluidity of *ratio* and emotion lead to the discovery of non-ideal situations that negatively influence physical (and subsequently emotional) ways of living. Based on the identification of the situation, the next step is learning. This is carried out in the form of popular epidemiology and mapping of diseases.

Based on the data collected, a story is constructed to tell the claims of the Madres de Ituzaingó, focusing on the discourse of rights: the right to life and health, which are constitutionally recognised.

'Paren de Fumigar' ('Stop Spraying')

Another type of resistance to the new trend of bioeconomy is the *Grupo de Reflexión Rural* (GRR), founded by members of varying disciplines such as economics, social sciences or agronomy as a platform to discuss the impacts of global capitalism on Argentina. Supporting the Madres de Ituzaingó, GRR founded the initiative 'Paren de Fumigar' ('Stop Spraying'), which soon gained support from environmental NGOs (e.g. CEPRONAT – *Centro de Protección a la Naturaleza*, i.e. the Centre for the Protection of Nature) and the UAC (*Unión de Asambleas Ciudadanas*, i.e. the Union of Citizen Assemblies). The aim of this initiative was twofold: first, the claim already made by the Madres de Ituzaingó was taken up, demanding a nation-wide buffer zone for glyphosate spraying around populated areas. And, second, the model of the bioeconomy is questioned in general, particularly the correlation between the introduction of the bioeconomy and national growth, development and subsequent prosperity.

Translating science: experiments on embryos showing the effects of glyphosate

Andrés Carasco, an embryologist from the CONICET (*Consejo Nacional de Investigaciones Científicas y Técnicas*, i.e. the National Commission of Scientific and Technical Research) appeared on the front page of the newspaper *Página/12*, speaking openly about his results showing embryonal malformations when exposed to glyphosate. While he was not the first to publish such results, it is argued that he was the first to make the results accessible in Spanish, readily understandable to lay people (Arancibia 2013, p. 87). Carasco decided to publish his results first in the newspaper *Pagina/12* (Aranda 2009), and was immediately criticised by Lino Barañao, the Minister of Science and Technology, because, to put it bluntly, the results were not scientific enough (Barañao, cited in Huergo 2009).[2] Barañao then defended the application of glyphosate based on global experience. Barañao received indirect (and surprising) support from the conservative newspaper *La Nación*, which clearly defended the application of glyphosate and criticised the work and procedures of Carasco (*La Nación* 2009a, 2009b; for a detailed discussion, see Motta and Alasino, 2013).

Concerned about the danger of mixing science and lucrative business opportunities, a petition called 'Voces de Alerta' ('Voices of Alarm') was drafted and signed by over 600 scientists, intellectuals, international NGOs and indigenous movements (Voces de Alerta 2009; Arancibia 2013, p. 87; Motta and Arancibia 2015).

This section has shown that Latin American and in particular Argentinian forms of environmental justice interpretation occur. While the classification presented above is useful to identify certain commonalities and differences among the cases, the following section focuses more on a theoretically-informed and analytical way of approaching social-ecological conflicts. In so doing, the particular context of the Chaco Salteño is chosen.

Notes

1 At this point it has to be noted that environmental justice in general has developed in urban surroundings, most of the literature is based in urban areas (Schweitzer and Stephenson 2007). Rural communities, however, have received less attention (Carroll Jones 2011, pp. 1–2; Nussbaum 2013).
2 One year later, the same results were published in the journal *Chemical Research in Toxicology* (Paganelli *et al.* 2010).

References

Acselrad, H., 2008. Grassroots reframing of environmental struggles in Brazil. In: D. Carruthers, ed. *Environmental Justice in Latin America: Problems, Promise, and Practice.* Cambridge, MA: MIT Press, pp. 75–97.

Agyeman, J., Bullard, R.D. and Evans, B., eds., 2003. *Just Sustainabilities: Development in an Unequal World.* London: Earthscan.

Alfie Cohen, M., 2003. Rise and fall of environmental NGOs along the Mexico-US border. In: B. Hogenboom, M. Alfie Cohen and E. Antal, eds. *Cross-Border Activism and Its Limits.* Amsterdam: Centre for Latin American Research and Documentation, pp. 39–60.

Arancibia, F., 2013. Challenging the bioeconomy: the dynamics of collective action in Argentina. *Technology in Society*, 35 (2), 79–92.

Aranda. 2009. *Pagina/12*, 2009. El tóxico de los campos. *Pagina/12* [online], 13 April. Available at: www.pagina12.com.ar/diario/elpais/1-123111-2009-04-13.html

Arellano-Yanguas, J., 2013. Mining and conflict in Peru: sowing the minerals, reaping a hail of stones. In: A. Bebbington, ed. *Social Conflict, Economic Development and Extractive Industry: Evidence from South America.* London: Routledge, pp. 89–111.

Barbarán, F., Rojas, L. and Arias, H., 2015. Sostenibilidad institucional y social de la expansión de la frontera agropecuaria. Boom sojero, políticas redistributivas y pago por servicios ambientales en el norte de Salta, Argentina. *Revista Iberoamericana de Economía Ecológica* [online], 24 (21–37). Available at: www.redibec.org/IVO/rev24_02.pdf

Bebbington, A., ed., 2013. *Social Conflict, Economic Development and Extractive Industry: Evidence from South America.* London: Routledge.

Benford, R.D. and Snow, D.A., 2000. Framing processes and social movements: an overview and assessment. *Annual Review of Sociology*, 26 (1), 611–639.

Berger, M., 2014. Redes de luchas ambientales en América Latina. Problemas, aprendizajes y conceptos. *Argumentos* [online], 27 (76), 193–215. Available at: www.redalyc.org/articulo.oa?id=59537777010 (accessed 21 July 2015).

Berger, M. and Ortega, F., 2010. Poblaciones expuestas a agrotóxicos: autoorganización ciudadana en la defensa de la vida y la salud, Ciudad de Córdoba, Argentina. *Physis Revista de Saúde Coletiva*, 20 (1), 119–143.

Borras, S.M., Franco, J.C., Gomez, S, Kay, C. and Spoor, M. 2012. Land grabbing in Latin America and the Caribbean. *Journal of Peasant Studies*, 39 (3–4), 845–872.

Bridge, G. and Perreault, T., 2009. Environmental governance. In: N. Castree, ed. *A Companion to Environmental Geography*. Chichester: Wiley, pp. 475–497.

Camacho, D.E., 1998. *Environmental Injustices, Political Struggles: Race, Class, and The Environment*. Durham, NC: Duke University Press.

Carroll Jones, C., 2011. Environmental justice in rural context: land-application of biosolids in central Virginia. *Environmental Justice*, 4 (1), 1–15.

Carruthers, D., 2001. Environmental politics in Chile: legacies of dictatorship and democracy. *Third World Quarterly*, 22 (3), 343–358.

Carruthers, D., ed., 2008a. *Environmental Justice in Latin America: Problems, Promise, and Practice*. Cambridge, MA: MIT Press.

Carruthers, D., 2008b. Popular environmentalism and social justice in Latin America. In: D. Carruthers, ed. *Environmental Justice in Latin America: Problems, Promise, and Practice*. Cambridge, MA: MIT Press, pp. 1–22.

Collado, P.A., 2015. Social conflict in Argentina: land, water, work. *Latin American Perspectives*, 42 (2), 125–141.

Daly, H.E., 1996. *Beyond Growth: The Economics of Sustainable Environment*. Boston: Beacon Press.

Dewey, J., 1954. *The Public and Its Problems*. Chicago: Swallow Press.

Faber, D.J., 1993. *Environment under Fire: Imperialism and the Ecological Crisis in Central America*. New York: Monthly Review Press.

Faber, D.R., 2005. Building a transnational environmental justice movement: obstacles and opportunities in the age of globalization. In: J. Bandy and J. Smith, eds. *Coalitions Across Borders: Transnational Protest and the Neoliberal Order*. Lanham, MD: Rowman & Littlefield, pp. 43–68.

García-López, G.A. and Arizpe, N., 2010. Participatory processes in the soy conflicts in Paraguay and Argentina. *Ecological Economics*, 70 (2), 196–206.

Giarracca, N., 2003. La protesta agrorural en la Argentina. In: J. Seoane, ed. *Movimientos sociales y conflicto en América Latina: [Seminario 'Conflicto Social, Militarización y Democracia: nuevos problemas y desafíos para los estudios sobre conflicto y paz en la región', Buenos Aires, entre los días 16 y 18 de septiembre de 2002]*. Buenos Aires: CLACSO – Consejo Latinoamericano de Ciencias Sociales.

Goldfarb, L. and Zoomers, A., 2013. The drivers behind the rapid expansion of genetically modified soya production into the Chaco Region of Argentina. In: Z. Fang, ed. *Biofuels – Economy, Environment and Sustainability*. Rijeka, Croatia: InTech.

Harrison, J.L., 2014. Neoliberal environmental justice: mainstream ideas of justice in political conflict over agricultural pesticides in the United States. *Environmental Politics*, 23 (4), 650–669.

Huergo, H., 2009. *El campo, la industria verde*. Available at: www.youtube.com/watch?v=xngdzZpgTbI (accessed 31 March 2015).

Kirsch, S., 2013. Afterword: extractive conflicts compared. In: A. Bebbington, ed. *Social Conflict, Economic Development and Extractive Industry: Evidence from South America*. London: Routledge, pp. 201–213.

La Nación, 2009a. Tierra arrasada. *La Nación* [online], 24 April. Available from: www.lanacion.com.ar/1121402-tierra-arrasada

La Nación, 2009b. Glifosato no, fueloil sí. La Nación [online], 8 May. Available from: www.lanacion.com.ar/1125563-glifosato-no-fueloil-si

Leff, E., ed., 2001. *Justicia ambiental: Construcción y defensa de los nuevos derechos ambientales culturales y colectivos en América latina*. México, D.F.: PNUMA Red de Formación Ambiental.

Leguizamón, A., 2014. Modifying Argentina: GM soy and socio-environmental change. *Geoforum*, 53, 149–160.

Lemos, M.C. and Agrawal, A., 2006. Environmental governance. *Annual Review of Environment and Resources*, 31 (1), 297–325.

Maiwaring, S., Viola, E. and Cusminsky, R., 1985. Los nuevos movimientos sociales, las culturas políticas y la democracia: Brasil y Argentina en la década de los ochenta. *Revista Mexicana de Sociología*, 47 (4), 35.

Manzanal, M. and Villarreal, F., eds., 2010. *El desarrollo y sus lógicas en disputa en territorios del norte argentino*. Buenos Aires: Ediciones CICCUS.

Martínez-Alier, J., 2002. *The Environmentalism of the Poor: A Study of Ecological Conflicts and Valuation*. Northhampton, MA: Edward Elgar.

Martínez-Alier, J., 2008. Conflictos ecológicos y justicia ambiental. *Papeles*, 103, 11–27.

Morello, J., Pengue, W.A. and Rodríguez, A.F., 2008. Una historia de producción depredadora y degradación socioambiental. ¿Cómo vamos hacia el Chaco del siglo XXI? In: W.A. Pengue, ed. *La apropiación y el saqueo de la naturaleza: Conflictos ecológicos distributivos en la Argentina del bicentenario*. Buenos Aires: Grupo de Ecología del Paisaje y Medio Ambiente Universidad de Buenos Aires, pp. 162–182.

Motta, R. and Arancibia, F., 2015. Health experts challenge the safety of pesticides in Argentina and Brazil. In: J.M. Chamberlain, ed. *Medicine, Risk, Discourse and Power*. London: Routledge, pp. 179–206.

Nussbaum, M.M., 2013. Embedding issues of environmental justice in the mainstream curriculum. *Environmental Justice*, 6 (1), 34–40.

OCLA, 2005. *Justicia Ambiental, un derecho irrenunciable* [online]. Santiago de Chile. Available at: www.olca.cl/oca/informes/justicia.pdf (accessed 20 July 2015).

Ospina Peralta, P., Bebbington, A., Hollenstein, P., Nussbaum, I. and Ramirez, E., 2015. Extraterritorial investments, environmental crisis, and collective action in Latin America. *World Development*, 73, 32–43.

Paes e Silva, H., 2012. Ambiente e justiça: Sobre a utilidade do conceito de racismo ambiental no contexto brasileiro. *e-cadernos CES* (17), 85–111.

Paganelli, A., Gnazzo, V., Acosta, H., Lopez. S.L. and Andres, E.C., 2010. Glyphosate-based herbicides produce teratogenic effects on vertebrates by impairing retinoic acid signaling. *Chemical Research in Toxicology*, 23 (10), 1586–1595.

Pagina/12, 2009. El tóxico de los campos. *Pagina/12* [online], 13 April. Available at: www.pagina12.com.ar/diario/elpais/1-123111-2009-04-13.html

Porto, M., 2012. Complexity, vulnerability processes and environmental justice: an essay in political epistemology. *RCCS Annual Review* [online], 4 (4). Available at: http://rccsar.revues.org/420 (accessed 25 February 2015).

Porto, M.F. and Milanez, B., 2009. Eixos de desenvolvimento econômico e geração de conflitos socioambientais no Brasil: desafios para a sustentabilidade e a justiça ambiental. *Ciência & Saúde Coletiva*, 14 (6), 1983–1994.

Reboratti, C., 2008. Environmental conflicts and environmental justice in Argentina. In: D. Carruthers, ed. *Environmental Justice in Latin America: Problems, Promise, and Practice*. Cambridge, MA: MIT Press, pp. 101–117.

Reboratti, C., 2012. Socio-environmental conflict in Argentina. *Journal of Latin American Geography*, 11 (2), 3–20.

Reed, M.G. and George, C., 2011. Where in the world is environmental justice? *Progress in Human Geography*, 35 (6), 835–842.

Roberts, J.T. and Thanos, N.D., 2003. *Trouble in Paradise: Globalization and Environmental Crises in Latin America*. New York: Routledge.

Schweitzer, L. and Stephenson, M., 2007. Right answers, wrong questions: environmental justice as urban research. *Urban Studies*, 44 (2), 319–337.

Souza, A., 2008. The gathering momentum for environmental justice in Brazil. *Environmental Justice*, 1 (4), 183–188.

Teubal, M., 2009. Agrarian reform and social movements in the age of globalization: Latin America at the dawn of the twenty-first century. *Latin American Perspectives*, 36 (4), 9–20.

Tudela, F., Paré Quellet, L. and Martínez, S., eds., 1997. *Semillas para el cambio en el campo: Medio ambiente, mercados y organización campesina*. México, D.F.: Instituto de Investigaciones Sociales, UNAM-IIS; Sociedad de Solidaridad Social 'Sansekan Tinemi'; Saldebas, Servicios de Apoyo Local al Desarrollo de Base en México.

Urkidi, L. and Walter, M., 2011. Dimensions of environmental justice in anti-gold mining movements in Latin America. *Geoforum*, 42 (6), 683–695.

van Dam, C., 2003. Cambio tecnológico, concentración de la propiedad y desarrollo sostenible. Los efectos de la introducción del paquete soja-siembra directa en el umbral al Chaco. *Debate Agrario*, 35, 133–181.

Voces de Alerta, 2009. *VOCES DE ALERTA. Página Principal, declaración* [online]. Available at: http://voces-de-alerta.blogspot.co.at/2009_05_01_archive.html

Weiss, G., 1999. *Body Images: Embodiment as Intercorporeality*. New York: Routledge.

Wright, A.L., 2005. *The Death of Ramón González: The Modern Agricultural Dilemma*. Austin, TX: University of Texas Press.

7 Chaco Salteño and the environmental justice incommensurabilities framework (EJIF)

The environmental justice concepts and their related popular counterparts presented have one feature in common: Claims-making (in a variety of shapes and forms) is a core feature; the presence of some form of conflictive situations (with varying degrees of severity) is given. Reboratti (2012) focuses on actors in particular social-ecological conflict situations. Čapek (1993), as well as Davoudi and Brooks (2014), explicitly centre their concepts around claims making, the former from a social movement perspective including underlying causal structures and the latter also considering ecological aspects but focusing on particular clear-cut temporal and spatial frames. Pellow (2000) and Elvers *et al.* (2008) highlight processes, the former on the basis of problem identification and the latter establishing robust processes. Fredericks (2011) sees social-environmental problems and concentrates on the subsequent forms of political reaction and policy development. And, finally, Flitner (2003, 2007) takes distribution of environmental goods and bads as a starting point to reveal different scales and dimensions of environmental justice based on scales of meaning and regulation and including elements of recognition. Similar aims can be observed with activist-driven popular concepts related to environmental justice. Three examples have been given: (1) popular epidemiology as a post-normal science approach including and empowering local communities to gather and create social-environmental data (that can be used for claims-making) that otherwise would not be available; (2) environmentalism of the poor to explicitly strengthen activism against disadvantaging local and indigenous communities; and (3) defence of the commons in order to preserve current social-environmental settings and their connected livelihoods.

All the concepts mentioned are useful in their own right and their particular contexts and perspectives. However, taking into account Ludwik Fleck, one aspect has not yet been studied: incommensurabilities of environmental justice (both research and activism) in relation to social-ecological change and conflict. Or to rephrase it: why certain situations do (not) produce claims making, even though it seems counter-intuitive from a particular thought style. Hence, to focus on this gap I develop an environmental justice incommensurabilities framework (EJIF) (Figure 7.1).

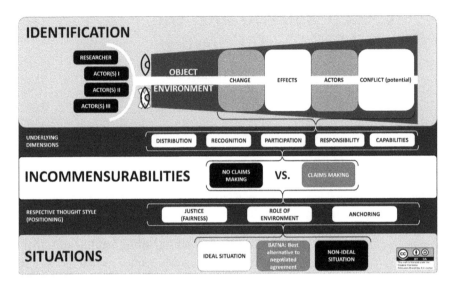

Figure 7.1 Environmental justice incommensurabilities framework (EJIF).
Source: Hafner (2016).

Going along with the environmental justice concepts described above, the EJIF is anchored in the issue of claims making. However, one major difference here is the multi-faceted perspective of the framework and the content it permits to be analysed. Three perspectives of this book are represented:

- the CLASSIC: Here, the narrow perspective of environmental justice research is considered. In this view, conflict potentials can be quantified predominantly based on the visualisation of distributive inequalities in relation to environmental goods and bads. As highlighted, (environmental) justice theories and normative understandings thereof are applied to the case study. Consequently, and simply put, conflict potentials should theoretically result in actors' claims making.
- the ALTERNATIVE: Here, the different local thought styles are considered, reconstructing their perspective of the same bio–physical environment used in the CLASSIC version. The actors identify conflict potentials on their own and have the decision sovereignty over whether to make claims or not. Consequently, different foci of actors can emerge, resulting in different thematic claims making based on the actors' membership in particular thought collectives. Incommensurabilities arise among the different realities of conflict (potential) perception.
- the COMPLETE: Here, I do not assume that claims actually have to be articulated or conflicts materialised. The rationale behind the complete is

to focus on the epistemology of thought styles not just among the thought collectives researched in the ALTERNATIVE, but also reflexively including the results from the CLASSIC.

At a more hands-on level, the layout of the EJIF allows a structured approach to the three perspectives. Thus, the following section offers a guideline on how to read the EJIF (Figure 7.1).

Identification

The CLASSIC: *researcher's (outside) perspective*

In order to unearth and compare incommensurabilities among different thought styles, the first step is the identification of a case that allows comparison. Environmental justice, as argued above, always has a connection to the bio-physical, offering a perfect entry point for the classic perspective.

   Much like entering a new thought collective, the researcher's first perspective on a new topic comes from the outside. Without major case-specific knowledge, the researcher uses familiar patterns and tools in order to make the transition from looking at a case and seeing something. Well aware of their own subjectivity, the first task of the researcher is to identify the their own perspective on a particular case: social-ecological change and environmental justice include two components: the social and the environmental. Bearing in mind Drummond's (2008, p. 180) first question on what humans do with natural variables, two questions have to be asked:

* *Change*: How far, if at all, have natural variables changed over a particular time and in a particular area? The identification of change occurs predominantly on the basis of scientific literature or databases. Consequently, a particular perspective of one scientific community (thought style) is taken up. The researcher new to the topic enters this thought style through the exoteric circle and relies (to a certain extent) on the presumptions and conclusions of members of the esoteric circle.
* *Effects*: Based on the evaluation of change, what kind of relationship between change and human interaction is observed? The question focuses on whether causalities of environmental change can be traced back to human intervention. The general idea here is closely linked to Elvers *et al.* (2008) and their analytical levels of impact and effects.

Next, the focus lies explicitly on the actors involved:

* *Actors*: Who is involved in changing the natural variables?; who experiences an impact based on actions of the former? Here, a connection – however very loose – is made to the elaborations of Reboratti (2012).

The last step of identification deals with outside-perspective conclusions on the results of the previous three categories:

- *Conflict (potential)*: What conflict potential can be identified according to the researcher's thought style and the information on change, effects and actors at hand?

The CLASSIC analysis of the four different stages of identification does not necessarily involve long-term fieldwork since it relies heavily on already pre-set concepts, classifications and indicators elaborated in the field of environmental justice. Additionally, it is heavily based on quantitative top-down analyses of the region under focus; involvement of locals in the research process is not necessarily required. This aspect, of course, has one major consequence: reduced visibility. The researcher is not considered to have identified all components of change, effects, actors and conflict potential; openness towards new perspectives (i.e. thought style expansions) is not considered relevant here.

Consequently, the characteristics of change, effects, actors involved and conflict (potentials) visible to the researcher are the basis for evaluating claims making situations.

The ALTERNATIVE: *actors' perspectives and thought styles*

The ALTERNATIVE approach draws on the same mechanisms as the CLASSIC. The same questions related to change, effects, actors and conflict (potentials) are used. The difference, however, is that the answer to those questions is based on the context of the respective (local) actors' thought collective background. A theoretic embedding in environmental justice research as in the CLASSIC version does not occur, visualising new thought collective realities and varying thematic emphases. Consequently, the results are possibly alternative claims among the actors studied.

Incommensurabilities

The COMPLETE: *comparison of researcher's and actors' perspectives*

What has happened so far? Based on the results from the researcher's outside perspective, nurtured by literature reviews and scientific debates on environmental justice, it is then conceivable to deduce possible areas for claims making – the trigger for conflictive situations. Once identified, the researcher's top-down approach has to be abandoned in favour of participatory bottom-up forms, thus going along with Fleck's praxis-driven comparison of different forms of cognition and thought styles.

Consequently, the results of (non-)claims making from the CLASSIC and the ALTERNATIVE are compared and contrasted.

The following questions are considered:

- *Claims making:* How far do open claims made by actors correlate with or differ from the researcher's results?
- *Incommensurabilities:* Why is there a difference and what forms of incommensurability are detected?

Having identified the differences of claims-making outcomes, discovering incommensurabilities is the core task. This is carried out both in the ALTERNATIVE (incommensurabilities among thought styles researched) as well as in the COMPLETE (incommensurabilities between thought styles researched and the results from the CLASSIC perspective).

In so doing, contextual details are necessary. To provide this additional information, two categories are added to the analysis: (1) underlying dimensions and (2) thought style positioning.

Underlying dimensions

The underlying dimensions of environmental justice are designed to reveal the thinking processes of the respective thought collectives in relation to concrete change, effects, actors and conflict (potentials). Thus, a close connection to the actual hands-on topics the actors choose to discuss is made.

The dimensions are visualised for each type of actors in the respective context:

- ALTERNATIVE: Focus on underlying dimensions of actors studied.
- COMPLETE: Focus on underlying dimensions of actors studied in the ALTERNATIVE and the results from the CLASSIC.

Once again, elements from already existing environmental justice concepts are referred to. The guiding questions for distribution, recognition, participation, responsibility and capability compiled by Davoudi and Brooks (2014, p. 2698) are considered helpful here. Additionally, special focus is laid on Nussbaum's (2013) elaborations on capability. In answering the questions from the actors' perspectives, their respective focuses and concerns are highlighted. Additionally, cultural aspects considered by Flitner's (2003, 2007) environmental justice matrix come in handy to grasp the underlying context of regionality, traditions and developed social patterns of interaction.

Thought style positioning

The second category used to understand the development of respective incommensurabilities deals with more generalised positioning towards the topics of justice (fairness), the role of the environment and the actors' thematic, traditional/cultural anchoring. Thus, the following questions are guidelines for the analysis:

- *Justice (fairness)*: What conceptions of fairness prevail? Do the actors follow an egalitarian, libertarian, utilitarian or a hybrid approach towards fairness?
- *Role of the environment*: How is the actors' form of thinking coined by their understanding of the environment? The actors' positioning can range from anthropocentrism via intermediate axiology to eco-centrism.
- *Anchoring*: How far do emotional bonds to traditions and/or cultural habitus influence the actors' thinking and acting?
- *ALTERNATIVE*: Focus on the thought style positioning of the actors studied.
- *COMPLETE*: Focus on the thought style positioning of the actors studied in the ALTERNATIVE and the results from the CLASSIC.

Situations

The most abstract category in the EJIF is termed 'situations'. The basic idea here is to identify the actors' main focus and/or starting point when thinking about/carrying out (non-) claims making.

- *Situation*: What is the actors' initial focus (i.e. solution): ideal situations, non-ideal situations, or the best alternative to a negotiable agreement (BATNA)?
- *ALTERNATIVE*: Revealing the initial focus of the actors studied.
- *COMPLETE*: Revealing the initial focus of the actors studied in the ALTERNATIVE and the results from the CLASSIC.

The EJIF is designed in a very open and a linear way. While the researcher's starting point is based on the change of natural variables over time, the subsequent elements, the actors' perspectives with their underlying dimensions and thought styles (positioning) are not followed the same way by all actors. Depending on the starting point (both in terms of the actors' perception as well as the researcher's fieldwork design), different focuses (be it distribution, recognition, social movements and activism, or ecological, just to name a few) determine the thinking processes, actions and ultimately the overall analytical design and outcome. Thus, laying bare how the actual path through the framework was taken, is crucial here.

Actors

Focusing on the EJIF, the identification of the actors is crucial in order to discover the connectedness and incommensurability of thought styles. This holds particular value for the discussion of hands-on social-ecological changes and varying perspectives on them. Thus, this chapter gives an overview of the pre-defined (by scientists) groups, from a macro-national level to (if relevant and/or possible) local scale. This is particularly important to *see* which actors are considered vital for the analysis of soy agribusiness conflict situations. Later, a more open and less thought style-based categorisation of actors is proposed.

Soy agribusiness actors

The main drivers for change in the research area are soy agribusiness actors (SAB). A classification of four different actors is given (Table 7.1): (1) traditional land-based actors; (2) new land-based actors; (3) non-land-based actors focusing on land; and (4) service providers.

Local soy actors in the area around Las Lajitas, in the department of Anta

While many of the above-mentioned actors are also involved in activities in the department of Anta, certain place-specific groups are identified. Las Lajitas, despite the vast soy expansion, still hosts a relatively 'small' community of approximately 60 producers. According to van Dam, there is a 'strong interaction among the village, ... the commercial centre and agrarian services in the region' (2003, p. 149; my translation). The self-definition of local soy agribusiness actors, according to van Dam (ibid., pp. 148–149) can be summarised as followed:

•   As pioneers, having created something out of nothing without the help of the national state.
•   They are the true 'non-absent' agrarian producers, with knowledge of the land, re-investing their earnings in the region.
•   They criticise the top-down mega-companies that try to enforce a system not suitable for the region.

Soy farmers have founded cooperatives to create a platform for technical exchange. There is Grupo Las Lajitas, a cooperative among producers that offers technical support and runs an experimentation site for new forms of cultivation and seeds. A second semiformal group is ProAnt, comprising newer actors in the soy business (ibid., p. 147). Central to both groups is the predominant focus on technical issues that are not provided by the local branch of INTA (currently a one-person office in Las Lajitas with little standing in the region), lobbying or political discussions are not core elements of the gatherings.

Despite the self-definition of the soy producers in Las Lajitas, van Dam (ibid., p. 178) sees Anta's nucleus of production as an enclave economy, where increasing land concentration is taking place, leading to rising

Table 7.1 Actors and interest groups in the Argentine soy sector

Actors	Description
Traditional land-based actors	
Traditional large land owners	• transition from cattle breeding activities to financial speculation • investment in new forms of GM-based/precision agriculture • land ownership and proper cultivation • size: >100,000 • policy: growth • examples: Alzaga Unzué, Leloir, Blaquier, Fortabat, Bemberg, Duhau, Ayerza
Medium-/large-scale producers	• increasing proportion of land rented to other producers • size: >500 ha • policy: persistence
Small-/medium-scale producers	size: 200–500 ha
Small-scale producers	size: <200 ha
New land-based actors	
Small-scale renters	• size: mostly <200 ha • survived disappearance of 50,000 producers in the 1990s • five- to sixfold income compared to proper production by leasing out their land • location: predominantly Pampas region
New large-scale owners from the industrial sector	• size: >100,000 ha • invest activities based on the foreignisation of their industries in the agricultural sector • policy: expansion • examples: Ratazzi, Terrabusi, Blanco Villegas
Absentee owners	• claims-makers (personal or heirs) stating that their land is occupied • significant time lag between occupation and claims making • sometimes false claims
Non-land-based actors focusing on land	

Investment groups, trusts, *pooles de siembra*[1]	• function as investment funds
	• from within and outside the agricultural sector
	• main task: land renting and management, distribution of profits at the end of each agricultural cycle
	• diversification of risk by using multiple
	  • production regions
	  • contractors (machinery and services)
	• internationalisation of business
	• including foreign investors
	• expansion of market into Mercosur
	• examples: Los Grobo, El Tejar, Cazenave, MSU-Uribelarrea, Lartirigoyen

Table 7.1 Continued

Actors	Description
Foreign investors in land	• size: >100,000 ha • policy: expansion • ratio: make use of comparatively cheap land, particularly in NOA and NEA • small-scale investments in the Pampas region • examples: Acecoagro-Soroso, Liag Argentina, Dreyfus
Land speculators and real estate intermediaries	Purchase of cheap land (land tenure often questionable) and resale at higher prices
Service providers Machinery contractors (*contratistas*)	• offer machinery and services for planting, fumigation, harvesting • get either share of production (value) or fixed prices • previously individual endeavours, now predominantly capitalized companies • in total, there are almost 10,000 contractors performing 80–85 per cent of harvesting and spraying
Machinery producers	• increasingly concentrated and globalized with transnational/local actors • local examples: Deutz, Ferguson, Zanello • international examples: John Deere, New Holland
Storing infrastructure and collectors (*Acopiadores*)	• intermediaries between producer and (international) buyer • deal with 80 per cent of overall production Other services • grain quality monitoring • business strategy consulting for producers • (including time and place to sell) • technical assistance • financing of producers • examples: AGD, Bunge, Noble Argentina
Biodiesel companies	• considered a growing sector; • large capacities already installed • examples: "Big Four" (UnitedBio, Viluco, Explora, Diaster), Rosario Bioenergy, Biomadero, AOM

Input sellers	• predominantly transnational companies selling seeds
	• market of agrochemicals is dominated by Monsanto
	• examples:
	  • transnational companies (seeds): Monsanto, Pioneer, Novartis, Dupont, Ciba
	  • agrochemicals: Monsanto

Technical assistance	• important role of private sector • national and trans-national companies • examples: AAPRESID (Argentinian Direct Tillage Producers Association), AACREA (Argentinian Association of Regional Consortia for Agricultural Experimentation)

continued

Table 7.1 Continued

Actors	Description
Exporters	• purchase of soy and derivatives from producers, intermediaries and the industry • high concentration (<10 companies) • high influence on collection, storage, inputs selling and production • examples: • soy beans (control of 85 per cent of export): Cargill, Noble Argentina, ADM, Bunge, LDC-Dreyfus, AC Toepfer, Nidera • soy oil: Bunge, LDC Dreyfus, Cargill, AGD, Molinos Río de la Plata • soy derivatives: Cargill, Bunge, Dreyfus, AGD, Vicentín, Molinos de la Plata

Source: Based on Arceo *et al.* 2009, Giancola *et al.* 2009, Aranda 2010, Giarracca and Teubal 2010, Dobelmann 2012, Goldfarb and Zoomers 2013, pp. 82–84, Leguizamón 2014, 2015.

Note

1 Relating to the *pooles de siembra*, the term 'financialisation', i.e. the increased focus on financial reasoning, financial markets and actors towards domestic and international economies is highly relevant (Arbolave 2003, Epstein 2005, Fieldman 2013, p. 226).

ecological problems and environmental bads. The 'Pampeanisation' of soy production has led the producers to become more vulnerable and dependent on other actors in the soy business (particularly service providers in the form of seeds and pest control).

Local (traditional) non-soy actors

Even though extraterritorial actors have an increasing impact on the economic, social or political processes of Latin American rural territories (Ospina Peralta *et al.* 2015, p. 41), Krapovickas and Longhi (2013, p. 41) competently highlight that numerous studies have been compiled about the effects of the agrarian frontier on the local population in the Chaco region (León *et al.* 1985; Teubal 2006; Paolasso *et al.* 2012). However, the *campesinos*, the indigenous population and rural small-scale farmers have not been sufficiently described. On top of that, I argue that the local community living in towns and villages is highly underrepresented when it comes to their characterisation as well as in terms of their dealing with social-environmental struggles and conflicts. This is particularly due to the fact that this group is highly heterogeneous, does not have much media coverage (unlike indigenous communities, for example), and are not traditionally anchored in the Argentine narrative of rural dwellers, like the *puesteros ganaderos* or *gauchos* further south.

Hence, the aim of this section is to identify the already established groups of actors: *Campesinos* (*puesteros ganaderos* and indigenous communities) and the 'defenders of biodiversity'. The 'local community' will be dealt separately in the empirical analysis, drawing on the on-site findings in order to categorise and contextualise them.

The campesino

The *campesino* is difficult to describe; it is not one particular actor but summarises a group of actors with different backgrounds. The rural dweller in the Chaco area is someone 'who lives scattered around the monte, who breeds cattle and/or has a plot with crops for domestic use, who sells his/her production when necessary, who carries out the activities of hunting, gathering and fishing' (Krapovickas and Longhi 2013, pp. 53–54; my translation). This definition is frequently applied in academic studies and development programmes alike (Wald 2015, p. 95). Bryceson (2005, p. 2) adds 'class' as another defining criterion, arguing that 'external subordination to state authorities as well as regional or international markets' is crucial to consider.

The puestero ganadero

The great majority of the rural population in the Chaco area are predominantly cattle breeders. They live on the *puesto ganadero*, an often precarious living area comprising a house, a watering place and farmyard and a fenced area of 2–4 hectares for natural pasture and the planting of corn. The type of farming is considered extensive and often termed *'ganadería del monte'*, i.e. a free-range method of cattle and goat breeding in the *monte* standards (Krapovickas and Longhi 2013, p. 55). Veterinarian control is not available, leading to the general assumption that the products do not meet certain quality standards required (León *et al.* 1985, p. 402).

Additionally, land tenure is complicated and in recent years, the uncertainty related to land use and land access has culminated in conflicts.

Indigenous communities

The main indigenous communities in the Chaco are Wichí and Toba (Qom). The majority of the communities are located in the northern parts of the Chaco Salteño. In the department of Anta, only a handful of communities still live in rural surroundings. The best-known one is the Eben Ezer Community in General Pizarro. Nevertheless, in most towns of Anta there are certain – often designated – *barrios* (neighbourhoods). They are characterised by marginality in terms of location and socio-economic standards.

The defenders of biodiversity

Langbehn (2013, p. 232) implicitly classifies the defenders of biodiversity in terms of place-based *'vecinos autoconvocados'* (i.e. 'self-organised neighbours') working on one particular case close to their home, and non-place-based NGOs such as Greenpeace, FARN (the Fundación Ambiente y Recursos Naturales, predominantly active in a legal environment), the Fundación Pro-Yungas (with its roots in ecological sciences), or the Fundación Vida Silvestre (part of the international WWF). In Salta, Greenpeace made major news coverage in relation to forest issues in 1998, protesting against the Gasoducto Norandino project (a gas pipeline from northern Salta to northern Chile) or in the early 2000s against the rapid increase of deforestation in Salta.

In terms of participatory processes, top-down measures are taken in the form of forums for sustainable/responsible soy. Here, the Round Table on Sustainable Soy (later changed to the Round Table on Responsible Soy, RTRS) is an initiative started in 2004 by 'a group of "concerned" producers, NGO's and companies ... [initiating] a series of multi-stakeholder forums' with the goal to strengthen corporate social responsibility (García-López and Arizpe 2010, p. 200). Five principles are highlighted: 'environmental responsibility', 'good agricultural practice', 'responsible community relations', 'responsible labor conditions', as well as 'legal compliance and good business practices' (RTRS 2010). However, organisations such as the World Wildlife Fund (WWF) or Greenpeace have been subject to criticism for cooperating with highly questionable multinational corporations like Monsanto (Wilshusen *et al.* 2002; Chapin 2004; García-López and Arizpe 2010, p. 198).

Effects of change and conflict (potential)

Whenever there is change, its effects have the potential to lay the ground for conflict. The first wave of conflict emerged in the nineteenth century due to the increasing degradation of the forest and the right to use forest resources. The main actors were indigenous groups belonging to the Wichí and Toba (Qom) on the one hand and settlers on the other (Murgida *et al.* 2014, p. 1388).

The 1960s marked another important milestone in the region: because of forest degradation the forest industry declines and becomes partially replaced by agricultural production (especially Phaseolus beans) and cattle grazing (ibid., p. 1388). Additionally, the construction of the Cabra Coral hydro dam (finalised in 1972) regulates the water flow of the Río Juramento, preventing major floods and allowing partial irrigation, improving agricultural activities in the region. The facilitation of agricultural expansion leads to new frames for interaction in the region. The following sections identify the most discussed effects of change in the advance of the soy frontier in the research area.

Modification of the campesino lifestyle

Bisio *et al.* (2010) highlight that agriculturalisation has had a huge impact on the modes of existence (see Latour 2013) of the *campesinos*, particularly when it comes to the livestock they breed and the numbers of animals they keep. The reason is predominantly seen in the fencing off of the land, thus, they have de facto less (commonly used, i.e. a common pool) land available. This is also reflected in the reduced access to fodder and watering places. Additionally, the social structure of the *campesinos* is adapting, particularly the formerly strong social networks (Cáceres 2015, pp. 129–130), which are particularly important, both place-based and non-place-based ones, as Silvetti and Cáceres (1998) highlight for cases in Córdoba, in Argentina, or Martínez (2004) for Ecuador.

Rural-urban migration

Closely connected to the modification of the *campesino* lifestyle, the side effect of the technification of agricultural production in general and soy cultivation in particular is that specified knowledge of how to carry out agriculture is now transferred by universities rather than through the traditional way through the community and/or family (Leguizamón 2014, p. 153). This feature goes along with an increased detachment from the rural space and the reduced necessity for great numbers of people to be working in the fields. As a result, rural-urban migration due to better educational (and health) opportunities is often cited (Leguizamón 2014, p. 153, Krapovickas 2016; for the Pampas region in particular, see Stratta Fernández and de los Ríos Carmenado 2010). In general, this migration pattern leads to increased farm sizes, a decrease in farm numbers and thus greater concentration of land (Teubal 2006; Gras 2009, 2012; Gras and Hernandez 2009).

The main effect, however, is noted in urban centres, where poverty is increasing due to the migration of the rural population to the urban areas, or as Carlos Reboratti puts it 'the agribusiness does not populate the land, but it empties it of population' (Reboratti, cited in van Dam 2003, p. 176; my translation).

Land tenure change

The expansion of soy to the NOA follows three main discourses: (1) availability of cheap land; (2) low levels of or even lack of regulations; and (3) the narrative of the 'empty land' (Borras and Franco 2012, p. 45). The general framework for soy expansion comprises extra-regional investors (including individuals and *pooles de siembra* alike) who have connections to local technicians (Goldfarb and Zoomers 2013, p. 81). Generally, access[1] to land for soy investment is relatively easy through purchase or lease; the land itself is

> [not necessarily] empty but probably difficult to control by locals, even if they held rights to the land. The relationship with the local people was, in fact, less personalized; investors were generally represented by

managers, which has both advantages and disadvantages when it comes to conflicts with the local communities and individuals with weak tenure rights.

(Goldfarb and Zoomers 2013, p. 81)

In this context, the 1990s are particularly relevant for the NOA region. Naharro *et al.* (2010, p. 133) talk about two new processes in the region: (1) the reactivation of the land market due to the increasing demand for soy production; and (2) Argentina's recognition of indigenous rights.

For the area of the case studies, i.e. the department of Anta, land concentration is an important factor: 12 per cent of the enterprises own areas ranging in size between 11,000 and 17,000 hectares, while two particular companies hold 63,000 hectares and 41,000 hectares respectively, and four businesses account for land sized between 35,000 and 38,000 hectares (Murgida *et al.* 2014, p. 1391). Not mentioned are public lots commissioned by the government of the province of Salta; here one agribusiness representative can cultivate on 100,000 hectares of land for minimal annual fees per hectare. As a result of this trend, the gap between the number of small-scale farmers and large-scale agribusinesses is widening. Additionally, extra-regional actors increasingly influence provincial decision-making, having effects on traditional smallholders and *puesteros* due to land sales and not respecting semi-formal/informal and traditionally grown uses of land (Delgado 2007; Slutzky 2007; Murgida *et al.* 2014).

Getting new land in Anta is a closely connected business circuit; this holds true for both purchase and lease (van Dam 2003, p. 172). In total, less than a handful of intermediaries (mostly living in the provincial capital Salta) organise land transfers. Their inside knowledge and personal ties to the production and land community are vital.

Land tenure conflicts: a thought style example

Shifts in land control are omnipresent in the research area (Goldfarb and van der Haar 2016). Venencia *et al.* (2012) describe a model to identify and visualise conflicts of land tenure in the Chaco Salteño. The components of this model are information on conflicts of land tenure, types of actual property (public or private), surface quantity of the land, actual land use, territories with claims by indigenous groups, territories with claims from *criollos* (i.e. locally-born people of European, particularly Spanish, descent), and data from the Forest Law.

Figure 7.2 presents the different levels of conflict, according to Venencia *et al.* (ibid., pp. 109–110). It is shown that particularly the northern part of the Chaco Salteño experiences high levels of conflict. This aspect is related to the high density of the indigenous population and the most dynamic expansion of the agrarian frontier. The department of Anta, however, shows medium levels of conflict, with only four visibly defined physical areas.

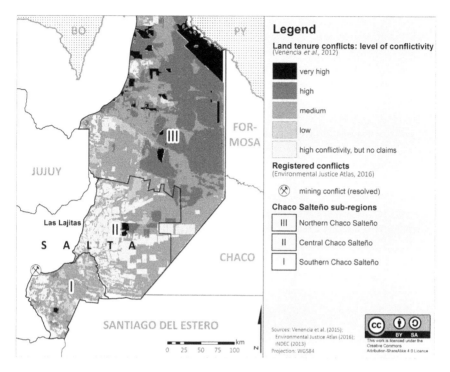

Figure 7.2 Conflict and land tenure in the Chaco Salteño.
Source: Hafner 2016.

At a second glance, the map has to be critically questioned. Venencia *et al.* (ibid., p. 110) have drawn a map containing zones of high conflict without claims making by indigenous and *criollos* communities. When looking closely at the map, almost the entire area of the research area is considered – with varying degrees – as conflictive. This aspect goes hand in hand with the dominant thought styles from an academic and/or environmental activist perspective: drastic and fast land use change leads to the situation that certain groups of actors are winners and others are losers. The presumption then is that the losers in the change are in fact aware of their situation. Additionally, as shown on the meso-level, the whole area is subject to land tenure (including social-ecological) claims making, i.e. the precondition to identify (environmental) justice conflicts. Hence, from the broad scientific perspective, the actors are considered to have full overview over the changes in their region, can contextualise their position in the new situations and articulate their nonconformity. Ground truth data, however, are missing in the analysis.

A second critique of Figure 7.2 is based on the categorisation of the high conflict without claims making. In its original publication, Figure 7.2 was split up into two maps, one of which shows the area of agricultural activity. Thus, the authors' assumption – bluntly put – is: fields for agriculture equal high conflictivity, but no claims making. This statement, however, clearly counteracts the land tenure conflict mapping, where underneath the non-claims categorisation, the area is in fact categorised as 'low level conflictivity'. Strictly speaking, this double categorisation shows, on the one hand, a major flaw in the analysis of Venencia *et al.*, but, on the other, beautifully illuminates the perspectives from which the conflict analysis is carried out.

Third, an additional piece of information is added to the results of Venencia *et al.* (2012). Conflicts (particularly social-ecological ones) are continuously monitored and georeferenced by EJOLT, 'a global research project bringing science and society together to catalogue and analyse ecological distribution conflicts and confront environmental injustice' (EJOLT 2016). Following the high conflict mapping of Venencia *et al.* (2012), conflicts – particularly in the northern part of the research area should be visible on EJOLT's environmental justice atlas (ejatlas). However, only one entry can be found on the atlas: a mining conflict in the surrounding of the town Metán, now resolved, where the locals successfully opposed the establishment of open pit mining for copper and silver (with elements of uranium). Biomass conflicts and/or land use change conflicts do not appear in the ejatlas.

In conclusion, the topic of (potential) land tenure conflicts is highly influenced by different thought styles and interpretation of facts and indicators. The maps of Venencia *et al.* (ibid.) have been used as one example to visualise such thought style developments, highlighting the necessity to include more perspectives and ground truth data.

GM soy-related effects

The introduction of GM soy in the 1990s was a major game changer in Argentina's agricultural landscape. The technological change led to two major forms of critique. From a global scientific point of view, the global distribution of environmental goods and bads is highly criticised by focusing on the role of the Global South and the Global North: 'GM crops are developed in the laboratory, usually in science-rich Western nations, tested in the field, and transported thence for commercial propagation in both naturally and socially variable environments' (Jasanoff 2006, p. 288). This statement bears close resemblance to the scientifically informed activist claims making represented in many environmental justice movements. The second criticism is more place-based and focuses on the north of Argentina. As Pengue (2005) argues, by far the greatest toll is found in the NOA, particularly in the provinces of Chaco, Santiago del Estero and Salta. This is explained by two factors: (1) the ecosystem varies greatly from the Pampas region; in the NOA, the most dominant ecosystem is the *monte*, supporting a unique and rich flora and fauna; and (2) this biodiversity is being drastically reduced by deforestation through bulldozing or fire (Leguizamón 2014, p. 154).

In short, particularly the second critique highlights the role of GM soy's introduction as a facilitator for change, leading to ecological effects (e.g. deforestation), which in turn cause social, economic and cultural changes.

Deforestation

Deforestation is not a new phenomenon in the study area (Boletta *et al.* 2006). However, as many studies show, the rate and acceleration of deforestation increased drastically with the introduction of GM soy in the region (Gasparri *et al.* 2008; Paolasso *et al.* 2012; Krapovickas *et al.* 2016). Long-term effects of deforestation on the carbon pool balance (Gasparri *et al.* 2008) or the ecohydrological imprint (Giménez *et al.* 2016) have not yet been exhaustively studied. However, as Bonino (2006) shows, losses are significant, particularly in the Gran Chaco, leading to a 'growing threat to natural ecosystems in the Dry forest (Chaco)' (Izquierdo and Grau 2009, p. 863).[2] The department of Anta can be considered a ' "hotspot" of Chaco deforestation' (Gasparri *et al.* 2013, p. 1611).

Gasparri *et al.* (ibid.), in their paper on Anta, analyse the correlation between soy production and deforestation. Their results show that pre-1997 marked moderate coupling of the two events, 1997–2002 brought a decoupling and from 2002 to 2010 was a strengthened correlation. Hence, it is seen that with the introduction of GMO seeds, deforestation is not a major problem, since the new seeds have to be planted on already prepared land in order to obtain optimum results. Additionally, low capital availability based on the national recession, combined with low international prices, is another factor highlighted by Gasparri *et al.* (ibid., p. 1612). After 2002, the trend follows a different direction, triggered by massive currency devaluation and thus increased attractiveness of land investment.[3]

Conflicts over deforestation: an example

The discussion based on social-environmental issues sheds light on the conflictive potential of deforestation, on the one hand, and the protection of the *monte*, on the other. One of the most prominent cases of conflict in the Chaco Salteño was observed in Pizarro; the impacts, underlying structures and contexts of this conflict have been widely discussed (Hufty 2008; Silva *et al.* 2010; González *et al.* 2012) and highlight the negative effects of non-protection. The conflict arose in the locality of General Pizarro in Salta, where the creole population (intensive land users), the indigenous Wichí community of Eben Ezer and the provincial authorities were involved. Contextually, the main issue here is the officially wanted abolition of a natural reserve (due to its failure to reach the requirements for a natural reserve) in 2003, theoretically allowing the clearing of land for soy production and the subsequent removal of the livelihoods of locals living off this particular land. With the help of scholars from the Universidad Nacional de Salta (UNSA), as well as the National Park Administration (NPA), the initial plans of the provincial government were prevented and a national park was considered the solution to the problem. However, members of the Eben Ezer community claim that the result de facto prohibits them from their traditional form of living, limiting their scope of action and territorial expansion (PER2).

The department of Anta ranks first in the province of Salta in terms of deforestation. Barbarán *et al.* (2015, p. 30) highlight the linearity of the correlation between deforestation, mortality rates and child malnutrition.

Fumigation

Fumigation is a core element of the biotechnological advance of GM soy and necessary for the business model currently in place in Argentina. Spraying of pesticide and herbicide is – unlike deforestation or land tenure change – not a one-off event, but occurs continuously in order to maintain production. Two challenges are observed. First, resistant pests, (such as Johnsongrass) as well as soy degradation, lead to the effect that Binimelis *et al.* (2009) call the 'transgenic treadmill', i.e. the steady increase in the use of agrochemicals to combat pest resistance. Second, the more agrochemicals are sprayed, the higher an impact they have on the surrounding environment. Those effects range from the reduction of biodiversity (both flora and fauna), also affecting small-scale farmers and household gardens, to cases of human health issues for both workers in the field as well as the local population living close to soy fields (Avila-Vasquez and Difilippo 2016).

Notes

1 As Ospina Peralta *et al.* (2015, p. 35) so clearly highlight, the concept of 'access' is more appropriate than 'property' in this case, since other and new forms of land use (e.g. concessions, leasing, etc.) are also taken into account.
2 This process occurs not only in the Chaco region, as Fearnside (2001), Mayle *et al.* (2007), Coy and Neuburger (2002), or Coy and Klingler (2011) show.
3 Similar patterns are found in Brazil, where at the end of the 2000s the BRL (Brazilian Real) was strong and the US$ weak, having the effect of reduced deforestation rates (Richards *et al.* 2012).

References

Aranda, D., 2010. *Argentina originaria: Genocidios, saqueos y resistencias.* Buenos Aires: Lavaca.

Arbolave, M., 2003. La renta de la tierra. *Márgenes Agropecuarios*, 18 (2016), 18–20.

Arceo, E.O., Basualdo, E.M. and Arceo, N., 2009. *La crisis mundial y el conflicto del agro.* Buenos Aires: Centro Cultural de la Cooperación Floreal Gorini; Página/12; Universidad Nacional de Quilmes.

Avila-Vasquez, M. and Difilippo, F., 2016. Agricultura tóxica y salud en pueblos fumigados de Argentina. *Crítica y Resistencia. Revista de conflictos sociales latinoamericanos*, 2, 23–45.

Barbarán, F., Rojas, L. and Arias, H., 2015. Sostenibilidad institucional y social de la expansión de la frontera agropecuaria. Boom sojero, políticas redistributivas y pago por servicios ambientales en el norte de Salta, Argentina. *Revista Iberoamericana de Economía Ecológica* [online], 24 (21–37). Available at: www.redibec.org/IVO/rev24_02.pdf

Binimelis, R., Pengue, W. and Monterroso, I., 2009. 'Transgenic treadmill': responses to the emergence and spread of glyphosate-resistant Johnsongrass in Argentina. *Geoforum*, 40 (4), 623–633.

Bisio, C., *et al.*, 2010. Los impactos de la agriculturalización en el Norte de Córdoba. In: N. López Castro and G. Prividero, eds. *Repensar la agricultura familiar: Aportes para desentrañar la complejidad agraria pampeana*. Buenos Aires: CICCUS, pp. 77–96.

Boletta, P.E., Ravelo, A.C., Planchuelo, A.M. and Grilli, M.P., 2006. Assessing deforestation in the Argentine Chaco. *Forest Ecology and Management*, 228 (1–3), 108–114.

Bonino, E.E., 2006. Changes in carbon pools associated with a land-use gradient in the Dry Chaco, Argentina. *Forest Ecology and Management*, 223 (1–3), 183–189.

Borras, S.M. and Franco, J.C., 2012. Global land grabbing and trajectories of agrarian change: a preliminary analysis. *Journal of Agrarian Change*, 12 (1), 34–59.

Bryceson, D.F., 2005. Peasant theories and smallholder policies. past and present. In: D. Bryceson, C. Kay and J. Mooij, eds. *Disappearing Peasantries?: Rural Labour in Africa, Asia and Latin America*. Warwickshire: ITDG, pp. 1–36.

Cáceres, D.M., 2015. Accumulation by dispossession and socio-environmental conflicts caused by the expansion of agribusiness in Argentina. *Journal of Agrarian Change*, 15 (1), 116–147.

Čapek, S.M., 1993. The 'environmental justice' frame: a conceptual discussion and an application. *Social Problems* [online], 40 (1), 5–24. Available at: www.jstor.org/stable/3097023

Chapin, M., 2004. A challenge to conservationists. *World Watch Magazine* [online], 17 (6), 17–31. Available at: www.worldwatch.org/node/565 (accessed 7 April 2016).

Coy, M. and Klingler, M., 2011. Pionierfronten im brasilianischen Amazonien zwischen alten Problemen und neuen Dynamiken. Das Beispiel des 'Entwicklungskorridors' Cuiabá (Mato Grosso)–Santarém (Pará). In: Innsbrucker Geographische Gesellschaft, ed. *Innsbrucker Jahresbericht 2008–2010*. Innsbruck: Innsbrucker Geographische Gesellschaft, pp. 109–129.

Coy, M. and Neuburger, M., 2002. Brasilianisches Amazonien. *Geographische Rundschau*, 54 (11), 12–20.

Davoudi, S. and Brooks, E., 2014. When does unequal become unfair? Judging claims of environmental injustice. *Environment and Planning A*, 46 (11), 2686–2702.

Delgado, O., 2007. La ruta de la soja en le Noroeste argentino. In: J. Rulli, ed. *Repúblicas Unidas de la Soja: Realidades sobre la producción de soja en América del Sur*, Huerquen, pp. 133–158.

Dobelmann, A., 2012. Neue Strukturen der Abhängigkeit: Das globale Produktionsnetzwerk der Gensojaproduktion in Argentinien. Ein Beitrag zur entwicklungstheoretischen Debatte. *PERIPHERIE*, 32 (128), 475–499.

Drummond, J., 2008. What I would like to see published in *Environmental Justice*. *Environmental Justice*, 1 (4), 179–182.

EJOLT, 2016. *Environmental Justice Organizations, Liabilities and Trade* [online], EJOLT. Available at: www.ejolt.org/ (accessed 25 April 2016).

Elvers, H.-D., Gross, M. and Heinrichs, H., 2008. The diversity of environmental justice. *European Societies*, 10 (5), 835–856.

Epstein, G.A., ed., 2005. *Financialization and the World Economy*. Cheltenham: Edward Elgar.

Fearnside, P.M., 2001. Soybean cultivation as a threat to the environment in Brazil. *Environmental Conservation*, 28 (1), 23–38.

Fieldman, G., 2013. Financialisation and ecological modernisation. *Environmental Politics*, 23 (2), 224–242.

Flitner, M., 2003. Umweltgerechtigkeit. Ein neuer Ansatz der sozialwissenschaftlichen Umweltforschung. In: P. Meusburger and T. Schwan, eds. *Humanökologie: Ansätze zur Überwindung der Natur-Kultur-Dichotomie*. Stuttgart: F. Steiner Verlag, pp. 139–160.

Flitner, M., 2007. *Lärm an der Grenze: Fluglärm und Umweltgerechtigkeit am Beispiel des binationalen Flughafens Basel-Mulhouse*. Stuttgart: Steiner.

Fredericks, S.E., 2011. Monitoring environmental justice. *Environmental Justice*, 4 (1), 63–69.

García-López, G.A. and Arizpe, N., 2010. Participatory processes in the soy conflicts in Paraguay and Argentina. *Ecological Economics*, 70 (2), 196–206.

Gasparri, N.I., Grau, H.R. and Gutiérrez Angonese, J., 2013. Linkages between soybean and neotropical deforestation: coupling and transient decoupling dynamics in a multi-decadal analysis. *Global Environmental Change*, 23 (6), 1605–1614.

Gasparri, N.I., Grau, H.R. and Manghi, E., 2008. Carbon pools and emissions from deforestation in extra-tropical forests of northern Argentina between 1900 and 2005. *Ecosystems*, 11 (8), 1247–1261.

Giancola, S.I., *et al.*, 2009. *Análisis de la cadena de soja en la Argentina*. INTA.

Giménez, R., *et al.*, 2016. The ecohydrological imprint of deforestation in the semi-arid Chaco: insights from the last forest remnants of a highly cultivated landscape. *Hydrological Processes*, 30 (15), 2603–2616.

Goldfarb, L. and van der Haar, G., 2016. The moving frontiers of genetically modified soy production: shifts in land control in the Argentinian Chaco. *The Journal of Peasant Studies*, 43 (2), 562–582.

Goldfarb, L. and Zoomers, A., 2013. The drivers behind the rapid expansion of genetically modified soya production into the Chaco Region of Argentina. In: Z. Fang, ed. *Biofuels – Economy, Environment and Sustainability*. Rijeka, Croatia: InTech.

González, A., Silva, A., de Viana, M.L. and López, E., 2012. Clearing Pizarro. *Environmental Justice*, 5 (2), 93–97.

Gras, C., 2009. Changing patterns in family farming: the case of the Pampa Region, Argentina. *Journal of Agrarian Change*, 9 (3), 345–364.

Gras, C., 2012. Los empresarios de la soja: cambios y continuidades en la fisonomía y composición interna de las empresas agropecuarias. *Mundo Agrario*, 12 (24).

Gras, C. and Hernandez, V.A., 2009. El fenómeno sojero en perspectiva: dimensiones productivas, sociales y simbólicas de la globalización agrorural en la Argentina. In: C. Gras, V.A. Hernandez and C. Albaladejo, eds. *La Argentina rural: De la agricultura familiar a los agronegocios*. Buenos Aires: Editorial Biblos, pp. 15–37.

Hafner, R., 2016. Figures [online]. Available at: http://roberthafner.at/figures (accessed 7 November 2017).

Hufty, M., 2008. Pizarro protected area: a political ecology perspective on land use, soybeans and Argentina's nature conservation policy. In: M. Galvin and T. Haller, eds. *People, Protected Areas and Global Change: Participatory Conservation in Latin America, Africa, Asia and Europe*. Bern: NCCR North-South, Swiss National Centre of Competence in Research North-South, University of Bern, pp. 145–173.

Izquierdo, A.E. and Grau, H.R., 2009. Agriculture adjustment, land-use transition and protected areas in Northwestern Argentina. *Journal of Environmental Management*, 90 (2), 858–865.

Jasanoff, S., 2006. Biotechnology and empire: the global power of seeds and science. *OSIRIS*, 21, 273–292.

Krapovickas, J., 2016. El extractivismo sojero y sus consecuencias humanas. Modelos de desarrollo en disputa en el Chaco Argentino. *alternativa. Revista de Estudios Rurales*, 5, 114.

Krapovickas, J. and Longhi, F., 2013. Probrezas, ruralidades y campesinos en el Chaco Argentino a comienzos del siglo XXI. *Estudios Rurales* 4.

Krapovickas, J., Sacci, L. and Hafner, R., 2016. Firewood supply and consumption in the context of agrarian change: the North Argentine Chaco from 1990 to 2010. *International Journal of the Commons* [online], 10 (1), 220–243. Available at: www. thecommonsjournal.org/articles/10.18352/ijc.609/

Langbehn, L., 2013. Conflictos y controversias por el Ordenamiento Territorialde Bosques Nativos en Salta. La cuestión ambiental y el control sobre el territorio. In: M.G. Merlinsky, ed. *Cartografías del conflicto ambiental en Argentina*. Ciudad Autónoma de Buenos Aires: Ediciones CICCUS, pp. 223–254.

Latour, B., 2013. *An Inquiry into Modes of Existence: An Anthropology of the Moderns*. Cambridge, MA: Harvard University Press.

Leguizamón, A., 2014. Modifying Argentina: GM soy and socio-environmental change. *Geoforum*, 53, 149–160.

Leguizamón, A., 2015. Disappearing nature?: Agribusiness, biotechnology and distance in Argentine soybean production. *The Journal of Peasant Studies*, 43 (2), 313–330.

León, C., *et al.*, 1985. El conflicto entre producción, sociedad y medio ambiente: La expansión agrícola en el sur de Salta. *Desarrollo Económico*, 25 (99), 399–420.

Martínez, L., 2004. El campesino andino y la globalización a fines del siglo (una mirada sobre el caso ecuatoriano). *European Review of Latin American and Caribbean Studies/Revista Europea de Estudios Latinoamericanos y del Caribe* [online], 77, 25–40. Available at: www.jstor.org/stable/25676133 (accessed 11 April 2016).

Mayle, F.E., Langstroth, R.P., Fisher, R.A. and Meir, P., 2007. Long-term forest-savannah dynamics in the Bolivian Amazon: implications for conservation. *Philosophical Transactions of the Royal Society B: Biological Sciences*, 362 (1478), 291–307.

Murgida, A.M., González, M.H. and Tiessen, H., 2014. Rainfall trends, land use change and adaptation in the Chaco Salteño region of Argentina. *Regional Environmental Change*, 14 (4), 1387–1394.

Naharro, N., Álvarez, M.A. and Klarik, M.F., 2010. Territorios en disputa: reflexiones acerca de los discursos que legitiman la propiedad de la tierra en el Chaco salteño. In: C.P. Medina, M. Zubillaga, M. de las and M.Á. Taboada, eds. *Suelos, producción agropecuariay cambio climáticoAvances en la Argentina*. Buenos Aires, pp. 133–154.

Nussbaum, M.M., 2013. Embedding issues of environmental justice in the mainstream curriculum. *Environmental Justice*, 6 (1), 34–40.

Ospina Peralta, P., Bebbington, A., Hollenstein, P., Nussbaum, I. and Ramirez, E., 2015. Extraterritorial investments, environmental crisis, and collective action in Latin America. *World Development*, 73, 32–43.

Pagina/12, 2010. Ayer la Rural, hoy Grobo. *Pagina/12* [online], 28 March. Available at: www.pagina12.com.ar/diario/suplementos/cash/17-4233-2010-03-28.html

Paolasso, P., Krapovickas, J. and Longhi, F., 2012. Agriculture and cattle frontier advance and variation of poverty in the northof the 'Gran Chaco Argentino' during the 1990s. In: V. Le Sandner Gall and R. Wehrhahn, eds. *Geographies of Inequality in Latin America*. Kiel: Im Selbstverlag des Geographischen Instituts der Universität Kiel, pp. 51–76.

Pellow, D.N., 2000. Environmental inequality formation: toward a theory of environmental injustice. *American Behavioral Scientist*, 43 (4), 581–601.

Pengue, W.A., 2005. Transgenic crops in Argentina: the ecological and social debt. *Bulletin of Science, Technology & Society*, 25 (4), 314–322.

Reboratti, C., 2012. Socio-environmental conflict in Argentina. *Journal of Latin American Geography*, 11 (2), 3–20.

Richards, P.D., Myers, R.J., Swinton, S.M. and Walker, R.T., 2012. Exchange rates, soybean supply response, and deforestation in South America. *Global Environmental Change*, 22 (2), 454–462.

RTRS, 2010. *RTRS Principles and Criteria for Responsible Soy Version 1.0*: RTRS.

Silva, A., *et al.*, 2010. *Desmontar Pizarro*. Salta, Argentina.

Silvetti, F. and Cáceres, D.M., 1998. Una perspectiva sociohistórica de las estrategias campesinas del noroeste de Córdoba, Argentina. *Debate Agrario*, 28, 103–127.

Slutzky, D., 2007. *Situaciones problemáticas de tenencia de la tierra en Argentina*. Estudios e investigaciones 14. Buenos Aires: Secretaría de Agricultura, Ganadería, Pesca y Alimentos.

Stratta Fernández, R. and de los Ríos Carmenado, I., 2010. Transformaciones agrícolas y despoblamiento en las comunidades rurales de la Región Pampeana Argentina. *Estudios Geográficos*, 71 (268), 235–265.

Teubal, M., 2006. Expansión del modelo sojero en Argentina. *Realidad Económica*, 220, 71–96.

van Dam, C., 2003. Cambio tecnológico, concentración de la propiedad y desarrollo sostenible. Los efectos de la introducción del paquete soja-siembra directa en el umbral al Chaco. *Debate Agrario*, 35, 133–181.

Venencia, C.D., Correa, J.J., Del Val, V., Buliubasich, C. and Seghezzo, L., 2012. Conflictos de tenencia de la tierra y sustentabilidad del uso del territorio del Chaco Salteño. *Avances en Energías Renovables y Medio Ambiente*, 16, 105–112.

Wald, N., 2015. In search of alternatives: peasant initiatives for a different development in Northern Argentina. *Latin American Perspectives*, 42 (2), 90–106.

Wilshusen, P.R., Brechin, S.R., Fortwangler, C.L. and West, P.C., 2002. Reinventing a square wheel: critique of a resurgent 'protection paradigm' in international biodiversity conservation. *Society & Natural Resources*, 15 (1), 17–40.

8 The case of Las Lajitas

Two approaches

A CLASSIC approach

The previous chapters aimed at the contextualisation of soy-driven social-ecological change in Argentina in general and the Chaco Salteño in particular. Viewed from a mainstream environmental justice perspective, all the above-mentioned changes and effects have the potential for conflict and claims making by the recipients of environmental bads based on maldistribution, misrecognition and non-participation.

So far, facts, data and information have been retrieved by relevant (scientific) literature and expert interviews, combined with (inter)national statistics. The subsequent compilation and analysis were carried out based on the author's thought style, expanded by the attempt to enter and present the thought style of the soy agribusiness in Argentina. When focusing on the effects of the research area's inclusion in the globalised soy agribusiness, a change of perspective was carried out in order to show – once again in the author's thought style – the basis for potential conflicts.

Context has been provided. The next step is to focus on the basic truth, searching for potentials for friction in the department of Anta, and even more so, focusing on the (non-)manifestation of conflict. In this sense, interaction among the different actors and the clash of thought styles will be at the foreground of the analysis in order to highlight the incommensurabilities of perceptions of social-ecological change. Simply put, the results of the following empirical analysis compare the thought styles according to their conclusion whether or not claims are being made.

On a first visit to the Chaco Salteño, three main areas of interest were identified (see Figure 7.2):

1   *The Southern Chaco Salteño*: This sub-region has a long-lasting tradition of horticulture, sugar crops, citrus and beans (Krapovickas *et al.* 2016, p. 233). Over the last 25 years, the major changes have occurred by an alteration in systems of agriculture (primarily towards non-tillage farming); deforestation, though visible, has not had as much impact as in the other two sub-regions.

2   *The Central Chaco Salteño* has experienced major land use change, particularly deforestation driven by agribusiness enterprises focussing on soy production. The focus of my research lies in this sub-region, since, as Krapovickas *et al.* (ibid., p. 233) highlight '[m]ajor environmental changes with socio-ecological effects on the local communities have occurred over a short period of time … [thus] locals' adaptation has been significantly shorter' than in area (1).

3   *The Northern Chaco Salteño* is considered a more rural area, with high forest coverage and not (yet) high levels of agrarian production. Future hot spots are already identified, particularly comprising factors of deforestation, indigenous land tenure and relocation of *puesteros* and *criollos* in favour of soy production.

In the end, I had to choose from among three different dynamics: either focus on (area 1), an established agricultural area where the general tradition of agricultural activity has dominated over decades (thus leaving – in my perception – little room for environmental justice claims) or place my major interest on a sub-region (area 2) where new and major changes are occurring, with major friction between actors, including indigenous communities, environmental NGOs, soy agribusiness representatives and social activists, i.e. the classic setting for environmental justice research carried out already *n*-times globally. Or I could focus on the intermediary part (area 3), where new dynamics of change have not yet faded, agribusiness is thriving, and little research has been done to focus on environmental justice issues with a broader set of actors in mind.

I chose the latter. The town of Las Lajitas, home to approximately 12,000 inhabitants (10,000 of whom live in the urban area) and nucleus of soy production in the Chaco Salteño, has become my base station and laboratory for my ideas.

In 1936, the region around Las Lajitas was connected to the national railway system; the Station 1126 marked the starting point for the foundation of the village of Las Lajitas in 1940. The main source of income derived from the extraction of sleepers, firewood and other forest-related goods, including the processing of charcoal. Nowadays, the self-definition of Lajiteños (i.e. people living in Lajitas) is best summarised as followed:

> In its majority, the inhabitants are criollos, some are of aboriginal descent. Spanish, Arabic, Turkish, Bolivian immigrants and their descendants have their roots in the region. Sharing culture and knowledge, they managed to build an entrepreneurial and progressive village that has been multiplying in the course of the time.
>
> (Escuela N° 4.510 'Antártida Argentina' 2010, p. 24)

Las Lajitas is located at the crossroads, both literally (in the form of the Provincial Routes 5, 30 and 52), being important for N–S transit and transportation of commodities, as well as figuratively, since new processes of globalised agri-business activities merge with traditional local forms of living. Out of this mix, and remaining in the environmental justice thought style, the potential for conflict is very high.

In order to develop my perspective on visually detectable conflict potentials in Las Lajitas,[1] I apply the visual method of shooting scripts (Collier and Collier 1986; Rothstein 1986), a set of questions guiding the act of taking photos in the research area (Rose 2012, p. 302). In other words, the photos 'provide a means by which photography can be grounded in a strategic and focussed exploration of answers to particular theoretically-generated questions' (Suchar 1997, p. 34). Following a common – however, not unproblematic – form of doing research (i.e. short-term, parachute-like research), the questions comprising the shooting script are:

- What representations of the agribusiness are found in Las Lajitas?
- Which conflict potentials can be visualised, based on macro-meso-level discussions on soy expansion? The core topics are related to GMO, fumigation, and issues of (denied) access to (public) land.

Having established the two basic questions, I took two days walking round all streets of Las Lajitas, taking geo-tagged photos and mapping as well as classifying the respective neighbourhoods according to their main (visual) function in relation to soy agribusiness. The second task performed in post-processing is to look at the photographs and highlight particular and visible environmental justice conflict potentials I can recognise based on other researchers' and activists' identification of environmental justice issues worldwide. It goes without saying that the majority of the visual potentials identified have a close relation to the most tangible underlying environmental justice dimension of distribution.

Figures 8.1 and 8.2 summarise the results of the mapping. Concerning infrastructure issues, the commercial and industrial areas of Las Lajitas are located in the southern and eastern parts of the town, which can easily be explained by the proximity to the major roads and exit points. Furthermore, the urban area is divided by railway tracks into a larger western and a smaller eastern area. This division can be observed in every urban area with railway access. This physical barrier is also resembled in the socio-economic status of the neighbourhoods. '*Del otro lado de la vía*' ('from the other side of the tracks') is considered a euphemism for less privileged areas. In the case of Las Lajitas, the eastern – and oldest – part is classified thus. While small-scale socio-spatial fragmentation is visible in all parts of the area, the most disadvantaged living conditions are found at the northern end along the railway tracks, located on *tierra fiscal* (state-owned public land) and thus not under the direct influence of the municipality of Las Lajitas. Going beyond the urban area, the town is virtually surrounded by soy fields, with two larger exceptions of land for animal breeding in the north-east and citrus

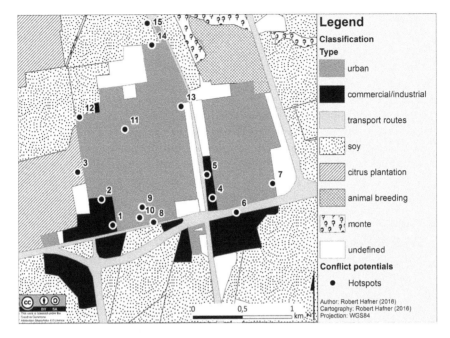

Figure 8.1 Author's first evaluation of (visual) conflict potentials in Las Lajitas.
Source: Hafner 2016.

plantations in the south-west, already highlighting the importance of the agribusiness in the region. Only small patches of *monte* are found north of Las Lajitas, which can be explained by the proximity to the River Río del Valle, the prohibition on deforestation in order to maintain areas of protection from the river.

The second piece of information that is represented on Figure 8.1 highlights the materialisation and geo-referencing of my perception of visual environmental justice conflict potential throughout the urban area of Las Lajitas. It is striking that the majority of the tags are located at the edge of the urban area, representing high metaphorical spill-over effects to residential sites. Table 8.1 gives more details on the perceived conflict potentials.

It is observed that particularly the southern part of the urban area is a cluster for businesses, valuing the proximity of Las Lajitas' main exit routes. Another interesting piece of information concerns the commercial/industrial area in the south-west. Located at the crossroads of the main national/provincial routes and separated from the rest of the urban area, this the self-defined *centro commercial* (commercial centre) has gained major popularity among agribusinesses. An increasing number of offices are established. The most expensive and most luxurious hotel of Las Lajitas (Hotel Las Lajitas) is also located in this commercial cluster. The relevance of this hotel for

Figure 8.2 Photos of conflict potentials of Figure 8.1.

agribusiness activity is highlighted through the pricing policy: Contrary to many tourist destinations, hotel prices are almost doubled during weekdays in comparison to weekends. Thus, one can say that the commercial centre is designed and used as an economic enclave physically detached from the rest of the town.

Table 8.1 First evaluation of (visual) conflict potentials in Las Lajitas

Nr.	Environmental justice evaluation	Description
1	Ownership of trailer: unknown Ownership of the plot: Municipality Las Lajitas Major EJ conflict potentials: • spillage of agrochemicals • noise • dust Probability of harm for neighbours: low	Right at the main entrance road to Las Lajitas, still in the commercial/industrial area, a storage area for heavy machinery (including sowing and harvesting equipment) is identified. My main focus here lies at the unlabelled silver tanker trailer. It is not visible, whether the trailer contains water or agrochemicals. In case of the latter, this would be an infringement of municipal law prohibiting agrochemicals to be transported or stored within the boundaries of urban space.
2	Ownership of plot: unknown Major EJ conflict potentials: • noise • dust Probability of harm for neighbours: very low	A machine park is located close to humble housings. Although still within the boundaries of the commercial/industrial area, negative EJ effects for the local neighbourhood cannot be ruled out. As opposed to picture 1, no tanker trailers have been seen.
3a	Ownership of the plot: unknown Major EJ conflict potentials: • spillage of agrochemicals • noise Probability of harm for neighbours: high	The plot is used for storage and maintenance of agricultural machinery, particularly *mosquitos* depicted in the picture. They are used for on-site fumigation. Technically, the area is outside the boundaries of the urban area of Las Lajitas, but the distance from the machinery to the nearest houses is minimal: a single-lane dirt street and a small ditch (approximately 2 metres) followed by a mesh wire fence. During my 14-month fieldwork, the working area has been expanded towards the north where households with low socio-economic status are found.
3b	Ownership of the plot: unknown Major EJ conflict potentials: • noise • emission of particulate matter Probability of harm for neighbours: medium	Expansion project of the industrial area. The sign says 'PLOTS FOR SALE'. These properties are ideal for the installation of storehouses, worksheds and areas for machinery since they account for excellent direct access from the main road without entering the urban area.

Table 8.1 Continued

Nr.	Environmental justice evaluation	Description
4	Ownership of the plot: Bunge Major EJ conflict potentials: • denial of access/trespassing • noise • transit Probability of harm for neighbours: very low	Along the railway tracks, the multinational company Bunge holds a fenced plot in front of the major silo, cutting off half of the eastern neighbourhoods from the western (central) ones, making it one of the most visible areas of agribusiness activity in the town. During harvest season, the plot is used as a parking space for trucks.
5	Ownership of the plot: Bunge Major EJ conflict potential: • emission of particulate matter during harvest season • smell • noise Probability of harm for neighbours: high	The most prominent and tallest construction in Las Lajitas is the soy silo located in the centre of the town, one block away from the main square. Currently operated by Bunge, it is used for storage of soy harvest. Due to the de facto location within urban space and its scale, the plant has a high impact on the local community.[1]
6	Major EJ conflict potential: • leakage of agrochemicals Probability of harm for neighbours: very low	The sight of a *mosquito* at the main road is not illegal, but since there is the urban area in its proximity, leakage of agrochemicals is a risk here.
7	Ownership of the plot: unknown Major EJ conflict potential: • leakage and/or remnants of agro-chemicals Probability of harm for neighbours: very high	This picture taken at the outskirts of Las Lajitas shows two sources of EJ conflict potential: The blue barrel in the middle, which is commonly used to store and transport agrochemicals and afterwards re-used privately for water storage. It remains unclear, whether the barrel has been used for chemical storage, washed or how it is used otherwise. The second source is the tanker with the writing 'FUMIGATION AND SOWING', indicating the previous/current use for agrochemicals. Considering its rusted state and major dents, it shows high risk potential for intoxication of its surroundings.
8	Ownership of the plot: unknown Major EJ conflict potential: • leakage and/or remnants of agro-chemicals Probability of harm for neighbours: low	The comparatively small storage plot is located within urban boundaries and holds predominantly harvesting machinery, including tanker trailers used for the distribution of agrochemicals, among others.

continued

Table 8.1 Continued

Nr.	Environmental justice evaluation	Description
9	Ownership of the plot: unknown Major EJ conflict potential: • noise Probability of harm for neighbours: very low	The plot is used for storage of agro-machinery.
10	Ownership of the plot: unknown Major EJ conflict potential: • leakage and/or remnants of agro-chemicals Probability of harm for neighbours: very high	In the middle of a residential area, a tanker trailer is parked. It is unclear, whether the machinery has been washed properly and/or is used for agrochemical appliances.
11	Ownership of the plot: public Major EJ conflict potentials: • leakage and/or remnants of agro-chemicals • high exposure to socio-economically disfavoured population, children Probability of harm for neighbours: very high	A tanker trailer is parked at a public space, close to humble housing sites. The danger of children playing with/on the machinery is very high, since access is not prohibited or hindered. It remains unclear, whether the trailer is used for water or other substances.
12	Ownership of the plot: unknown Major EJ conflict potentials: • exposure to agrochemicals during their application • emission of particulate matter during harvest season • smell • noise Probability of harm for neighbours: very high	The proximity of housing to soy fields is high, being separated by only a dirt road. No buffer zones have been established. The application of agrochemicals is in question, as are the potential direct effects on the local neighbours. This area is characterised by one-room houses and plastic-covered sheds with high numbers of household members.
13	Ownership of the plot: Grupo Segovia Major EJ conflict potential: • noise Probability of harm for neighbours: very low	The locally-based Grupo Segovia is one of the most visible companies in Las Lajitas, offering agroservices as well as cultivating fields. This plot depicted is used as an open air show- and storage room for tanker trailers and other agricultural machinery. Please also note the writing on the red trailer saying "DANGER INFLAMMABLE".

Table 8.1 Continued

Nr.	Environmental justice evaluation	Description
14	Ownership of the plot: unknown	Pictures 14 and 15 show a classic environmental justice situation. The neighbourhood consists of IPV social housings distributed by the Province of Salta. The location of those housing complexes is directly exposed to nearby soy fields; no barriers or buffer zones are established, making the houses and their inhabitants directly vulnerable to agribusiness activities.
15	Major EJ conflict potentials: • exposure to agrochemicals during their application • emission of particulate matter during harvest season • smell • noise Probability of harm for neighbours: very high	

Note
1 According to an interview with Mayor Fermani, use of the silo has to be stopped by 2018/2019.

Contextualisation

In this chapter I have assumed and portrayed a particular – and deliberately narrowly defined – role and perspective of a researcher by focusing on the visual/physical representations of environmental justice conflict potentials in Las Lajitas. The basis for the construction of this perspective has been twofold. First of all, I have tried to completely dive into the mainstream activist environmental justice thought style. This also indicates that my assumption of the place was that non-ideal situations for locals have to be present (thus following an ex-post approach). In other words, I *saw* the conflict potential by means of the context of the environmental justice thought style and thus created my personal reality. This does not indicate by any means that I was making up the conflict potentials, but rather followed the schemes of the thought collective's thought style. Procedurally, the method applied was coherent and led to the above visualisations. Second, the above-stated aim was to identify the visual, fixed and tangible features of soy agribusiness. Therefore, the main focus of conflict potentials was on distributive features; physical manifestations of participation or representation, for example, could not be found, leading to another crucial characteristic of the above-described methodology: No actors were in the picture, no stakeholders interviewed or members of the community talked to. Other approaches have to be used in order to obtain insights into actors' perspectives.

Re-contextualisation: adding the social component

Still in the narrow thought style, and based on the conflict potentials shown above, my next task was to identify actual claims making and resistance to the hotspots of injustice I identified. The basic almost common denominator revolved around the use, storage and potential of leakage of agrochemicals.

Naturally, I considered the first point of information the local hospital to look for official data on possible correlations between the application of agrochemicals and the incidence of diseases among the locals. No official data were available for my concern, but I was left with the following quotes from the SOC group:

> The topic is the following, we do not have a before and after … many people talk about allergies because they live close to the silos. But the silos are there basically since the village has started to grow. So, no, because I do not have medical statistics how it had been.
>
> (SOC1)

> If you ask me about 'allergies of the skin', we are the same in all the area…. Yes, there has been less fumigation, for sure, but the allergies are still here.
>
> (SOC1)

> In terms of malformations, we have periodical meetings about child mortality. They are not very different in places with great plantations … they are within the expectable level, on a national level.
>
> (SOC1)

In conclusion, no statistics are available, neither for nor against the application of agrochemicals. As an official representative of the hospital, SOC1 refrains from clear statements or personal perceptions. Recalling the case of the Madres de Ituzaingó, my quest was to find out to what extent popular epidemiology had been carried out in Las Lajitas. Unlike in Ituzaingó, no initiative to highlight or document increases in illnesses has been taken in the town. Nevertheless, persons related to health issues mentioned (informally) 'the increase in illnesses is not high high [*sic*], but it is through the conversation with the close relative of the patient … the doctor asks in which zone (s)he lives and … there is the deduction' (SOC2), meaning that there are heightened senses of correlations, but even if there were evidence for maldistribution of environmental bads (the classic foundation for environmental justice claims making), no organised entity is in sight to take on the task of contextualising claims:

> There are no environmental activists. There are none. Yes, there may be people complaining about the collecting site, the silos, the fumigations, asking where the tanks are disposed of. But there is no great activity against, nothing, nothing organised.
>
> (ASC1)

Reflection

Having applied the thought style of environmental justice (activism) to guide the conceptualisation of the first part of the empirical study, it has become apparent that the conflict potential identified and the expected claims making (which is the central trigger for change in the field) did not match at all with the empirical findings so far.

With reference to Erving Goffman's (1990, pp. 113–115) stage metaphor, certain actions are designed to be carried out on the front stage; they are clearly visible to every spectator. The interesting structures and actions, however, are carried out off-stage, where the performers are allowed to drop their façade, articulate their beliefs and share their ways of thinking. So far, from the perspective of locals, I have not *seen* what was going on in the village; I was a lay person *looking* around, without the place-specific contextualisation and frame. I had to look behind the curtains, live the daily life, get to know what was going on in order to understand regional dynamics beyond the front stage plays such as:

ME: Does one talk about taking away the silo?
ASC2: No, no … there is no conflict … there is one that practically does not work.

Or:

ASC3 (quite nonchalantly): When they are pesticide spraying, we are surrounded. People do not complain.
ASC4: But that is nothing new, this has happened already 20–30 years before.

An ALTERNATIVE approach

So, the next task is to go beyond the CLASSIC to include the ALTERNATIVE perspective by asking the questions: what do people care about?, what do people complain about?, and what goes beyond the mere articulation of discontent?

In order to answer those questions – and to avoid the trap of bipolarisation between representatives of the soy agribusiness and actors opposing agricultural activities, five actor categories[2] have been established (Table 8.2).

A prequel to the EJIF: four thought collectives unearthed

The environmental justice incommensurabilities framework (EJIF) is used as a tool to systematically analyse different thought styles and compare them with one another. Since the main idea is to understand incommensurabilities among the groups of actors, it is first necessary to identify the respective thought styles and backgrounds. Or to put it differently 'it is not enough for

Table 8.2 Classification of actors used in the EJIF

Type	Description	Acronyms	# of interviews
Soy agribusiness	The majority of the members of this group are farmers, members of *pooles de siembra*, and/or agro service providers	SAB	12
Local administrations, support and control institutions	Those actors range from local politicians, members of the public sector, representatives of the police, environmental enforcement groups as well as representatives of INTA	ASC	14
Schools and education entities	This category comprises representatives of schools, i.e. headmasters, teachers and librarians	EDU	8
Social entities	Members of social entities are considered hospital staff (both administrative and medical), members of health centres, social workers that work directly "in the field", visiting households, heads of religious organizations with social projects in the region (e.g. soup kitchens)	SOC	8
Local perception actors	This group comprises locals with whom I spent significant amounts of time and thus gained insights into their ways of thinking and acting	PEL (Las Lajitas) PEM (Coronel Mollinedo) PER (regional)	37

Note
* The number of interviews represents only those that were directly used in the subsequent analysis.

researchers to identify where people are (both socially and spatially) – they must also question where they/we are coming from, going to and where on these paths research encounters have occurred' (Crang and Cook 2007, p. 10).

In so doing, the following pages contain five different 'stories' of thought collectives, where individual elements and histories are core elements, but should be seen as a representation of the collective memory of particular groups. Where needed, contextualisation and interpretation are provided. However, the main goal is to let the interviewees 'speak for themselves' as much as possible, capturing what Ludwik Fleck (2008, p. 91) called the 'peculiar magic of thought' (my translation). This approach considers Maristella Svampa's *Los que ganaron* (2001) to work with direct quotations, but opts for a more radical version to strengthen the core topics within the thought styles. Additionally, Max Weber's 'Idealtypus' (1988), though in a less stringent form, has been influential to highlight central aspects of the thought styles' particular realities.

1 Soy agribusiness actors (SAB)

'IF YOU WANT TO GET SOMETHING DONE, DO IT YOURSELF'

Soy agribusiness actors have had a major influence on the shaping of the region. Their general self-perception circulates around the fact that they have pushed forward the soy frontier, towards new and more difficult territories for doing business.

> This is an area – I always compare it with Buenos Aires – here you have an order of sowing that is much more violent than over there. In Buenos Aires/Santa Fe (Humid Pampa) you can start sowing soy from October to the first week of December. You have a comfortable 60-day period for sowing. Not here, here it starts raining in November, you have to sow your entire surface until the middle of December. Because if you reach January, the return is minor. Here it is much faster, the plagues are much more difficult, there is pasture resistant to glyphosate; it is much more difficult to produce here. And you arrive here in December, here with giant seed drills, everybody working flat out. And it is very competitive, this sector in Argentina. And here, I tell you, it is even more competitive. It is more complicated.
>
> (SAB1)

The South–North and core–periphery movement is clearly visible. Those who started sowing early on focused on the land close to the urban area. The main choice of crop was beans, since there have already been high levels of expertise in the southern region of the Chaco Salteño, particularly around Rosario de la Frontera, south of Las Lajitas (SAB2, SAB3). Only with time, soy and corn have become of increasing interest for the farmers themselves. This on-site perception goes hand in hand with the macro-analysis of soy field expansion.

Thus, local soy farmers take great pride in the fact that they thrive under substantial pressure and bad conditions: Transportation costs are high, agricultural seasons are shorter than in the Pampas region, and most importantly, technical support from outside the field is very low. Here, the main source of complaint is directed towards INTA. While quite appreciative and collaborative in the 1970s, INTA was a respected partner in finding new varieties of corn and sorghum suited to the region so they did not have to depend on the production of beans ('We were conscious that working in agriculture we have to do non-monocultures. We did not want to, we did not have to, we were conscious of that'; SAB6). However, today's perception of INTA is that they are only working for small-scale (family) farmers; soy farmers feel left out. The main concern articulated deals with the fact that INTA technicians do not understand the problems and pressing issues today's soy farmers have to face:

> How many people from INTA are working in the fields nowadays, and how many are sitting there in Cerrillos [INTA's main office close to Salta Capital]? They are all there drinking mate.
>
> (SAB2)

> Here they have opened a technological information office a month ago. They held a meeting and said, 'Well, now you will have a local window so that you, the producers, know what INTA is doing.' So I said: 'No, you are wrong. This is a window for you to know what we are doing and what we need.'
>
> (SAB2)

Another indicator of the strong dissent among the actors is highlighted by a concrete project carried out by the Grupo Las Lajitas: 'We have established an experimental site. 600 sites in an area of 100,000 ha, sized 25–30 ha, that we have set up, but not INTA' (SAB2). This strong sentiment that INTA is out of sync is also replicated for the soy farmers' relationship with universities, particularly the Universidad Nacional de Salta where 'they have our sector pre-conceptualized as a sector that is going after the profit, that we don't give a shit about sustainability and natural resources' (SAB2). This negative sentiment is deeply embedded in the local farmers' thought style: Possible cooperation in search of finding solutions to pressing issues (e.g. the rise of the water table) is doomed from the start, pointing fingers at the farmers and blaming them for having caused the problems in the first place. Farmers are well aware that their activity changes the environmental conditions:

> We know that it will not equally work out. It is impossible replacing a system as complicated as a forest with a system that is simple as in most of the cases of two crops, soy and corn, to function alike.
>
> (SAB2)

With respect to the perceived institutionalised prejudice from INTA and the Universidad Nacional de Salta, lack of recognition is the main issue for large-scale farmers: 'But we are not the wrong component. They chose sides' (SAB2). This latent friction was noticeable with all the representatives of the soy agribusiness.

Continuing with the notion, 'if you want to get something done, do it yourself', the Grupo Las Lajitas was founded to provide technical information and training to its members. Access to the group has traditionally been open;

they started to compile publications and tried to find financing among the soy producers and service providers (including Monsanto or Bayer), and then distribute the information free of charge. Today, the group comprises about 12 companies, with the prospect of increasing its size (SAB2). Its structure and work focus are based on the members' individual needs for problem solving, i.e. organised as a form of self-help group. This feature distinguishes Grupo Las Lajitas from the nation-wide CREA (Asociación Argentina de Consorcios Regionales de Experimentación Agrícola), dealing with technical innovation and crop experimentation. However, the latter is considered to work with a more closed methodology and on a national level, leaving out the particularities of doing agriculture in the area of Las Lajitas. Other associations that are visible are CREA ganadero (focused on cattle breeding), CREA Anta (the department branch of CREA), Asociación PROGRANO and the Sociedad Rural de Salta (Rural Society of Salta). Members of those unions share similar thought styles revolving around the notion of 'we are working for the *campo* [i.e. the productive part of rural space]'. However, the connection to nation-wide organisations or national headquarters of unions and interest groups is less developed, highlighted by the fact that the soy frontier in the Chaco Salteño does have different characteristics and needs to be compared to the rest of the country's productive industry. This relationship experienced a major change in 2008 during the lock-out, when the core interests of all members of the soy industry were at stake:

> Here in Salta we have a very good relationship with the regional Agrarian Association. At the national level it was not like that until 2008. In 2008, we united because it was natural, because it made no sense being divided.
>
> (SAB6)

THERE WILL BE (OUTSOURCED) GROWTH

One core axiom of the agribusiness thought style is based on the element of growth. 'The farmer tends to – if he can – grow; and he tries to grow in the field he is familiar with and knows. It is to do more of the same' (SAB2). Thus, growth is considered in the form of territorial expansion and/or increase in yield per hectare. It is clear that deforestation plays a central role for development: 'We have the vision that everything has to be deforested' (SAB6). However, it is recognised that 'those with a more environmentalist perspective put pressure on that all the forest should be preserved' (SAB6), leading to the BATNA (i.e. best alternative to a negotiated agreement) position that 'the equilibrium is in the middle' (SAB6). Thus, the final agreement resulted in the forest classification and the allotment of 15 million ha for agriculture, 1.5 million ha for cattle breeding (which have been reduced since it was not expected that yellow zones would expand that far). Conflicts related to deforestation are not perceived around Las Lajitas, since it is an already 'super-developed' (SAB10) area, with 'an impact of deforestation that is very humble concerning hectares' (SAB10).

The other form of growth lies in innovation. If needed, technical cooperation among producers is not uncommon (as with the example of Grupo Las Lajitas), particularly in the application of new methods (most prominently during the introduction of non-tillage farming) and local adjustments of technological packages. However, the expansion of business does not occur vertically. The secondary sector is very little developed, since the farmers are 'producers, and imagining them as industrials, it is a world they do not manage' (SAB2).

Thus, it comes as no surprise that outsourcing is – much like in any other agribusiness regions in Argentina – an omnipresent feature:

> Everything work-related is outsourced: sowing, harvesting, fertilisation, fumigation, extraction, packaging. The companies come from Jujuy, Salta, Buenos Aires, Santa Fe, Cordoba, Tucuman. For harvesting, they are coming from the south, from Buenos Aires. One always tries to keep the people; the contractors have to have everything in order.
>
> (SAB4)

Unlike in the south, only locally operating contractors do not exist due to the short productive season. The contractor 'buys a machine, sows for one person. When he finishes, everything else is already sown. He has to store away the machine for next year' (SAB2).

One of the most labour-intensive tasks outsourced is the actual clearing of the land and preparation for agricultural production. The contractors (mostly individuals from the region) often hire day-to-day labourers to carry out the groundwork, while heavy machinery is applied by stable personnel or once again subcontracted to other companies. In all cases the actors involved highlight that every worker has to be legally employed. Since the owner of the land is equally responsible for the workers to have their papers in order (a task carried out by the contractors), high priority is given to the question of who to work with by the farmers. In terms of provision of labour, most work is available during seasons of high profit:

> The idea is, whenever you are doing well, invest … here you have greater risk, it is a marginal area; and the types of investment are different. In the Pampa you buy land in instalments, here you buy land for development.
>
> (SAB1)

COME RAIN OR COME SHINE: THE PROBLEM WITH WATER

The core variable for soy farmers is water (SAB2). The quantity of rain defines the level of success:

And then there is always the topic of water. This year we are below the historic average of rain in the field. It rained 400 mm and it should have rained 600 mm. We have had years with 750 mm and more than 3,000 kg of soy per hectare, and with 400 mm 1,000 kg.

(SAB4)

Here you have soil that does not forgive you if it does not rain for 20 days. With rainfall of 50–60 mm in February, it would have been a record harvest. It did not rain and you get 1,300 kg of soy when the norm is over 3,000 kg. Last year it was 800 kg.

(SAB1)

Last winter made us cry because of the drought. Hopefully, it will not be like last year. It is serious and critical.

(SAB5)

However, water surplus, particularly due to the increase in the water table, also poses a major threat to a significant number of soy fields around Las Lajitas, making the entrance of heavy machinery almost impossible, thus creating major operational problems. Some affected farmers started to construct dams and drainages to keep the water out, but a macro-level focus was missing. INTA insisted on working to focus on the river basin, but

many times there is a discourse they are repeating, but when it is time to settle on defining a methodology: 'Focus on the basin' – but they do not tell us how it is done. We are suffering from the absence of an academic agreement.

(SAB2)

Additionally, strong lobbying is carried out to co-finance adaptation measures, or at least trying to reduce property taxes by the amount farmers have to invest in fixing ground water issues.

A direct consequence of both scenarios, besides the loss of income, is the increase in land lease and the high reduction of deforestation development and investment. 'It does not work, because you won't be getting any profit for the first years' (SAB4). Another major concern for local small to medium-scale producers is the increase in competition from outside of the region: 'When it does not rain, they come from other places to buy good land at a very low price' (SAB5), fearing worse working conditions and negative impacts on their own plots due to other styles – more shaped by real estate investment – of business. From the perspective of local soy farmers, about six big players from the provinces of Cordoba and Santa Fe have expanded their business towards Las Lajitas, and they 'take a bit of the cake' with them (SAB4). An interesting aspect here is the fact that even business insiders, technical managers and farmers are not sure whether other big players are acting in the region. However, a big distinction is made between those who do farming for a living (most of the local farmers define themselves as such, since it is more 'legitimate, more authentic, the interest in production', SAB2) and those who see agriculture as a real estate business, as in the case of CRESUD. This company has its main operation at the easternmost frontier of Las Lajitas, where the conditions for soy production are highly unfavourable; but 'CRESUD will be applying pressure until it can sell [the properties] not for cattle breeding but for agriculture' (SAB2).

TRIAL AND ERROR: WHY ORGANIC FARMING DOES NOT WORK

All soy fields in the region are cultivated with GMO. Some farmers have tried to follow the organic route, but failed:

> It has been an adventure, I have made organic soy and I tell you, it was not sustainable. The extensive organic production was a practical joke, because instead of using agrochemicals, one uses mechanical controls. You don't know what this was for the soil. The worst damage we have done to the soil has been with organic production, the turning-over of the soil … it is criminal what you are doing with the organic material … it is much worse than non-tillage farming.
>
> (SAB2)

The term 'sustainability' is predominantly used when talking about soil. The main preoccupation is that the soil quality is diminishing, depending on the different locations, but the concrete drivers have yet to be identified. Absolutely degraded areas, however, do not exist in the perception of the local farmers. If there were some, they would 'take them instantly' (SAB2).

Additionally, there is hardly any ecological problem seen with (aerial) fumigation. However, struggles with bureaucracy are highlighted. Aerial fumigation has become much more difficult, having to register each flight at the local environmental office and having to notify and let neighbours sign off beforehand (SAB4). Claims are being made that this procedure takes too long in cases where fast fumigation has to occur to counteract sudden pest strikes, endangering the yield of the upcoming harvest.

FROM CATTLE TO SOY AND BACK: THE ANCHOR EFFECT

Another aspect of regional change has to do with the interrelation between cattle breeding and soy production. 'When I arrived in this area, there have been installations of cattle breeding. You could see cows. Here, the cows have been carried/run like that [towards the east]' (SAB2). The advantage of cattle breeding in the region is the fast use of the land, cattle are held either on pasture or *bajo monte* (under semi-cleared forest) (SAB4). Consequently, 'whenever there is cattle breeding, there is always more *monte*' (SAB4). Two main strategies can be identified: first, cattle breeding is used as a means of income during the transition phase from *monte* to deforested and prepared land for crop production. 'The idea is to deforest new places, medium term to try if agriculture works, but at the beginning, it is for cattle breeding' (SAB2). Thus, it is considered a temporary place-based activity that constantly moves at the forefront of the soy frontier, particularly towards the dryer areas east of Las Lajitas. Second, cattle breeding is used as a coping strategy to deal with seasonal climate changes. 'On the land, I want to do agriculture – cattle breeding. I am going to define it depending on how the weather is behaving. We are going to sow pasture on our plots' (SAB1).

For the majority of the local farmers, the combination of cattle breeding and agriculture has one great advantage: When doing the necessary crop rotation (which is the most predominant form in the region) to maintain soil coverage, soy is alternated with corn. Since the prices for corn are set in the harbour of Rosario (not to mention the stock exchange in Chicago), and corn has higher transportation costs than soy (for one tonne of corn transported, half of the cost has to be used to pay the transportation, according to SAB2), it is considered a low-profit business. However, when breeding cattle, parts of the corn can be used for fodder, adding value and generating higher returns. This holds particularly true for locally-based feedlots (there are still very few feedlots found in the department of Anta, predominantly around the area of Joaquín V. González). Nevertheless, only three of the biggest farmers in the region (Las Lajitas SA, Anta del Dorado, Agroagil) actually apply this mix of cattle breeding and soy/corn farming, often explained as 'the people who are cattle breeding, they do it because it is something they like. It is a subjective decision' (SAB2).

As well as it being something farmers prefer, cattle breeding can be also associated with the anchoring effect (Chapman and Johnson 1999; Mussweiler and Strack 1999; Mussweiler and Englich 2005), i.e. if an initial decision is made, one tends to come back to this very result in subsequent decision processes, thus acting like an anchor.

CERTIFICATION: THE NONSENSICALITY OF SENSE AND SANITY

From a European perspective, it is surprising to see that certification of soy only plays a minor role in the research area. One big company, Vilucco, offers RTRS-certified crops. Though proud to have certification, the local managers mention the high bureaucratic effort to maintain the certification. Reasons for non-certification are manifold. From the perspective of RTRS, the Chaco Salteño does not provide enough companies eligible for the process (due to deforestation measures carried out after the Forest Law of 2008), complemented by the fact that RTRS is not considered to have the manpower to expand beyond the Humid Pampa, their core area of operation in Argentina (SAB8). Additionally, RTRS is a members organisation, depending on the soy agribusiness for financial support ('I am only an employee', SAB8), hence the rules and regulations for certification are perceived to be barely above the already legal norms. Taking this aspect into consideration, non-participating soy farmers do not see basic advantages for certification, the costs prevail (SAB9).

> The certification does not go far enough for me. I mean, it is what they are doing. There is not enough information to give your signature that you are sustainable.... They charge you five US dollars per hectare and they give you a seal. It permits you to sell to Europe, and it serves the customers for their conscience.
>
> (SAB2)

CONFLICTS: SOMETHING OF THE PAST

Soy farmers hardly mention open conflicts or conflictive situations. Salta Forestal, however, is always cited as a negative example of regional development. During the provincial governorship of Juan Carlos Olmedo, he established a project to develop large areas of *tierras fiscales*, covered in *monte*. The 99-year concession for almost unlimited usufruct was handed out to a group of businesspeople close to Olmedo: 'Instead of alternatives, he handed over 350,000 ha – with people and everything – to two persons: Olmedo and Cervera' (SAB2). People were (forcefully) relocated and most of the land cleared for agribusiness. 'There are many families living in conflict there' (SAB2), but hardly any public notice has been taken of the injustices. The general conception here is that this conflict has been handled incorrectly and works as a bad example for development in the soy community. Another conflict situation was located north of Las Lajitas, in General Pizarro, where similar constellations have been in place. However, 'they did not want to make the same mistakes, there have been more actors involved, there was Greenpeace, it came out on TV' (SAB2). Resistance against deforestation has been enormous, also due to the fact that a local indigenous community of Wichí (*Eben Ezer*) had been directly affected, creating even more publicity.

But resettlement from the (former) *monte* to villages does not necessarily connote negativity, but is generally perceived as a positive step towards development:

> There have been people living next to the river, they had their land in there [in the *monte*] over there. So now they are happy to live here [in the village] ... some happy, others no. Because the change from the retreat alone in the *monte* and now living with neighbours, it was ... well ... but when people felt what it was like living in a village, with running water, taps, electricity, having the secondary school nearby, having a grocery store, a butcher, having a primary school....
>
> (SAB6)

SOCIAL RESPONSIBILITY: SOMETHING OF THE PRESENT

The businessmen also have to take care of the common good.

(SAB7)

There are two types: people who have good intentions and people who want to make business.

(SAB2)

Few owners and operators of soy farms live in the area around Las Lajitas. In an act of self-reflection, producers from outside articulate that they are 'in debt to the village'. 'Here it has been bonanza for the last seven years. I have not extracted as much in Buenos Aires as I have done here' (SAB1). There is a strong notion that the producers should give back to the community, but

> [they] are going to be jerks. They do not have any obligation either, because well … they should have a moral obligation. But, well, I say that I come here with a land of 6,000 ha, I come here to eat, at night to eat barbecue, to play the guitar, and I see people living in a different way. What one could help, one should help.
>
> (SAB1)

The articulation of claims like the above follows a very specific pattern that has been replicated by the majority of the interviewees. From a semantic standpoint, claims are always directed towards 'them', the 'others' separating the producers into 'the bad ones' (i.e. the others) and the 'good ones' (including me, the good soy producer). External soy producers then go about making their connections to the town of Las Lajitas, highlighting their personal, social involvement (even though it is mainly reduced to a handful of restaurants and bars), legitimating their claims making. The last component of the claim is a call for action, uttered in a neutral way: 'one has to do something'. Summing up, the problem is identified ('them'), the personal involvement is legitimised ('I participate'), and – vague – general solutions are proposed. One such solution to 'give back to the community' is considered the establishment of a school of agriculture in Las Lajitas. The plot was donated by a soy farmer, and the construction co-funded. This perceived best-practice example is based on the education of locals so they could then work as technicians for soy farmers, i.e. a win-win situation. The farmers invest in locals who then have the potential to become part of the business. However, it has to be borne in mind that the number of employees per 1,000 hectares ranges from one to three persons.

2 *Local administration, support and control actors (ASC)*

THE STORYLINE: HOW THE *CAMPO* HAS BECOME THE VILLAGE

In the beginning, people lived in the *monte*, carrying out hunting and gathering. Then,

> we have started to work on the natural environment. The cattle breeding movement starts ... not agricultural, but cattle breeding – *bajo monte* ... you put up a *puesto*, a place where you go and settle – now they are called *fincas*.
>
> (ASC5)

Puesteros were scattered over vast areas of land, making cheese, looking for honey, keeping goats for eating. And 'they never came to the village' (ASC5).

With the introduction of cattle, everything changed:

> It began opening up to what is agriculture. Putting cattle in the virgin *monte*, there is a change. Agriculture began, and so did deforestation ... but not great extensions, one cultivated corn, pumpkin, some wheat, beans and chickpea – all for the people in the area.
>
> (ASC5)

The actual shift from the production of beans to soy, it is argued, is due to sanitary problems, making soy easier to handle. The cultivation of beans then was pushed increasingly to the north, towards the eastern parts of the department of Orán and the area around the department of San Martín (ASC4).

While cattle breeding is considered a central trigger, deforestation in the last 12 years has been the main driver for change. Developing deforestation in the region is difficult, disadvantaging the medium-scale farmers, even though forests are predominantly classified as green areas. 'Deforestation does not push forward any more because there are *lotes fiscales* [i.e. state-owned public lots] that have already been commissioned. So they have their problems, no individual can come and deforest unless it is a commissioned company' (ASC4). However, anyway, 'the land has changed a lot ... they have deforested a vast quantity. Here, there was a lot of *monte*. Now, there is almost no *monte* any more' (ASC6). A direct social consequence is the decreased use of firewood by locals:

> Before, you had the *monte* nearby and you extracted firewood. Deforestation of the zone has changed as well. The quebracho tree, a native plant, is killed by glyphosate.
>
> (ASC9)

Some locals still use firewood, but very few – because there is none.

(ASC1)

The production of soy started on a small scale in the 1980s in Rosario de la Frontera and Las Lajitas. 'Now, the soy boom has been produced here. Here it began to grow in progressive form' (ASC4).

MIGRATION PATTERNS: DO YOU STAY OR DO YOU GO?

Three basic migration stories are found in Las Lajitas: (1) the people who have lived in the *monte* and now migrated/were encouraged or forced to migrate to the urban area; (2) soy farmers and their employees, moving from the South to the soy frontier; and (3) temporary migration of 'soy tourists'.

CONFLICTS OF ONE-OFF EVENTS: SOMETHING OF THE PAST

> In Anta, there have not been conflicts like in the North. They go longer back, they were predominantly with *criollos* when they made land sales to investors coming from other parts of the country or foreigners. They bought large areas; the plots were cattle breeding areas from 150, 200 years ago until 30–40 years ago … and everything cattle breeding in the *monte*. So it was not like there was no population, nor that there was any production, it was carried out with the *monte*.
>
> (ASC4)

The change of land tenure included particular contractual clauses, ensuring the smooth operation of land use change:

> When the land was sold, there was always the clause 'empty space'. So when the investors came, everybody had to leave the land. But that is not something new, it has already happened 20, 30 years ago. It has accelerated a couple of years ago because there was a massive sale of land.
>
> (ASC12)

Hence, this type of often forced migration leads to a fast-paced re-arrangement of individuals' lifestyles. 'The minority got a place where they could take their animals and continue their way of production. The majority had to sell, often kill their animals and move to the peri-urban areas' (ASC4). Continuing with the thought style's chain of causality, challenges for the ASC group arose:

> This was the growth that was experienced by all the villages here, par-ticularly in the department of Anta in the last 15 years. Basically, those precarious settlements that were being transformed into neighbourhoods, with certain services … a growth of the chaotic form … and with enormous pressure on the municipalities to offer services. And an

important burden is that the people left their productive circle. Before, they had been learning, generation by generation, the profession of cattle breeding in their system – cattle breeding in the *monte*.

(ASC12)

SOUTHERN ETHICS TO THE NORTH

Since I have come the village has grown in size … I have been working with an owner who had a *finca* here, he worked there [in Buenos Aires] and came over here. He asked me if I wanted to work in another company there, or come to the fields [around Las Lajitas].

(ASC6)

Such migration stories are common for people living in Las Lajitas and occupying (secondary) posts in the local administrations or volunteer organisations (e.g. firefighters). However, the overall population is shrinking again; at the beginning of the soy boom, the population increase was due to the influx of people from the service industry (ASC7). 2012 was a key year when the socio-economic characteristics began to change. Plot sizes increased, the children of small-scale farmers are not interested in agriculture; the land is sold (ASC7).

SOY TOURISTS AND THEIR LOCAL DETACHMENT

Soy tourists are considered representatives of the agribusiness staying only for the short term in Las Lajitas and being otherwise detached from the town. The main concern of ASC is that 'there are many large *fincas* … they are all people from abroad that do not leave any money in the village' (ASC6). Hence, the relationship with representatives of the soy agribusiness is characterised by ambivalence:

The farmers … ehhh … you have everything with the farmers. There are some that are conscious of what they are doing, applying all the norms, and there are others that don't. Those ones have local managers that make the economic difference; they do not care what they are doing.

(ASC9)

At irregular intervals, municipal representatives meet with farmers for an exchange of ideas. The above classification of actors is reflected here as well:

Here are about 60 farmers, half of whom I talk to, the others I do not even know, they are from Buenos Aires, from Cordoba, Jujuy.

(ASC9)

The farmers that do most for the locals are those who are living here most of the time, or are more permanently here…. Some that live here are those who give the most support, because their children go to school, they need the hospital. They already see the other side and are aware of the necessities of the communities. And those who do not live here, they send their manager and they do not care much about what is going on in the village. I say, they are tourists and they come one or two nights, once or twice a month.

(ASC9)

THE CONSEQUENCES OF ABSENT WATER: WHEN IT DOES NOT RAIN, IT POURS

As seen with the soy agribusiness actors, perceived changes in water supply are a core trigger for action. Even though on a regional level, precipitation is increasing, the perception is different:

Water for individual consumption is no problem. The issue is for agri-culture. Here, it rains 1,000 mm per year. The issue is when it does not come – like last year when it rained 400 mm – there is no production. There is a moment when the plant needs a certain amount of water, and if it does not rain, it does not have humidity [*sic*]. This happens predomi-nantly during sowing in December and January when there is most heat in the area. The sun is burning, and if there is no water, the plant does not move.

(ASC9)

Every time it rains less. If it does not rain more, they will be excavating wells everywhere to get some water, they will be making channels. Until now, the ground water level is not falling since the water comes from the hills, the mountain. I saw a map of hydrological resources and there is quite some water. Yes, it is about 30 metres below surface; there are other places where it is at 9 metres.

(ASC1)

Also the communication gap – that is interestingly enough experienced by the soy agribusiness actors alike – with research institutions is wide: 'Environ-mental issues are studied by the Universidad Nacional de Salta, but I don't know what they say' (ASC8).

However, the major concern here is not the provision of water for agri-culture, but the effects new projects have on the local community:

There are a lot of great investments in irrigation infrastructure. But in all those areas you have problems of changing ownership of land: The closing of country roads; the majority has had access to the river, but now they are closed with fences. This generates many social problems, because the *fincas* are very large. Sometimes they are some kilometres long. It is crazy. The people have to walk around in that case.

(ASC4)

Additionally, the absence of water is considered to have other – often invisible – secondary effects: 'The climatic influence is present, but nobody talks about it. If it does not rain this year, there will be more incidents' (ASC8). There is a fear, particularly among police, that droughts have a direct influence on criminal activities in and around Las Lajitas:

The village lives depending on the costs of how the [agricultural] field is doing.

(ASC8)

When it does not rain, development is plummeting, because there is no work, and then one feels the lack of work and the economic problems thereof.

(ASC9)

In Las Lajitas, the topic is complicated; there is not much work any more. Apolinario Saravia has horticulture. There is work, seasonal work, of course. That is what does give life to Saravia.

(ASC10)

FUMIGATION: THE FIGHT AGAINST WINDMILLS OF
(MIS-)KNOWLEDGE

For ASC members, the handling of fumigation plays an important role. GM soy production seems inevitable:

Well, soy production is the most profitable at the moment and everybody runs towards the cultivation of soy.... Here it is difficult to cultivate anything organic, because in one way or another it will be contaminated, by the neighbour, by someone else, what do I know? Everybody sprays pesticides. And since there are great extensions of land, many times terrestrial fumigation is not enough and they have to do it by plane. And the planes, depending on the wind, they carry the product for 5, 6, 10, 20 kilometres.

(ASC9)

And ASC 'are in the middle' (ASC9), meaning that no major influence from the executive powers can be implemented; the only way of interfering is by municipal ordinance:

From an environmental standpoint, we have ordinances that are sometimes even superior to provincial ones, where we try to protect the environment – above all, the environment of the village. So to speak: 'Do not fumigate with glyphosate here above us but have an ordinance that means having to ask permission.'

(ASC9)

The reasoning behind stricter legislations is the fear that

there are many illnesses related to genetic modification and genetics that – in reality – we do not know anything about yet. There is not one study that tells me that it was glyphosate. It seems that there is not much desire to continue investigating glyphosate.

(ASC9)

It is striking, that the greatest opposition to and criticism of soy agribusiness actually comes from local politicians in charge.

They say [glyphosate] is disseminating when it falls to the ground. But it is not like that, because there are new things appearing every week. There is a girl who was born without a brain. And we thought she would die instantly … and she lived for many months. And we know that there is something that cannot ever function. What it is the reason, we do not know. I cannot say that it is glyphosate, but.…

(ASC9)

He shrugged his arms without continuing his sentence, as if nothing could be done.

There are claims by people who have become ill due to a physical effect. Yes, nothing more.

(ASC1)

They told us that there were barrels [of agrochemicals] stored in private homes, but there has been nothing. And next time they tell you … well, maybe they are correct, but.…

(ASC11)

There are serious health problems, but what are we to say? As we say here: The one that gives us food, signs the contracts. You are not going to be against them, either.

(ASC10)

So it is considered only logical that no local resistance is forming: 'Agrochemicals … nobody talks about them. You see them in the *campo*. About the climate, nobody talks about it, of the connections' (ASC8). The only thing that holds true in their perspective is change: 'Change in the region? Yes, climate change, illnesses, let's say ... it is an issue because of all the fumigation. One notices in the village? Of course ... when they are spraying we are surrounded. People do not complain' (ASC3). Local claims are more felt on a day-to-day basis:

> Those who come here they complain about the fumigator passing. But now they don't pass by because it is forbidden in urban areas. It is prohibited fumigating from the human zone to 500 metres, no matter what. From 500 to 1,500 metres, only land-based fumigation and aerial fumigation is allowed from a distance of 1,500 metres onwards.
>
> (ASC1)

> There is a policy of executive control, of fining. We do not permit mosquitos in our village. But they bring them in here to fix a tyre or something ... they do not clean it and they come with poison. They come with chemical products. And they are contaminating the children, the locals. It is a fight because a chemical product kills you in the long run. The people do not notice that it is killing them, they note it in the long run. If only it was something fast....
>
> (ASC9)

Even though a newly established Environmental Secretary has been established at the municipal level, their controlling powers are highly limited, being only three people patrolling and handling the bureaucracy of fumigation control.

MONEY, WHERE DO YOU COME FROM, WHERE DO YOU GO?

> The village does not live off the *campo*. Only indirectly. When they are moving all the agricultural machinery, it is fair to say that, of course, the farmers, the *finqueros*, the owners of the land, they do use the local shops to buy food, some products they need for their machines, much like their employees. But, this year when it has not rained in the fields....
>
> (ASC9)

This way of thinking goes hand in hand with the notion that the agribusiness is seen as a very unstable field of employment, offering only temporary work for locals:

> During harvesting season, a *finca* can take up to 100 persons. But, in reality, it is a very unstable work because it depends on rain, depends on the climate. Those who have feedlots, well, it is a different form of management already, they need people all year round to take care of the animals. Here are no factories, the workforce depends a lot on agriculture.
>
> (ASC9)

Or to put it even more directly:

> The people here do not get the money. The people from the agribusiness get the money. The village does not live off the *campo*. Here, some work in cattle breeding, in the hospital, the municipality, in the schools. But all in all, there are a lot of people who do not have work.
>
> (ASC3)

> There is no work for women ... everything is for men.
>
> (ASC13)

> The topic of the universal salaries, it is a big topic. Uh, there are a lot of people. The good thing is that the children have to go to school in order to get the universal allocation per child.
>
> (ASC13)

Social plans are predominantly considered critical, having the potential to institutionalise a lifestyle driven by demanding money and services without doing any work:

> Here are many young people that have nothing to do, because they are all subsidized. And they are all lazy, consuming paco [a cheap but very devastating drug] like hell. There are many ruined kids.
>
> (ASC6)

> There is work available but no kids that want to learn. It is a shame. We are a village of 15,000 inhabitants and have only 11 firefighters. But the kids don't want to participate. They ask how much is paid ... how they piss you off. It is voluntary. Voluntary!
>
> (ASC6)

Besides social plans, there is a major claim against unjust distribution of the money retrieved from the *retenciones*. Concerns are uttered that due to the co-participation (i.e. re-distribution of *retenciones* and other company-related taxation to all the municipalities in Argentina), where other (neighbouring) municipalities have greater financial benefits due to larger numbers of inhabitants:

> For example, in the Andes, they give them a percentage of the soy [*retenciones*] even though I think they do not even recognize a soy plant. And with that money they finance determined works, such as roads, schools, education ... Las Lajitas has all the effects of soy, but the money goes somewhere else. You do not see the money.
>
> (ASC6)

URBAN SPACE AND CONCRETE/ACTIVE POWER

Two success stories of the ASC are continuously told. The first being the establishment of the non-fumigation distances around the urban space, and the second, the potential removal of soy silo operations from the village:

> Now there is a deal between the silo and the municipality; they have to withdraw their activities from the urban area within five years. When they constructed it, it was on the outskirts of the village. And now they are obliged by the municipality to leave. It generates smell, particulate matter, noise. Last time I felt a mix of decomposition and burning smells. It heats up a lot and with the heat, gases and alcohol are created.
>
> (ASC1)

However, the need to balance positions is strongly felt, putting claims and negative effects into perspective – 'One feels the particulate matter, the trucks, but only during the season, two months back to back and then it is over' (ASC2) – highlighting the ASC internal struggle: 'It is a challenge of this work. You have to look for the equilibrium because you are always stuck in the middle' (ASC1).

Thus, the solution was to establish a master plan with the credo: 'Keep the agribusiness out of the urban space'. Therefore, a commercial park was established at the entrance of the town.

THE ELEPHANT IN THE ROOM: SECONDARY PROBLEMS NOBODY
TALKS ABOUT

Secondary problems, including criminal activities such as prostitution and child prostitution, are hardly ever mentioned, and if so, put as a problem from the past: 'There was a problem with a girl, but this has changed. That type of problematic person has changed' (ASC8). Or put in other words: 'In the past, there were problems with child prostitution, but not any more. They have grown up' (ASC9).

3 Social actors and schools (SOC&EDU)

THE STORYLINE RETURNS: HOW THE *CAMPO* HAS BECOME THE
VILLAGE

Unlike the previous two thought styles, SOC&EDU have more removed from the physical aspects of change and evolution in and around Las Lajitas.

> Soy has generated more harm than benefits. Climate change, in the past, it was a dry climate, now we have a humid climate; the companies that have arrived; and one of the things that wears out the soil is soy, for sure.

There has not been a re-cultivation so that this soil returns to having the strength and nutrients.

(EDU2)

Due to the thought style anchored in social and educational realms, it is natural that social and health aspects are in the foreground:

My father was one of the first to live here. He knew a bit about the history, how it was. It started with sawmills, then cattle were bred, afterwards has come the active sector you see today.... There is always the two parts ... but in these days we suffer a lot the change, we note it many times. Sawmills, cattle breeding, agriculture – everything happened in 50 years. There are people who have lived through all this.

(SOC4)

The conception of change is marked by ambivalence:

[The *campo*] is an area where it has been depopulating ... due to the technology. There are large fields, many machines and one needs few people. So what has happened?

(EDU3)

In the past we were in the *monte*. And now we cannot find the *monte*. And where are we going to work? There is no work with the axe. The production of what is called the city, that is what you see. It is a problem that affects the adult, the adolescent as much as the child.

(SOC4)

There are people who live in a very risky state. There are many settlements. So many people have come from the ex-*monte*.

(EDU1)

There is a gap, of course. There are poor people, there are businesspersons, people who have a good job in agriculture, engineers. So there are people in a good economic situation.

(SOC3)

Las Lajitas has grown a lot during the seven years that I have been here. The three avenues are asphalted, lights set up, everything developed behind the cemetery. It has grown a lot. When I arrived it caught my attention that it was a village that had four eateries.

(SOC1)

It is an area with great potential. The development you see is very important inasmuch as how the *campo* is spilling over, including what is consumed. Shops, little shops, pharmacies, supermarkets, they all settled in this area.

(SOC3)

The public face of Las Lajitas has changed as well, building 'spaces where you can socialize with the families. The have constructed a significantly sized plaza, although without flowers and without as many trees.... It is the social part, a public space' (SOC1).

TWO SPEEDS OF DEVELOPMENT CLASHING

While physical change is recognised, normatively interpreted (both positively as well as negatively), the locals' lifestyles are not adapting to the new situations. This is particularly noted by external medical volunteers who regularly visit the region:

> You see very little change. It is difficult to fight against the years and decades of the same rhythm of the people and everything ... it is difficult changing this mentality. The political side does not do much either, so it is difficult to ... people are waiting for us to attend them, to do something. But one does not see [change] from the political side, one does not see that they modify things a lot.
>
> (SOC5)

Viewed from the inside:

> The village is big, it has grown a lot, but the village is not seen as it was seen in the past. Including the people. The people themselves are suffering. We are suffering the transformation from village to city, and all that attracts growth: In the past, we all knew each other. Now we go out to the main plaza over there and we do not know each other.... People are emigrating or they are coming from other places or cities. The growth is due to a lack of work, due to poverty.
>
> (SOC4)

One component that indeed has adapted is the shift of personal preferences and the desire to increase their perceived living standards: 'The problem is that people were more satisfied with what they had. Now they want a car, a good kitchen, etc.' (SOC4).

One of the results of the two speeds of development colliding is thus the discontent among locals, the feeling of being left out. Drug use (particularly among the younger generations), alcohol misuse and domestic violence (particularly during low seasons and droughts) are the consequences. Additionally, religious (evangelical) groups have experienced a major upswing in members. 'Members of the Catholic community drink alcohol; members of the evangelical do not. Many members of the Catholic community with a lot of problems have converted to the evangelical ones' (SOC1).

LINKING CHANGE TO HEALTH ISSUES

Regional (physical) change is linked to health issues. However, absolute clarity on the actual extent of the relationship between agribusiness and illnesses is neither confirmed nor denied. The thought style revolves around secondary sources (i.e. 'friend-of-a-friend'), statistical probabilities and observations carefully embedded in semi-context without definite quotes:

> In the past, there was virgin *monte*, now everything is deforested. One sees many questions that are influenced by herbicides and all the things they are using, in other words: There are allergies, at some point it was said to be cancer. It can be because suddenly there have been young people with stomach cancer, throat cancer … according to some studies, they are directly related to this type of activity.
>
> (EDU1)

> Here you find a lot of allergies, a lot. Fumigation is one more factor. Not the only one. There is some aerial fumigation that I know of is not done in the form that is protocolled due to the distance to the town.
>
> (SOC3)

> Environmental people have come to say that it was not allowed to do aerial fumigation, but here they are continuing with it.
>
> (SOC6)

> But it is not that I see it all bad … it is also not the way where we can say that we are intoxicating ourselves. We probably have to correct something, but it is not something possessing our health. In fact, I do not consider it, no. There are other factors much more important to health. That way, one should correct distances a bit, but it is not like planes are passing by over our heads.
>
> (SOC3)

> And this thing with the feedlots, it is said to be a health problem, but nobody does anything. My God, that smell!
>
> (EDU2)

WORK, OR GET FAT

> The people here have been growing up with the *monte*, not so much the last generation…. And there have been people who had little fields and they sold them to companies, big businessmen, multinationals.
>
> (EDU2)

Here you find companies from Australia, from Buenos Aires, those kind of places. And they have millionaire revenues, millions of dollars.

(SOC3)

With soy, it is a south–north movement, because in the south they do not have that kind of return like here any more. It's people that come and they already know how to produce soy. They come and they go.

(EDU1)

In the perspective of SOC&EDU, those few people who do find work in the agribusiness lack critical reflection on the sector:

People are not interested in what [the soy agribusiness] is doing, they are not interested in it. They do not have an idea whether if it does good or bad. What is it that interests them? If they have work or not.

(EDU4)

Working opportunities are considered to be scarce and almost entirely limited to the agricultural sector:

The number of people who move to other places for work is not significant. Maybe you go into the *campo*, with some new farms, when you have to remove the roots [after deforestation] – technology does not remove them for you. This is what you have to hire people for. This is where you need a workforce, in the new fields.

(EDU3)

Other people are

nothing but municipalities' public employees. As a woman, you work in the municipality, or you work in the schools, or you work in the hospital. The woman does not have much field of action. If you are not a housewife, you are gone. You are at home, you dedicate yourself to drinking mate and you get fat like this. Because one observes many people, there is a lot of obesity, including the young ones. And it happens to me as well, due to the great heat we are having, one remains locked up inside … it is a humid heat and it beats you, you do not leave. One does not leave, there is not much physical activity. People do not leave to go for a walk.

(EDU3)

SOCIAL CONTAINMENT OR STUDYING FOR WORK?

The official institutions are central for the local community, particularly in terms of education:

The official part does play a major role here, the kids have a lot of help. Children that do not have the scholarship, they cannot do anything, they can only work in the fields.

(SOC7)

The school has a cantina, so it is important to pick up the kids so that they come to eat. The kids eat before going home. For many parents this is important, having food secured.

(EDU3)

The parents, what are they working at? They do odd jobs. Very few are working on farms. And what happens when they work on the farms? They move. Therefore, the father is gone all week. The mother stays, alone with the child. Like in the city – children being alone. And lately I see many grandmothers taking care of the children.

(EDU3)

This general perception is enforced when looking at a remote (publicly funded) boarding school:

In Las Lajitas there are three primary schools, but they still come here. Because here they have food, a bed, all elements a child needs to be OK, to have a better quality of life. That is everything they do not have at home. This is the issue here.

(EDU5)

We have had children with many problems here. We have children that have taken drugs, we have children that live on the street, we have children in bad shape, we have abused children. The school is a social containment. One has to look for ways that the children continue studying.

(EDU5)

When I asked: 'Is the situation in Las Lajitas getting worse?'

Well, here, those who we have here, there are many children that are brought up by their grandparents … and they have their father … [prolonged silence].… Let us say that when they are at school, they are doing well.

(EDU5)

The boarding school is surrounded by soy fields and the farmers regularly pass by the school, but never stop or donate anything: 'The farmers do not help us. There is no contact with the farmers, the only thing we see are the pickup trucks that come and go' (EDU5).

4 *Local perception actors (PE* = PEL + PEM + PER)*

This thought style represents local actors, the 'common' people who are not classified as being SAB, ASC, or SOC&EDU. The main idea behind this group is to capture central features of what PE* are predominantly concerned with.

THE STORYLINE FROM BELOW: NOSTALGIA AND RESIGNATION

The thought style of PE* is marked by strong comparison between the good past and the bad present:

> All this, in the years from the 1950s to the 1960s, including until the 1970s, the owners were all *criollos* from here. But they did not know what they had. They did not pay taxes − just like their grandparents − they did not know anything, not even how to write. Then other people came, they paid taxes. When they [the *criollos*] found out, they had to leave. All the new people have been made owners of the land.
>
> (PEM1)

> He did not have the papers, nothing. So they took all his land, all the land.
>
> (PEM1)

> It is not like in the past, they have already sold the farm, they have owners already, they have already fields for sowing. Everything deforested.
>
> (PEL3)

> Back in the days there was a lot of hunting; there was cheese, *quesillo* − my mother made everything − we ate *locro*. We did not look for honey … well, a little bit, yes. How delicious the honey was! But it is not coming back. Now there is no honey, no hive, there is nobody who does it like that … you have to have balls.
>
> (PEL2)

> You cannot hunt here, there is almost nothing left. There in the countryside, yes: pigs, rats, deer, … there is everything. But we hunted very little. Sometimes the patron tells us that he would like pork, so we go hunting.
>
> (PEL11)

> In the past, we extracted honey from the *monte*. But now, where do I get it from? It can be detrimental. It generates so many things … here we have winds, we do not have cover, they make us a tornado because we do not have a shelter, there is no curtain. I don't know what they from the government are doing.
>
> (PER1)

Another highly present topic is firewood. While natural gas is generally considered a step up the energy ladder (Krapovickas *et al.*, 2016, p. 221), the emotional attachment to firewood persists, reflecting perceived better times that have gone. 'We used to cook with firewood, now with gas. Firewood is already gone …' (PEL2). 'Yes, we are still looking for firewood. Sometimes we go into the *monte*. We do not buy it. But you have to ask for permission to enter' (PEL7).

Finally, the growth of Las Lajitas is attributed to the farmers, however, always with clear hints of resentment and envy: 'The village is growing because the wives and children of the farmers stay in Las Lajitas; the men work on the farms. If you see construction, it is the farmers who build the big houses close to the plaza' (PEL6).

WORK, WORK, UNTIL YOU CAN WORK NO MORE

Very few claims are made by the PE*. One claim deals with work: (1) in the service business:

> When the big brands arrive, the multimillionaires, they make my father go bankrupt. My father, and my grandfather, they were the owners of the first gas station. So, what has happened? When this cereal company came, ESSO arrived as well. And their owners were the same owners of the soy plant and silos. So they delivered fuel to, for example, the farmers and they paid them back in soy, they made barter. So my father could not compete. And he went bankrupt. The big companies make the others go bankrupt. My father did have good business before, but when they arrived.…
>
> (PEL4)

(2) Or work directly in the fields:

> In the past, there were not as many fields, it was an era of development. There were farms, big farms, with good plains, they are nice, one can sow better. Now they are deforesting with bulldozers, in the past, it was done all by hand.
>
> (PEL2)

> In the past, the countryside was for work. One knew what to do. This is going to end because there will not be any more, so one has to come here [to the village].
>
> (PEL3)

> There are only few people left in the countryside – now it is pure soy.
>
> (PEL1)

Those still working in the campo, describe it like this:

> They give you 20, 25 ARS per hectare, 40 hectares per day, sometimes
> 30, it depends. Accommodation? A stall, only a stall in the fields. When
> you leave for the village, you have to spend money on accommodation.
> And then there are weeks when you do not work, and you get bored.
>
> (PEL13)

> But sometimes they [from the agribusiness] give some work, otherwise
> they give you some little work in the village. Furthermore, when it goes
> bad in the fields, it is indeed noted in the village. There is less business
> for the hardware store.... Even in the pedestrian streets, you see fewer
> people, when there is a drought, there is no soy.
>
> (PEL4)

> Somewhat yes, the drought has affected us. Many have sold their land,
> they went to shit, were left with nothing. Now I don't know, it seems to
> be turning nice again.
>
> (PEL5)

> My children, they are all working already. Sometimes they go far away,
> but they keep coming back. They go with the patrons from here. The
> contractor comes and picks them up.
>
> (PEL8)

> Sometimes the work is for sowing or for whatever it may be. Sometimes
> for cleaning the land, this is what has been the most. Now there is almost
> no *monte* any more.
>
> (PEL5)

Other work opportunities are scarce, the second largest employer is considered the municipality:

> The municipality of Las Lajitas only has 10–15 fixed employees. The
> others have a contract of one to three months. And the municipality is
> the biggest employer here. The dependence on the mayor is very high. If
> you are against him, you lose your work.
>
> (PEL9)

> This village is a humble one, and a stupid one at that. Because it is 20
> years that they [the mayor and the municipality] are doing whatever they
> want, that is what the delegates have said in Apolinario Saravia.
>
> (PEL10)

WHEN THE HUMAN INTERFERES WITH THE NATURAL

Fumigation is the most tangible topic of human-environment interrelation and claims-making. An ambivalent relationship is observed, based on the reason for pesticide/herbicide spraying:

> They do not fumigate here. This is the land for the little horses, for the little animals. It would be nice to fumigate it, because of the insects. There are always mosquitos, *zancudos* [type of mosquito].
>
> (PEL3)

versus:

> We are now six years on our own piece of land. And there were fields before; but now they apply more poison. Here, they have re-forested, 6 metres, but the very poison did not let the plants grow. All the poison that is not used in other countries, here they use it as if it was water.
>
> (PEM2)

> The smell is everywhere when they pass by fumigating. They do not do anything to the plants. There are some [agrochemicals] that harm the children, harm the skin, others are harmed in their head, like that. For example, to her, yes, she was caught by vomiting and fever during fumigation season.
>
> (PEL7)

As a third option, environmental bads are simply ignored: For example, the silo in the middle of Las Lajitas is hardly ever mentioned. When directly asked, the thought style revolves around statements like: 'The silo? It does not affect us. The only thing that comes here is in winter, with the grain-drying machine. When the drying machine goes, the sun goes away' (PEL12). Particulate matter is released into the air, but 'it does not bother us. Why not? No, because one is already accustomed to it. But many people have said that it does bring many illnesses. The doctors themselves have said so, respiratory illnesses' (PEL12).

The second environmental problem present in the PE* thought style is the flooding of the village: 'Here, everything was flooded, the Barrio San Antonio, Barrio 50. It can be that the water comes from the dam. They irrigate the limes. The dam belongs to the farm' (PEL7). However, active claims against the farm, for example, are never directly uttered.

THE ELEPHANT IN THE ROOM II: SECONDARY EFFECTS THAT ARE MOSTLY IGNORED

Two themes are identified: first and economically driven, the actual disproportion between soy farming and horticulture is claimed: 'There are too few small farms that grow plants for daily needs, there is no irrigation system. Only large soy fields destined for export' (PEL9).

The second issue deals with social effects of soy production:

> What I did see was during the season of the harvesters, when people from out of town arrived, well, the girls were always pregnant.
>
> (PEL4)

> They say that prostitution is a problem, towards the north of the village, down where the eucalyptus trees are … including child prostitution.
>
> (PEL6)

THE ENCORE: FILLING THE DATA GAP OF PEL

A recurrent theme in this book is the emphasis on the importance of context. Environmental justice activism and research tend to have a clear focus on one particular conflictive situation, take it as a starting point and anchoring focus; a broader contextualisation of actors' thought styles – particularly that of PE★ is hardly carried out. While this relatively narrow focus may prove fruitful for other situations, the case of Las Lajitas needs additional data to be able to understand the reasoning for no claims making and the absence of locals' resistance.

For this purpose, participatory projects with children and adolescents in Las Lajitas were designed to gain additional insights into the local social fabric. The results can be interpreted in two ways: first, procedurally, since questions from the questionnaires were elaborated in several student workshops with as little bias as possible, the types of question asked give an insight into themes that the younger generation focused on. Second, substantially, as the dynamic of data collection is altered from social interaction between me, the external researcher, and locals, to local youth with their parents, siblings, grandparents, or neighbours. The idea behind this approach is to achieve a greater sense of connectedness and preparedness to answer questions more hands-on and with fewer mental filters.

Focusing on the positive reasons for living in Las Lajitas, three results are interesting here. First of all, with some limitations, the regional characteristics as well as the town's embeddedness in its surroundings are little represented. This goes even more so for the mentions of the *campo*; for comparison, the river is a little more relevant to locals. Infrastructural settings and social embeddedness are of great importance. Here, second, the town square represents a major anchor for locals to identify with the town. Thus, the overall perceptual focus of tangible elements shows a clear centring towards the inside of the village. Consequently, the outer parts of Las Lajitas are very little mentioned. Third, and most strikingly, Las Lajitas is characterised as tranquil, with great potential for a quiet, uneventful life. This description is also mirrored in the attribution of Las Lajitas being a village rather than a town, even though the number of inhabitants has reached approximately 12,000.

In total, Las Lajitas is connected with predominantly positive connotations. This result is also reflected by the inverted approach of identifying negative characterisations of the village. Of 75 interviews, only approximately 20 per cent identified local problems: Social troubles, waste, smoke, air contamination by soil and particulate matter from the soy silo, effects of the spraying of poison and water contamination are the core themes that bother locals. The connection, however, between change and effects, the identification of actors related to the problems at hand, were very seldom talked about.

In order to improve the credibility of the results, I follow Baxter and Eyles (1997, p. 512) by approaching the topic from an additional angle. Here, cooperation with the local younger generation proves fruitful. In several workshops, the idea of experiencing the town and its surroundings was worked on. The rationale behind working with children aged 10 (in the fourth form) is twofold. First, they are very enthusiastic about the method of actively experiencing their surrounding in new ways, leading to good and rounded results. Second, on a more abstract level, ten-year-olds are still more embedded in the thought styles of their parents; they take up the thematic issues talked about in their homes and – to a great extent – reproduce them in the hands-on activity. Thus, the participants can be seen – with certain limitations – as an indicator of PEL trends. Instead of directly asking the ten-year-olds about the good and bad of Las Lajitas and its surroundings, they were given the task to represent this question in the form of individual drawings.

First of all, the distribution of the locations the children preferred to draw shows that the urban area represents the closest spatiality to the majority of them (42 per cent), followed closely by the depiction of the rural (36 per cent) and the combination of the rural and urban (22 per cent). Here, the narrative of the adults is reflected inasmuch as the tales of the past and the romanticisation of the non-urban spill over to the younger generation: grandparents' houses in the countryside, old *puestos* in the *monte* or rural activities like fishing or livestock breeding are common pictures. Second, highlighting environmental components of the drawings, distant background elements include suns, clouds or mountains, whereas rivers are connected to activities. Trees, but even more so flowers, are predominantly drawn in the urban setting, located in the central town square. This infrastructure element plays a core role not just in the perception of the adults, but also for the children, shown in the frequency and representation of size in the kids' artworks (mostly in combination with the playground located in the town square). Third, another interesting aspect is the invisibility of shops, representations of the agribusiness (including the soy silo and workshops or garages), while other – emotionally closer elements such as the library, the football field or social housing do appear. The latter is a good indicator that the children are aware of the implications of social housing, being distributed by the official hand. Fourth, almost every drawing shows locals and their activity; animals are rare in the urban space, which is also a reflection of the prohibition on keeping livestock in the urban area. Finally, problems are rarely drawn, and if so, only in the rural-urban and rural area. While at first sight, this could be interpreted as implicit problems with the agribusiness surrounding Las Lajitas, the only two thematic issues are waste and smoke (in return, related to the burning of waste).

Complementing these results, I follow Rodaway (1994, p. 3) in his thinking that understanding actors' sensuous experience is the basis for the cognition of the socio-spatial fabric. In order to discover Las Lajitas' underlying dimensions on what is actively and passively recognised by the PEL members, vision, sound and smell are the three most relevant senses.

Focusing on the visual experience, the high level of recognition of the town square is striking – a feature that has already been shown in the analysis above. This urban centre is the predominant anchor of the PEL group and their core focus. Public infrastructure, like the sports facility, the school or the church, is highly visible. Another interesting detail in this category is that 'many people' as well as 'fights' are above the threshold of visibility, indicating certain levels of physical violence in Las Lajitas. Going beyond the urban space, very few elements are noticed, particularly when it comes to (socio-) environmental settings: The sun, the stars and the mountains in the distance are recognised. However, no direct connection to the soy agribusiness is made. Besides the observation that many cars circulate (being mostly pickup trucks), neither the soy silo (located in the middle of the village), (agri-) business representations in the form of offices, shops, workshops or garages, nor the soy fields encircling Las Lajitas appear here. Relating to sound perceptions, noises from inanimate objects are most present: cars, pickup trucks and hooters, machinery and construction-related noise. Loud music and radio transmissions make up the second category. In combination with the visual result 'fights', the sonic equivalence 'screaming' is often mentioned[3] – marking yet again the underlying social tension in Las Lajitas. Focusing on the olfactory, a resulting dichotomy is shown. On the one hand, fresh air and flowers (predominantly referring to the flowerbeds of the town square) portray a pleasant urban ambience. However, on the other hand, smoke, the smell of gasoline and exhaust fumes contaminate the air. Once again, no direct connections are made to the activities of the soy agribusiness, even though the soy silo, for example, emits significantly tangible particulate matter.[4]

The lack of regional embeddedness in defining the place where the PEL group lives is also reflected in the locals' awareness of environmental change (42 per cent; $n = 75$) and problems (43 per cent; $n = 75$) thereof. The most interesting piece of information here is the actual absence of the participants' deciding whether environmental change/problems occur or not: 50 per cent in both cases do not show an opinion, fostering the argument of the process of disconnecting the urban from the rural space.

Or to relate it to Lefebvre's (1991) or Soja's (1996) terms, the lived space has experienced a narrowing-down from the rural and rural-urban space to the urban, following the pre-settings of the perceived space (i.e. in this case the objective transformation of the physical rural space to the legalisation of locals' exclusion from it) created by the effects of the regional soy frontier expansion. Two remarks are important here. First, in this process, PEL should not be considered to be solely passive actors – or to put it bluntly, victims – driven by large multinationals in the soy agribusiness. Even though migration has had negative effects on many PEL livelihoods, they are the ultimate actors who make decisions and strategies (within certain boundaries) to strive for the capabilities needed for the life that PEL members want to live. Second, the fluid nature of scalar interactions is prominent here. PEL decision-making structures are not influenced solely by the local level, but made up of a multiplicity of scalar interactions, both directly and indirectly.

Coming back to local perceptions of environmental change, the first striking result is that 58 (46 + 12) per cent ($n = 75$) of all environmental change issues are in fact of a social-environmental nature. Consequently, the role of the environment is clearly defined by human interactions with and strong influences on the environment. Second, the distinction between one-off and recurrent social-ecological change shows that the latter is almost four times more present in PEL's minds. Here, the temporal component of events acts as an indicator. The highlighted one-off events deal with deforestation and fence construction, which are both activities that reached their peak 10–15 years ago. Recurring events are – by their very nature – still noticeable and have a direct impact on PEL. Third, waste is a recurrent issue in Las Lajitas, ranging from contamination to incineration and smoke, highlighting the implicit dissatisfaction with the actors (i.e. ASC) responsible for the organisation of waste management, including its collection and disposal infrastructure. Fourth, classic environmental change noted by PEL is characterised by ambivalence: On the one hand, droughts are very visible; on the other, more rain is experienced. As previously shown, precipitation has slightly increased by approximately 2–3 millimetres in the area around Las Lajitas, but simultaneously, weather extremes have increased, explaining the incommensurable perceptions of PEL. Finally, fifth, 12 per cent of all environmental change focuses on exclusively urban change, once again demonstrating the broad definition of environment by PEL. This category is particularly interesting since the connotations of thematic issues are more centred on procedural change with no or very little normative evaluation.

Moving from change to problems, PEL's problem evaluation shows one particular underlying dimension: problems are – with very few exceptions – connected to human action, causing negative effects. Comparing the perception of environmental change with environmental problems, it is seen that the mental move from change to problem decreases the visibility of the environment by half from 30 to 15 per cent. Focusing on activities by the soy agribusiness, the opposite effect – although on a limited scale – occurs: The agribusiness is made responsible for 26 per cent of the change, but for 28 per cent of (socio-) environmental problems, with fumigation being the most visible one. Nevertheless, contamination shows the highest level of concern among the PEL; issues with waste stand out once again, followed by water contamination.[5]

As a final result, the thought style of PEL is anchored in the past. This, however, does not mean that the future does not play a role in the way of PEL's thinking. Three pieces of information are observed ($n = 75$). First, PEL are well aware of the fact that Las Lajitas is dominated by high levels of socio-economic fragmentation – 63 per cent share this view – that is expected to continue and be reinforced. However, the dominating thought style of SAB also penetrates PEL's perception, particularly in terms of growth and wealth. Only 3 per cent see Las Lajitas as a poor place. Thus, the narrative of eco-nomic growth and increased wealth (without focusing on the redistribution of it), reinforced by SAB, is clearly visible. Growth is also central in terms of migration. The majority see Las Lajitas as a big city in the future, particularly by those who consider it a rich place or socio-economically fragmented. Another interesting detail here is that the influx of foreigners is correlated with urban growth and an increase in wealth. Once again, the SAB thought style of the advantages of the soy agribusiness shine through.

EJIF: soy production, environment and claims

The four storylines presented above are considered the dominant thought styles in the research area. They showed the different realities and foci of the four thought collectives SAB, ASC, SOC&EDU and PE*. The next step is to apply the first part of the EJIF (i.e. 'identification') to them. The respective perceptions of change, effects, actors and conflict potentials will be revealed (Figure 8.3).

Change

One criterion of comparison lies in the normative evaluation of change. A clear picture is observed: SAB have internalised the strongest notion of pro-gress, fostering the ideal of pioneering a region, thriving under harsh con-ditions in order to develop a remote region without external help from official actors or other entities. A strong sense of personal achievement is present. Furthermore, the before-and-after comparison relies heavily on aspects of physical, environmental rather than social change. Altering the physical setting is deeply rooted in the SAB's embeddedness in pliant anthro-pocentrism, seeing nature as quasi-instrumental (Vincent 1998, pp. 125–127).

The second group, ACS, are still positive about regional development, although concerns about security, distribution of goods and bads are present (aspects that are considered to have functioned better in the past). SOC&EDU are also located between the present being better, particularly in terms of infrastructure, access and mobility, but major concerns for cul-tural and social value change are uttered. Finally, PE* show the opposite

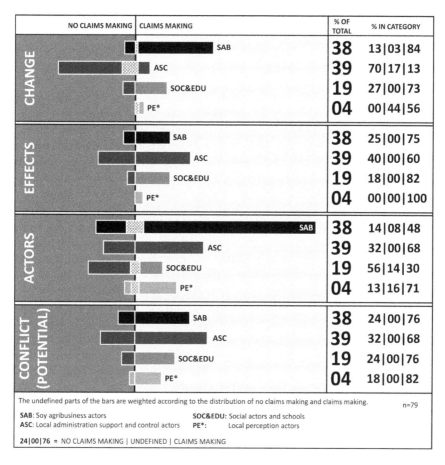

Figure 8.3 Actor groups' levels of claims making.

perception of the soy agribusiness actors. Their anchoring is clearly focused in the past, relating to the way of living in/being surrounded by *monte*, reflecting high levels of nostalgia.

While relevant for the understanding of the interaction of thought collectives, the perception of change does not allow a deeper understanding of respective claims making. Here, I want to highlight the difference between noticing change (procedural component, free of normative evaluation), temporal-normative anchoring of change and the final category of claims making (i.e. in common terms, the 'blaming' of particular situations and processes on actors).

Figure 8.3 is based on the correlation of codified interview pieces of the four relevant actors in the EJIF. Each bar represents the perspective of the respective group of actors, classified according to direct evidence in the particular field (i.e. change in the region due to soy agricultural activities) correlated with claims making, no claims making and claims-undefined mentioning. While the sections of the bars representing no claims making and claims making are clearly positioned within the respective fields, the third category is weighed according to the ratio between claims making and non-claims making.

First of all, during talks with members of SAB and ASC, it is striking that topics concerning change do play a fundamental role. As previously highlighted, both actors consider change predominantly of an environmental and physical nature, stressing the 'cleaning/clearing of the land off *monte*', setting the new areas in value, etc. However, the extent of claims making is diametrically opposed. On the one hand, SAB often complain about the infrastructural and environmental difficulties of their business activities, ranging from the struggle with droughts and floods to lack of access to the land and executing the then newly obtained land rights. ASC's discussions, on the other hand, are marked by absence of claims making in the past. Even though changes are mentioned and temporally-normatively anchored (e.g. the most dominant factor being deforestation), the potential of claims making is very seldom executed, in the sense: 'Change is change, it is what it is.'

The second group of actors, SOC&EDU and PE★, shows fewer mentions of environmental change that are or would be considered eligible for claims making. This can be explained due to the nature of the professional engagement with social actors, where environmental change is not a core feature of their thematic focus (SOC&EDU), as well as the form of storytelling observed in PE★. The engagement with PE★ was greatly influenced by oral history, where the personal path of life stands in the foreground of the conversation. Environmental change does play a role here, but is considered a frame with insignificant level of influence in their daily lives.

Effects

Small-scale regional climate change due to deforestation, increased risks of floods in urban areas, deteriorating health conditions due to soy production in the vicinities of towns and villages are considered effects of change. To get a more hands-on idea of daily effects that the soy agribusiness has on locals in Las Lajitas, five activities traditionally carried out in the region are investigated (Figure 8.4): looking for firewood and honey, fishing, hunting, as well as horseback riding. One prevailing trend is obvious: all the activities were carried out more in the past than now. This trend is used as an indicator that rural life and the engagement with the non–urban environmental space are decreasing.

It goes without saying that this development is contextualised by the fact that due to the advance of the soy frontier the *monte* has been cleared and access to it is prohibited. This holds particularly true for the issue of firewood, looking for honey and hunting. Access to the river, although made more

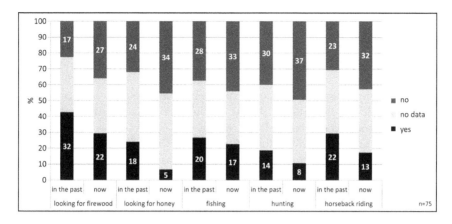

Figure 8.4 Non-urban activities carried out (past vs. present) – results from participatory student project.

difficult, is still possible and fishing now is a pastime activity rather than a fundamental means of providing food.[6] The decrease in horseback riding accounts for the fact that owning livestock (including horses) is prohibited in urban areas of Las Lajitas. Consequently, most people who have migrated from the rural to the urban space had to get rid of their animals – and mode of rural transportation.

Figure 8.4 also compares the distribution of effects and (non-)claims making among the four actor groups. While the main focus of claims making related to change has been on SAB, the effects of change are felt more by ASC. This result is partly influenced by the fact that the majority of ASC de facto have personal migration histories to the region, coming from provinces like Buenos Aires or Cordoba, where a great tradition of resistance against large-scale agricultural activities is firmly rooted.

SOC&EDU show similar patterns to SAB. The first group focuses on the social effects of environmental change, socio-spatial fragmentation, relocation of rural dwellers and socio-economic problems due to lack of work are vividly discussed. The latter group portrays – interestingly enough – the environmental effects of environmental change, keeping socio-spatial issues at or below the horizon of visibility. Finally, when it comes to PE★, the pattern observed in change continues to be valid with effects. Very few claims are made to portray the effects of soy cultivation, and if so, they are found at a very subliminal level.

Actors

Environmental justice, as defined so far, only works when claims are being made. In order to pinpoint conflictive situations, concrete actors or actor groups have to be identified. In the case of Las Lajitas (see Figure 8.3), it is interesting to see that SAB does name by far the most actors and relates them to specific claims. This means that SAB has the highest verbalised capacity to link negative outcomes of change and effects to particular actors. This is, additionally, closely linked to the aspect of tangibility. As previously identified, SAB is most concerned with environmental effects of change that can be measured (e.g. through loss of production compared to previous years, because of floods or droughts, misuse of fumigation), facilitating the identification of actors to be making claims against.

ASC has another 'comparative advantage' for claims making since its representatives do have – by their professional status – direct contact with and thus knowledge of relevant actors most likely to influence the regional setting. SOC&EDU show a different picture, highlighting the fact that the majority of the actors named and theoretically being possible to include in claims making are not mentioned at all. An increased disengagement between causers and change/effect is observed. PE★ do not fall into this pattern, showing the highest occurrence of claims making on the overall scheme from change to conflict (potential).

Conflict (potential)

The last (environmental) category is the amalgamation of change, effects and actors. This should lead to ultimate claims making – and conflictual situations – resembling the schemes observed in other environmental justice resistance situations. For the case of Las Lajitas, Figure 8.3 shows the comparison of (non-)claims making among actors in relation to conflict (potential).

ASC identify most conflict (potentials), due to the often-cited challenge of 'being in the middle' and 'having to react to shortcomings by other actors and/or environmental disasters' (ASC1). SAB here are most concerned with the lack of problem-solving of environmental problems, and the lack of a skilled workforce. SOC&EDU see health and poverty issues combined with criminal activities as the greatest source of conflict in Las Lajitas. Additionally, the influx of 'new people from the city' (SOC4) as well as the metaphorical conversion of the town into a port during harvest season (coupled with an increase in prostitution and subsequent soaring of STDs among women; SOC1) make up a large proportion of claims making. PE★ claims circulate predominantly around past events of perceived injustice (e.g. relocation from the *monte* to the village) and deforestation. Most current issues are located in the social space and are work-related.

Incommensurabilities unearthed

So far, the results presented are puzzling. First, based on the CLASSIC approach of the deliberately narrow environmental justice (activism) perspective, the core conflict potentials circulate around the themes of

(1) primary effects: agrochemicals, noise pollution, particulate matter and smells; and (2) secondary effects caused by deforestation and the availability of water. However, as stated, no concrete trigger for resistance could be found Second, with the help of participant observation, in-depth interviews, oral history approaches, Jane's Walks and informal talks, I could show that the question from the first approach – why no claims making occurs in Las Lajitas – showed an absolutely different thought-style-based reality than those of the perspectives presented in the ALTERNATIVE one. All four actor groups identify conflictive situations *and*, in more cases than not, *do* make claims about it. The incommensurability of thought style-driven realities – among the one in the CLASSIC and the four thought styles in the ALTERNATIVE perspectives – becomes ever so clear: The CLASSIC's initial conflict potentials that I have unearthed are all represented in the other four thought styles. However, the degree of concreteness/abstraction varies greatly. Since I initially lacked contextual knowledge, in the CLASSIC I was only able to see physically harmful sites prone to distributional injustice, thus remaining in the environmental space. The concentration on and identification of actors were treated in a secondary manner.

EJIF: from claims to conflict? Involvement of actors in environmental justice claims making

The next step is to go more into detail on the main topics of environmental justice. Based on the thought styles, the most prominent themes are listed in Table 8.3.

Those 11 issues, naturally, do not have the same relevance for and impact on each actor group, fostered by thought collectives' foci. This is highlighted in the following section.

Thus, on the following pages, the connections among topics, claims-issuing as well as claims-receiving actors will be presented in a multi-dimensional model. Claims have two components: a topic and an addressee. Figure 8.5 (and Figures 8.6–8.16) present this scheme. Claims-makers are always concrete actors. They take up an issue that is placed in either the

Table 8.3 Environmental justice issues in Las Lajitas

Environmental space	Social space
• climate change	• crime
• deforestation★	• operational support
• water issues★	• health
• pollution★	• work
• fumigation★	• poverty
	• social responsibility

Note
★ Those issues are also identified in the CLASSIC environmental justice analysis.

environmental or the social space (see Table 8.3). While the former is deeply grounded in the physical realm, the latter is rooted between the physical and the virtual, understood as a platform for second-level effects of environmental change. Additionally, both the environmental and the social space have a classification of problems according to the perceived form of concreteness/ abstraction. If claims are made, the issues are then connected to the addressee(s) of claims making. Depending on the context, the addressee is classified as being a concrete actor(i.e. named), intermediary or abstract actor (i.e. the soy agribusiness).

Finally, all three levels of environmental and social space and actors are interrelated by the respective thought styles' perceptions. Three forms of connectors are identified: (1) awareness of problems; (2) active claims making: identification of those who caused the problems; and (3) active claims making: responsibility for problem solving.

The abstract multi-dimensional model is also complemented, where useful, by relevant paragraphs from my field diary (see Boxes 8.1–8.9). The purpose of this exercise is twofold: on the one hand, additional context should be provided to situate the topics in the regional setting. And, on the other hand, the abstract analysis should be grounded and connected to real-life cases, making my arguments more tangible and understandable. Thus, the boxes are an add-on feature, or additional sensory- and perception-based stepping stone towards the cognition of particular realities.

Category (1): climate change and crime

Climate change and crime are two topics that fall into category (1) awareness of problems (Figure 8.5). The focus is on social-environmental problems that are present in the actors' perceptions. However, no significant connections have been established to re-connect the problem to actors.

First, changing climatic conditions (Figure 8.5a) are central in almost any conversation in Las Lajitas. The category acts as a nonconcrete middleware that translates sensible events like increased humidity, stronger winds, or droughts into an abstract form of explanation for the occurrence of such events. Another common feature is to use climate change as an opening to talk about regional progress:

> I have noted a lot of change, in climate, as much as in the social part as well. Happy, because imagine this being a small community and the people, how they are.... We are conscious that the advancement has been due to the farmers.

> (SOC2)

It is interesting to observe that a discursive shift occurs from a negatively connoted topic to a paralleling one with more positive attributes, replicating SAB's thought style of growth, progress and development.

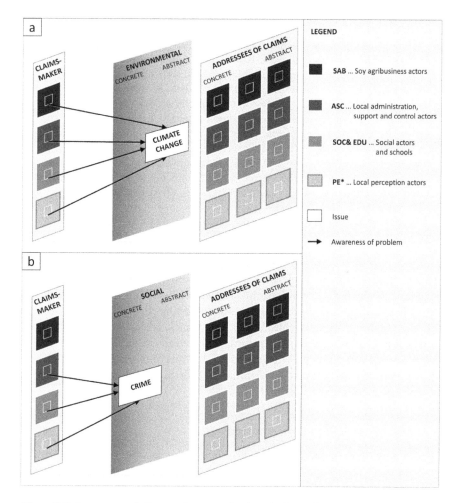

Figure 8.5 Awareness of climate change and crime in Las Lajitas.

Second, criminal activities (Figure 8.5b), such as illegal waste incineration or fumigation, robberies, (domestic) violence, prostitution, etc., are identified as problems by all actors but SAB. Even though crime rates are relatively low compared to major cities, like Salta Capital or Buenos Aires, even in relation to Apolinario Saravia (ASC2), an increase in non-legal activity is perceived (Box 8.1).

However, the re-connection to one of the four actor groups is hardly ever made. If actors are mentioned indeed, they are referred to as 'people from somewhere else' or 'from the city' and thus excluded from the actual local-level visualisation. The non-identification of crime as a problem by SAB is explained by the high level of disengagement with the urban space in Las

---

Box 8.1 Field diary: crime and the tale of the drunk

Sitting in the town square during a break from carrying out interviews, I come to talk with a middle-aged man, who is also enjoying the shadows from the trees. Drunkenly, like many unemployed men who roam the streets of Las Lajitas, he reminisces about the good old days when the town was still a village, when everybody knew each other and issues of insecurity never came up. But nowadays, he argues, security is decreasing constantly. Especially theft, he says, is on the rise. And prostitution – pointing towards the north where the big eucalyptus trees grow – prostitution over there, it is a problem. And drugs, oh, drugs, they have arrived as well. Further details are not revealed by him, either to conceal information on illegal activity or simply due to his drunken state of mind. But crime, he reassures me, crime is rising. One can read about crime in Las Lajitas in the provincial newspapers. The only news, the man claims, that the town is making, is related to crime. (Las Lajitas, 22 October 2013)

Lajitas, particularly on a physical level (e.g. most of the time spent in the region is on the farms, or due to the characteristic of being a 'soy tourist').

The advantage of this implicit sense of being aware of problems, but midway ignoring them or shifting to other topics, which is carried out by all four actor groups, is thus the missing connection of problems back to the actor level. From an outside perspective, this makes it seem as if the claims-making process has stopped in the middle of the process, but has to be seen as a problem-coping mechanism.

Categories (2) and (3): environmental issues

The following thematic concerns show a broader spectrum of actors' actions and reactions: Unlike in category (1), the reconnection of problems to actors via claims making both towards initiators of bads and those responsible for dealing with injustices (mostly ASC) occurs.

DEFORESTATION

Deforestation is a unique category when it comes to its characteristics. It is most distinguished as a one-off event, meaning that the forest is – due to lack of re-forestation – only cleared once. As a result, the impact is both visible in space and almost point-like fixed on the temporal axis. The four different thought styles all considered the tearing down of the *monte* a crucial event. Furthermore, changing land tenure, deforestation and open conflicts are connected, particularly referring to the cases of Salta Forestal and General Pizarro, both relatively close to Las Lajitas.

Besides those examples, conflicts that erupted in the research area are not mentioned. As Figure 8.6 shows, it comes as no surprise that SAB are not

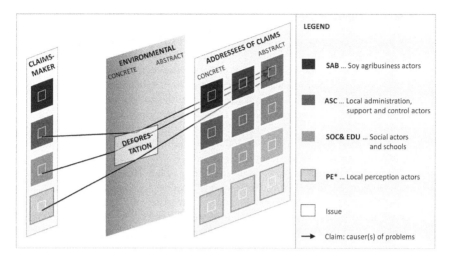

Figure 8.6 Claims making and deforestation.

active claims makers, recalling SAB's vision of entire deforestation for regional progress (SAB6). The most interesting piece of information, however, lies in the direction of the other actors' claims making.

All three groups consider the causers of deforestation within SAB, but on a highly abstract level. 'The agribusiness' or 'the *sojeros*' (loosely: those from the soy business) are blamed for the removal of the *monte*. The chain of causality is given, but there is a lack of direct/physical actors' identification (Box 8.2).

Summing up, deforestation is a concrete task, but due to the fact that it has already happened over the last 15–20 years around Las Lajitas, it is slowly moving from the actual visceral experience of deforestation to the narrative. Thus, the topic of deforestation shows a mental relocation from the concrete to the abstract.

WATER

Water is a broad category that is interpreted differently by the actor groups. The main distinction can be made over the question of surplus or lack thereof. The provision of water for households is excluded from this category for two reasons: both ASC as well as SOC&EDU, including PEL, confirmed that so far no shortage of provision of running water has been observed in Las Lajitas.[7] Concerns are more related to either water for irrigation (in the case of SAB), or floods in urban areas (PEL).

PEL are most susceptible to floods, particularly in the northern parts of Las Lajitas (Barrio San Antonio, Barrio 50) including precarious housing sites along the railway tracks (Box 8.3).

Box 8.2 Field diary: deforestation and a horse with no name

On one of my extended walks through Las Lajitas – it was the season of droughts with hot winds carrying dust through the empty streets – I saw an old couple sitting on plastic stools in front of their wooden house, the roof covered in a mix of corrugated metal sheets and plastic cover with the imprint of a local agribusiness, greatly resembling a traditional *puesto* in the *monte*. Seemingly interested in what a foreigner was up to – particularly in their neighbourhood and not in a fancy 4×4 pickup truck like most from out of town, but walking ('under the hot sun nonetheless!') – they invited me to join them and drink mate in the not-so-cool shadows of a lone tree.

Their story turned out to be quite interesting: They have been living in the same spot for decades, having already settled before any neighbourhoods had been established, only the Barrio Funavi, on the other side of the train tracks. Surrounded by *monte*, their land – not owned by them, but they were being tolerated – was used to breed cattle for milk production. Milking the cows was the task of the wife, who stayed at home with her 14 children, while the husband was away doing business. Being a merchant, he bought staple goods – 'flour, sugar, potatoes, everything' – in the village, packed his horse-drawn tumbrel and made his way to remote *puestos* in the *monte*. He had known everybody in the *monte*, he proudly affirmed, everybody from here (i.e. Las Lajitas) to the east, walking 90 leagues, taking him 10–12 days for one round trip. And the *puesteros* paid him in coal and animals (both alive and dead) – a classic *trueque*, a barter. Upon returning to the village, all the goods from the *monte* were sold to locals. 'It was a good deal,' the former merchant confirmed. However, business then started to decline, *puesteros* sold their land, left for the village and the land began to change, any bit of land was cleared for agriculture, for soy. 'Thank God, we have our pensions now,' said the old man, getting up and leaving the premises. Left alone with his wife, she explained his emotional attachment to the countryside, the *monte* and its animals. After having stopped his merchant travels, they also had to give up their cattle since their breeding area has turned into a new neighbourhood; and no animals were allowed in urban spaces. The only attachment, the old man still has to his former lifestyle is one horse. Tethered outside the village, he visits it every day, riding for a while alongside the river (where entrance to the land is still permitted), reminiscing about the good old days. When asked the horse's name, the response was accompanied with giggles: 'The horse's name. It has no name!' (Las Lajitas, 22 March 2014)

Additionally, it is striking that social housing sites (IPV housing) are more affected by high water levels due to their location. In this particular case, claims making against SAB occurs, however, not directed towards concrete SAB, but rather on an intermediate level between concrete and abstract SAB (Figure 8.7). To put it in other words, the names of the SAB potentially co-responsible for floods (due to deforestation and/or the construction of dams) are unknown; only vague spatial references are given. Additionally, for the first time, claims

Box 8.3 Field diary: snakes and ladders

Today's notorious walks take me to the precarious housing sites alongside the train tracks in the north of Las Lajitas. Access is difficult, so I decide to take the tracks, hoping that the bi-monthly train does not pass by in the next couple of minutes. On the left-hand side, towards the west, wooden frames, sometimes with more, sometimes with less plastic coverage (and the almost omnipresent imprint 'SOLO USO PARA AGRICOLA' ('sole use for agriculture'), border the tracks, that admittedly have seen better days as well. It surprised me, it was quiet; nobody could be spotted for some interviews or short small talks. A couple of metres further, already leaving the urban surrounding, I finally come across a seemingly old woman (it later turns out she is only 61), watching over a bunch of children running around. And so the conversation starts. I get to know the mother of 13 children and grandmother of nine, some of whom she is bringing up herself (the mother is 'working in the South', which I learned to decode as working in prostitution). So the humble grandmother, seemingly happy that somebody from 'out there' was interested in her person and her situation, poured her heart out. The following hours were filled with her fate of living and working in the *campo*, in the fields, not being able to provide continuous school attendance for her children (or not getting together her grandson's admission fee of 30 ARS to attend primary school), situations of health (see Box 8.5) – and her struggles with water. The woman praises the mayor of Las Lajitas for helping her 'all the time', in fact, she obtained a one-room house in the IPV housing, even though she had to pay for some of it. When health issues affected her, and she could no longer work in the fields, no income was coming in; the IPV house – though connected to water and electricity – was cut off from the water supply since the bills could no longer be paid. That is why she and her grandchildren moved back to the disadvantaged housing site. A garden hose, coming from the nearest proper house, provides her with water for daily use.

However, being back at her old living place certainly has its drawbacks, the woman said. Then she paints a metaphorical picture of the last floods that had come through the town, hitting her home hard. In a last-minute mission, she packed all her scarce belongings into improvised cupboards and ladders, just high enough to not get entirely wet. When the water level went down, she wanted to make up her bed, unfolding the mattress. To her unpleasant surprise, between the sheets a family of poisonous snakes had nested to get away from the floods. (Las Lajitas, 23 March 2014)

---

about problem solving are heard (see category (3)). Even though the cooperation with ASC during post-disaster situations is predominantly praised by PEL, concerns exist about the lack of action to prevent floods in urban areas; unlike with claims towards potential causers of floods, calls for action are directly posed to the municipality in general and Mayor Fermani in particular.

SAB have a different angle on water. The core concern is related to irrigation of agricultural land, especially during the drought seasons. While the

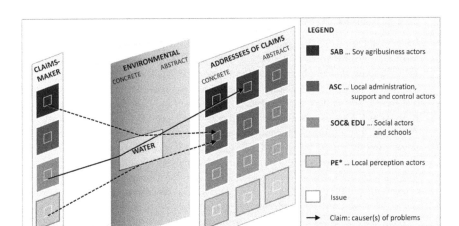

Figure 8.7 Claims making and water.

main thought style element 'if you want to get something done, do it your-self' is still held, claims against both INTA and the universities (particularly the Universidad Nacional de Salta) are uttered for failing to provide solutions for irrigation as well as against the local municipality's incapacity to provide hands-on plans to alleviate droughts, even if only on a fiscal-administrative level.

POLLUTION

Pollution includes the emission of waste, particulate matter or noise in and around the urban area of Las Lajitas. Here, the only actor group actively engaged in claims making is PEL (Figure 8.8). Claims of category (1) are directed against both very abstract actors of SAB and PEL. In the first case, noise and particulate matter are in the foreground, particularly during the harvesting season. The major concerns deal with the influx of large quantities of trucks and the increased circulation of pickup trucks within the urban area. In the latter case, PEL complain about littering in the streets and the connected mindlessness of fellow PEL.

Thus, the greatest problem of pollution derives from the (mis-)handling of waste. The responsibility for solving issues of pollution is attributed to the ASC and generally refers to the municipality as the organ responsible for clean-up in urban spaces. When it comes to SAB-related issues, claims are vaguer and weaker, often shoulder-shruggingly accepted that nothing could be done or referring to the claims that PEL were already accustomed to such environmental bads.

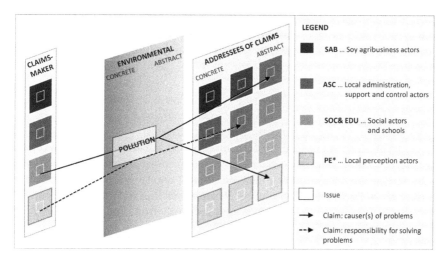

Figure 8.8 Claims making and pollution.

FUMIGATION

Besides deforestation, fumigation is the greatest source of conflict potential, both from a meta-level of environmental justice research and activism, but also from the locals' perspectives (Figure 8.9). ASC share a technical approach to claims making against a mid-abstract causer of problems. Theoretically, the actors emitting agrochemicals are known by ASC. However, in terms of daily

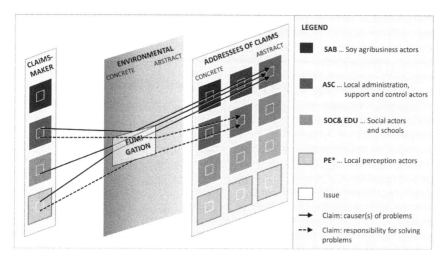

Figure 8.9 Claims making and fumigation.

noncompliance of rules and regulations concerning the application of pesticides and herbicides, the authorities consider themselves understaffed and thus not able to fully control the vast area around Las Lajitas. An interesting detail lies in the fact that ASC act on the assumption that fumigation is misused to the disadvantage of the environment and locals alike. Bluntly put: 'Every law has its loopholes' (ASC1).

SOC&EDU and PEL also make claims (Box 8.4) against SAB, however questioning fumigation on a more abstract, generalised level, focusing on the possible effects of the dissemination of agrochemicals.

Lack of – or very critical – information on the effects of spraying are major concerns. The intensity of claims making, however, is relatively low, also considering the recent implementation of legal regulations on fumigation distances to urban spaces. Nevertheless, demands for improvement of the current handling of fumigation are uttered predominantly from PEL (also carried out through reporting of illegal activity by citizens to the Las Lajitas Secretary for the Environment), but concrete actors of ASC are hardly mentioned or claimed against. An interesting aspect here is that ASC do see ASC in a pivotal role to act against unjust effects of fumigation, although often referred to other departments or institutions at other scales than the local one.

Categories (2) and (3): social issues

Due to the nature of non-tangibility, social claims making is less exercised than its environmental counterpart. Additionally, the thematic array is much wider and covers more actor group-specific topics.

OPERATIONAL SUPPORT

The first set of claims is issued by SAB towards ACS and has to do with operational support (Figure 8.10), i.e. the administrative and/or technical

---

Box 8.4 Field diary: no plants, no effects of fumigation

Strolling through Las Lajitas, it is eye-catching that very few houses have gardens, let alone flowers in their backyards. At most, I can see some trees planted in hard, light brown soil. Upon asking locals for the reasons – water scarcity for households has never been confirmed – the most common answer was that it was simply not the local cultural habit. When finally coming across one household with more plants, I once again asked the same question of why no one else followed suit. The woman, mid-fifties with a small child on her arm, replied that it was quite hard to grow something in that neighbourhood (her house is located on the NW corner of Las Lajitas) due to the fumigation. When the mosquitos passed by, she said, all the leaves shrivel and dry out. (Las Lajitas, 1 December 2013)

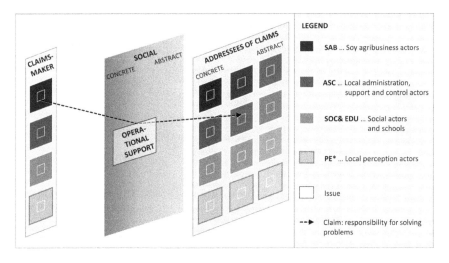

Figure 8.10 Claims making and operational support

help to ease agricultural production in the region. The receptors of claims making are predominantly universities (even though names were never referred to) or unspecified departments of INTA.

A common story is told among SAB, comparing farming conditions between the USA and Argentina, particularly the soy frontier in the North-west: Unlike in Argentina, the entrance level for farming without prior knowledge is very low in the USA. Due to the fact that each region has, according to SAB, well-established climate, soil and weather monitoring systems, trial and error in soy farming is de facto eliminated. Contrary to the USA, SAB, from their perspective, not only have to create the monitoring data themselves, but also face a harsh social climate against them from knowledge/technical institutions, leaving problem solving entirely to SAB.

HEALTH

The correlation between soy production – and in particular the application of agrochemicals – and increases in illnesses is a widely discussed question (Chapter 5), also in Las Lajitas (Figure 8.11). While the wide array of opinions is found, with SAB representatives' thought style being that with the right dosage of glyphosate, for example, nothing bad happens, and international environmental NGOs' interpretations stating the exact opposite, very few actual correlated claims are made in the town. Interestingly enough, those do not come so much from SOC&EDU, but rather from PEL. Even more surprising is the fact that no actual claims making against potential causers of problems occurs. It is rather projected abstractly onto

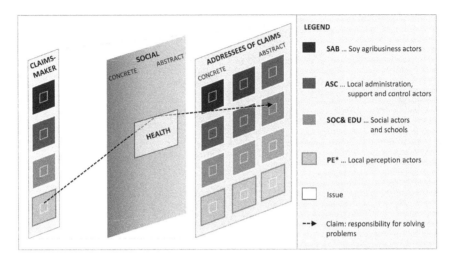

Figure 8.11 Claims making and health.

ASC, claiming that not enough is done to provide medical care in general; in particular, demands are for the provision of (free) medical drugs (Box 8.5).

WORK

Work – or the lack thereof – is omnipresent in Las Lajitas. The main sources of income are, as previously highlighted, either from the agribusiness sector or through odd jobs in the municipality. Exemplifying the spatial distribution, an approximation to the employment structure looks like the following: it is

---

Box 8.5 Field diary: health, a question of local administration

Thinking back to the 61-year-old grandmother living in the precarious housing area alongside the train tracks, discussed in Box 8.3, her situation perfectly condenses local conditions in relation to health. The woman has been working in the fields almost all her life, being exposed to agrochemicals. Now, she says, showing me her foot with a giant infected hole in it, she is suffering and anxiously waiting for a recovery. For more than two months her foot had been like that. Nobody knows what the reasons for her condition could be, let alone how to cure it. They had thought, she noted, that she was diabetic, but it proved to be a wrong diagnosis. She is also suffering from cardiac and circulatory troubles. But nobody, she claims, nobody besides the doctor [name withheld] is helping her And when she finally was able to walk a bit again, she could not retrieve her medication, because the local administration was on unlimited strike. (Las Lajitas, 23 March 2014)

Box 8.6 Field diary: the hidden work opportunities

Over the years of living in Argentina, I have come to know the ingenuity of the alternative (work) market. Las Lajitas is no exception. During my stays in the town I predominantly rented a cheap room in a motel that was located fairly centrally. The owners, a mother and her three daughters were well embedded in the local community, working on maintaining and expanding their hospitality business. Whenever I was accompanied by colleagues and fellow researchers, we used to stay on the upper floor, with an open corridor and perfect view to the parking lot. At the beginning, we did not think much of the fact that during the night trucks were pulling up, staying for a couple of hours and then leaving. This recurrent habit, however, started to make more sense when I realised that they always parked in the same spot, right next to the reception. In another stay in Las Lajitas, when working alone, I was assigned the room behind the said parking spot. While the room itself did not show any difference from the others, the TV did: It was the only one with the Playboy TV channel.

In a later conversation with the owner, it became obvious that she engaged in the business of prostitution. She praised her 'friends' from the South, particularly one Swede, with fabulous blond hair who always comes to visit her during harvesting season. (Las Lajitas, 5 May 2014)

---

seen that of those having a job (around 70 per cent), approximately two-thirds work in the urban area of Las Lajitas. In turn, the *campo* does not provide many opportunities (any more), making up only 15 per cent of the active workforce.

A great number of locals (about a quarter of all Lajiteños), however, are unemployed and live off one or several national social plans.

Even though bearing Box 8.6 in mind, claims towards causers of the problem of lack of work opportunities are made by PEL against the local municipality (and the mayor personally), or the semi-abstract actors in SAB (Figure 8.12).

On the contrary, SAB claims responsibility from PEL (in abstract forms) for not wanting to work, preferring to live off social plans. Here it becomes obvious that two different thought styles clash, creating two diametrically opposing realities in relation to work.

POVERTY

Socio-spatial fragmentation is present and visible in Las Lajitas, particularly the differentiation between socio-economically disfavoured (often relocated people from the *monte*) and economically well-off actors, predominantly from SAB. Even though – from an outside perspective – the connection between soy activity and poverty exists, no claims are made against actors potentially responsible for the current situation (Box 8.7; Figure 8.13).

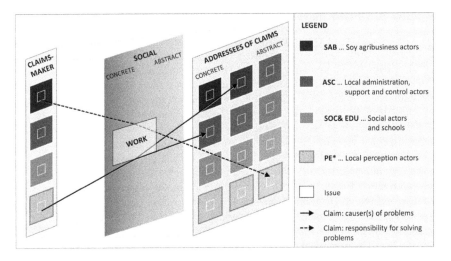

Figure 8.12 Claims making and work.

Box 8.7 Field diary: Gauchito Gil, wine and Coca-Cola; and youth and poverty

Having just arrived once again in Las Lajitas, I decided to go for a quick walk to stretch my legs after a long bus ride. Without a clear target, I headed towards the peripheral, sketchy areas of the town. Going along a small dirt street and before exiting to the national route, I crossed a small brook. There I saw a group of three young men in front of a small roadside shrine to Gauchito Gil (the most famous gaucho saint in Argentina), sitting in the grass, their barely functioning mopeds lying next to them. Instead of the otherwise obligatory mate, they were passing around a cut-open Tetra pack of wine, blended with Coca-Cola. They called to me, already quite verbally impaired – the wine had already taken effect – to come over and sit with them. 'You are a foreigner, right?' was the first question asked, followed by: 'Which agro-company do you work with?' Seemingly stunned that even though the first assumption was confirmed but the second one denied, they wanted to know more about me. Not quite sure what to do with the information they received, they returned repeatedly to the first two questions, seemingly having forgotten that we had already been through this bit of conversation. Shortly after, the main topic was women, where to get them from, which types they preferred. I kept quietly interested, pretending to sip the wine-Coca-Cola mix (which would have given me a massive headache the day after) before passing it back to the men. At some point, one started to talk about his three sisters, who were all 'offering services' that he organised, I only had to say a word and it would be done. Saying thank you, I declined. But it gave me segue to a new topic: socio-economic fragmentation of the town. My hosts' opinions surprised me: Yes, there was both poverty and wealth. The latter, they explained, derived mostly from the soy industry. 'You can spot them in the village, all the houses that are big and neat, for sure, there lives someone from the agro.' I was intrigued about their situation, but they only shrugged and commented that there was no place for them in the agribusiness (without holding too many grudges about that); they could live a poor but happy life off what the municipality and the social plans provided for them. 'And the best thing is: you do not even have to work for it.' However, the state could do more for them financially, all three agreed. (Las Lajitas, 12 April 2014)

Or to sum it up in a different way: 'The people have ... well, humble people conform. It is like noting an air of resignation. Having food, having drinks and done' (SOC3).

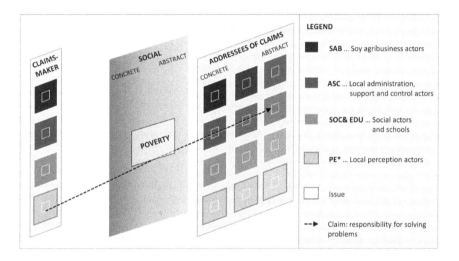

Figure 8.13 Claims making and poverty.

The only ways of claims that can be heard are from PEL against the abstract level of ASC. Thematically, demands are made that too little financial means are made available to PEL, predominantly issued through social, housing, or pension plans. A clear decoupling of cause, effect and demands by people affected occurs.

SOCIAL RESPONSIBILITY

Social responsibility is a category claimed by SAB, ASC and SOC&EDU. The idea behind those claims is an abstract demand for utilitarian fairness, i.e. claiming that soy farmers (though not concretely identified which ones) should contribute to the local society in order to redistribute some of SAB's revenues to the community in order to satisfy local needs (Figure 8.14). The most common translation of social responsibility is manifested in the form of

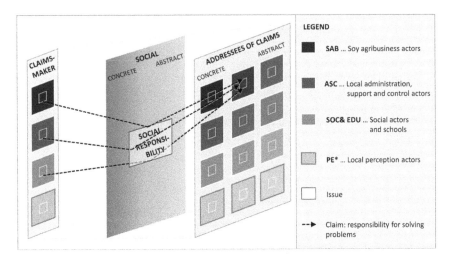

Figure 8.14 Claims making and social responsibility.

donations to some local primary or secondary schools and hospitals (particularly from local farmers living in Las Lajitas and benefitting from the investments as well), or contributions to the tertiary-level technical agrarian school.

Other drivers for social responsibility as well as particular foci are found as well, especially dealing with employees' well-being (Box 8.8).

EJIF: claims but no conflicts – a contextualisation

So far, in the CLASSIC perspective I have demonstrated that the results of the pre-EJIF analysis for Las Lajitas showed no active claims making in the town. With the application of the first part of the EJIF, however, a different picture has been drawn, highlighting the articulation of discontent along the four main thought styles. Chapter 7 revealed the thematic issues and the direction of claims. The next step is to deal with the question why claims do not translate into the materialisation of open conflicts and resistance.

Four angles of argumentation are identified: (1) I take up the often-cited notion of 'culture' to highlight the thought collectives' take on the question of claims making but no conflict eruption. (2) I focus on the characteristics, shapes and relationalities among the four thought styles to show the importance of dominating narratives of the thought collectives' esoteric circles (particularly SAB) on other thought collectives (especially PE★). Based on this analysis, (3) the underlying dimensions of social interactions are presented to identify features responsible for the PE★'s non-resistance. Finally, (4) a closer look at the patterns of addressees of claims is made, revealing the system of environmental justice proxying.

Box 8.8 Field diary: Doroteo Segovia, religion and social responsibility

Doroteo Segovia is one of the most recognised soy agribusiness persons in Las Lajitas. Whenever I was talking to employees of Grupo Segovia SA, they insisted that I had to meet their boss for he was considered a very special person in all respects. All said and done, a colleague and I headed to the headquarters in the south-western part of Las Lajitas, close to the bus station. Before entering the enormous property covering an entire block, I had already spotted an oversized painting of a religious figure leaning at the side of a wall. The second thing I noticed was a big, green football field, and what seemed like a hallway and a huge barbecue grill for making *asado* (Argentine barbecue) inside. I was impressed.

Inside the office, we were – after waiting a while – led to a conference room with a big, dark table and a marvellous view of the green garden with well-tended trees and flowers. Segovia enters, a middle-aged man, with a vibrancy of serenity. Sitting down, one of the strangest interviews I have ever conducted started. Asking questions was almost impossible; every introductory sentence was questioned by him, carefully painting a picture of him being the small and humble man, grateful for the gifts God had decided to grant him. Without detailed comment, he set up a laptop showing photomontages of his whereabouts, his struggles as a child of Bolivian immigrants, poverty and his striving to make something out of his life – until the success of Grupo Segovia SA was secured. But, he repeated, 'the most important thing of the region is to be grateful for life'. This gratefulness, in his opinion, is deeply embedded in the company's and his personal social responsibility towards the community. Being a good friend of the Monsignor of Salta, Segovia asked him what he could do, what he had to do for the community: Build a temple, a church. However, since the community was important, more people should contribute to the church. And that is how Las Lajitas got a new religious landmark.

Giving back to the community is also defined very much defined by offering social benefits to the company's employees, be it with regular *asados* on the premises (hence the big barbecue grill), football tournaments, other social events or support for employees in disadvantaged situations. (Las Lajitas, 10 October 2013)

Cultural components of the PE* thought collective

The first response to not understanding actions, or non-actions for that matter, is often to look for answers in the 'culture'. Thus, it is worthwhile exploring its relevance in Las Lajitas. The first challenge, however, is to grasp the concept itself. In so doing, I follow Hall's definition:

> Culture, it is argued, is not so much a set of things – novels and paintings or TV programmes and comics – as a process, a set of practices. Primarily, culture is concerned with the production and the exchange of meanings

– the 'giving and taking of meaning' – between the members of a society or group. To say that two people belong to the same culture is to say that they interpret the world in roughly the same ways and can express themselves, their thoughts and feelings about the world, in ways which will be understood by each other. Thus culture depends on its participants interpreting meaningfully what is happening around them, and 'making sense' of the world, in broadly similar ways.

(Hall 1997, p. 2)

Hall's characterisation of culture has a strong tendency to use 'culture' as a conception that is context-laden and – implicitly – includes Fleck's (1980) argumentations of thought styles and thought collectives. So what are the cultural characteristics referred to in the research area?

The first distinction often highlighted is the fact that locals (predominantly *criollos* who have been living in the region for generations) 'do not have a culture of cultivating, they have a culture of animal breeding and gathering' (ASC5), because 'here, if they do not eat meat, it seems like people cannot be fed' (ASC9). This perception is fostered in the urban areas:

Domestic agriculture does not exist [in the villages]. There are people who live in the *campo* – in the *campo*, yes. But the people that have come migrating to the villages, they don't.

(SOC3)

Almost nobody has a vegetable garden … it is not a custom.

(PEM3)

We do not have a garden; this plot only serves to amplify a house.

(PEL3)

A clear distinction from migrants coming to the region is made: 'The culture of the migrants is different…. You go back to the history of the past, to the times of the migrants and you will see that agriculture was taught' (ASC5). These flashes of comments show the general perception of PE★'s tradition-based habitus of non-agricultural activity in the region. Being still anchored in the past, the activities carried out then are still positively evaluated and cherished, leaving little readiness to accept change.

Second, PE★ are considered to be highly receptive, still entangled in the classic patron-peon system of the landlord watching over his labourers, making major decisions and controlling core aspects of the peons' lives (Box 8.9).

It is like the people from here do not have aspirations. One is born like that and one will die like that.

(EDU1)

Box 8.9 The case of Coronel Mollinedo

The village of Coronel Mollinedo is located 25 km north of Las Lajitas, with approximately 800 inhabitants. The location is quiet; immigration is not an issue. The most interesting feature, however, is the fact that this village along the train tracks and also hosting a local train station, was founded by a soy farmer's family, Elizalde. While officially part of the municipality of Apolinario Saravia, the de facto management of the village is still in the hands of this family. Whenever there are lots needed for village growth, Elizalde decides whether or not to donate parts of his land (the village is surrounded by the family's territory). Another very common business deal is that Elizalde provides materials for construction, local support for struggling individuals, etc. in return for services (e.g. changing and repairing tyres of agricultural machinery for free), or a workforce when needed. Elizalde is considered by most of the inhabitants as the patron in the classic sense of the term.

This is what exists here; this is the mentality of here.

(ASC6)

We do not understand much, since the village is small [in a metaphorical sense], we do not want to equilibrate upwards.

(SOC4)

This refers to the perceived inability to take part in the new dynamics of the soy frontier development:

The people are very submissive, not like in the South, the people from Buenos Aires that are complaining about everything. Not here, they subsist. If they need medicine here, they go to the municipality, the hospital … they are struggling, they are carrying on.

(SOC3)

It was some work to get accustomed. We were not accustomed to the village. It is a different life, but now we are already accustomed.

(PEL3)

Like in the old days with the patron:

people are waiting outside the municipality, waiting to receive: national programmes, social cards, bags of food.

(ASC5)

They have built houses with the money from the government. And well, here it goes along with the culture, it is what they wanted. They did not need it … they wanted it.

(EDU4)

It becomes obvious that representatives of other thought styles, or people from other regions have a hard time understanding local structures. Once reasons for particular local habitus cannot be found, the conception of 'culture' is used as a means to justify locals' behaviour, particularly in terms of non-claims making:

> I should not say what I am going to say. The thing is that I have lived in a different province, in Santa Fe. And I saw what is distributed in a village where everybody is Italian, mixed with Spanish. And they have a different work culture, a different social culture that does not exist here [in Las Lajitas]. So you come with different ideas. Almost everybody from the [municipal] secretary is from Santa Fe; they live a more organised way, the neighbour watches more the front [of his house], he has a different relationship. Here it is as if, I don't know … it is difficult changing the culture.
>
> (ASC9)

However, 'societies are always messier than our theories of them' (Crang and Cook 2007, p. 14). The conception of 'culture' is widely applied by PE★-different thought collectives to describe their perception of a contextual metaframe for the regional social sphere. Additionally, due to the non-tangibility, breadth and vagueness of the conception, I consider argumentations with 'culture' as alternate routes towards intellectual frame-bridging.

The interrelation among thought collectives

Thought collectives are central in Fleck's (2008) epistemological considerations. In order to understand the underlying dimensions of the four thought styles in Las Lajitas, the definition and positioning of the members behind those thought styles are necessary.

SAB has shaped Las Lajitas and its surroundings, having made the town the nucleus of soy production in North-western Argentina. The esoteric circle comprises soy farmers, agribusiness representatives and service providers from both within the region as well as from the South or abroad. This particular connection reinforces global narratives of soy production: soy reduces poverty; soy creates jobs; soy leads to development. The thought collective represents scenario (4) according to Fleck (2008, pp. 96–97). The esoteric circle (i.e. the elite's position) is significantly stronger than the exoteric one, thus supporting the cornerstones for regional success upon their followers.

ASC, SOC&EDU as well as PE★ are all very much a part of SAB's exoteric circle. This following is either based on the fact that they are financially dependent on SAB ('We will not bite the hand that feeds us'; PEL13; SOC7), showing signs of resignation and followership ('Here are serious health problems. But what shall we say here? You will not be against [soy production] either'; PEL9), or pure fascination by the capabilities of SAB ('A wonder what they have done'; ASC14).

ASC represents a very particular thought collective where both circles are almost identical and equal, as described by Fleck (2008, pp. 96–97) as scenario (1). The orientation of this group is very open and directed towards the present-future. Members of ASC are concerned about the trust of their lay people, an aspect that is understandable considering that most ASC jobs depend on the results of local elections. The thought collective is always described as being in the middle, which becomes very clear in this context. On the one hand, ASC need the SAB for financial revenues (be it through SAB donations at the local level, or indirectly via national allocations of soy-export-related *retenciones*). On the other hand, ASC do have to position themselves as a command and control organ actually working for PEL to improve their livelihoods. This ambivalence of this position also derives from the majority of members being part of the esoteric circle, facilitating faster interactions and alterations of standpoints.

SOC&EDU are a smaller and more heterogeneous thought collective. It is more difficult to become a member of this collective (particularly because of the very nature of having to have professional training); the orientation is towards the past-present. An interesting feature here is that many members of the SOC&EDU esoteric circle also belong to the esoteric circle of ASC, which is also considered a source of friction in both thought collectives.

Finally, PEL is a thought collective with a very flat hierarchy. However, the main focus here lies on the glorification of the past, while implicitly maintaining SAB's main credos of development.

Soy agribusiness activities: underlying dimensions of social interactions

Figure 8.15 shows the positioning of the actor groups in relation to activities based on the soy agribusiness. The first general trend is the close coupling of SAB with ASC (GROUP I) as well as SOC&EDU with PEL (GROUP II). While the first couple is concerned with setting the stage (i.e. physically in the form of the advance of soy and socially through actively changing the social setting), the second pair is more associated with the handling – if at all – of the effects caused by the first.

In terms of relevance, it goes without saying that SAB are ranked the highest, with soy production being their core business activity. Similarly, and for the same reasons, spatial and temporal anchoring is the main domain of SAB and ASC.

One basic feature distinguishing PEL from the other actor groups is the fact that PEL are considered more holistically involved. SAB, ASC and SOC&EDU here are portrayed in their dominant role as professionals, while PEL also – if not to say particularly – include private daily life. Visceral elements are much more important in terms of effect, affect and perception. Thus, the sensory engagement with soy production's effects are highest in this

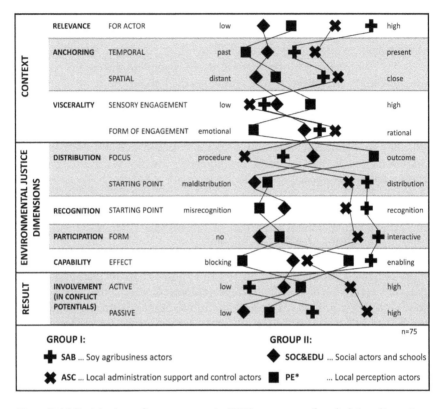

Figure 8.15 Positioning of actor groups in EIJF's category of underlying dimensions in relation to soy-based activities.

group, even though it was seen in Chapter 3 that other topics related to waste (mis-)management are much more concretely experienced.

Shedding light on environmental justice dimensions, the two supra-groups share an almost dichotomous positioning. While the focus on procedural distribution is the domain of ASC, particularly in setting and guarding the rules of support and control, PEL are most concerned with the outcome of distribution. This also explains the starting point for the thought style on distribution and recognition: While GROUP I is characterised by an *ex-ante* approach towards justice (i.e. ideal situations), GROUP II implicitly favours the *ex-post* version with the focus on non-ideal situations.

The most interesting aspect here, however, lies in the ambivalent positioning in the category of capabilities: PEL appear twice, creating a thought-style-internal incommensurability. On one side, the inclusion of the region around Las Lajitas into the globalised soy agribusiness has brought major changes in terms of lifestyle for PEL, dominated by rural-urban migration and subsequent alterations of situations related to (non-)working situations. New demands from PEL regarding their changing way of living also shape the composition and evaluation of PEL's capability situation. Referring back to Schlosberg, it is essential that the measuring of justice is not judged by 'how much we have, but whether we have what is necessary to enable a more fully functioning life as we choose to live it' (2009, p. 30). As a result, the blocking factor is formed by both decreasing opportunities for work (taking this as an example), but also highly influenced by the increase in desire to have a more financially rewarding lifestyle. On the other hand, PEL are – in the exoteric circle, i.e. as lay persons – highly involved in SAB's overarching thought style. Thus, the positive connotation of the soy agribusiness is subconsciously embedded in PEL's way of thinking, making it harder to oppose something that is perceived as 'good development'.

As a result, the involvement in conflict potentials is mostly located on the lower half of the scale; only ASC have high numbers of active and passive roles in conflictive situations.

Addressees of environmental justice clams and the implications thereof

One of the common features of environmental justice conflicts is the identification of both particular sites (e.g. toxic waste disposal sites, production plants, or airports) that have negative effects on their surroundings and their operators to whom claims are directed. However, as seen in Chapter 7, the situation in Las Lajitas is more complicated, dealing with a multiplicity of actors (more than 60 SAB have their field of operation in the municipality), varying degrees of visibility (SAB living in the town vs. soy tourists), and activities generating conflict potential that are recurring, with no or very little immediate impact on the local community. Furthermore, the spatial distribution of source and target of environmental bads is inverted, compared to original environmental justice spatialities (Figure 8.16). In traditional environmental justice settings, a smaller point of emission of bads is distributed to its surroundings. As a result, traditional environmental justice activism and research take those sites as the starting point for further activity.

However, typical soy agribusiness spatialities function differently, with soy fields having large extensions, surrounding urban spaces. Thus, the point of departure for an analysis is not the actual source of environmental bads but rather the target, i.e. the actors affected themselves.

As much as environmental justice claims vary in their degree of abstraction, the addressees of those claims range from concrete persons or companies to the abstract notion of 'the soy agribusiness', for example.

Two main trends are seen. First of all, SOC&EDU are very rarely confronted by claims from the other actor groups, being perceived as disentangled from regional dynamics of change. PEL is predominantly blamed by SAB and ASC – on an abstract level – for lack of initiative and willingness to work. The contextualisation of such claims does not occur in the form of direct connections as highlighted through the SOC&EDU thought style

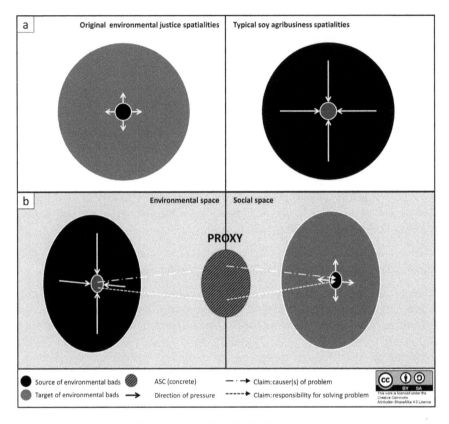

Figure 8.16 Directions of environmental bads' distribution.
Source: Hafner 2016.

(i.e. the lack of being able to adapt to new speeds of regional change due to the inclusion of the region in the globalised soy agribusiness and the forced change of PEL lifestyles), but is rather explained by ASC's distribution of finances through social plans (thus making claims against ASC both for causing the problem and for not fixing it). Thus, it comes as no surprise that in the arena of actor groups, one of the most striking results is that ASC – the municipality as an institution and in Mayor Fermani as a real person – is by far the most concrete recipient of blame and the one held responsible for problem solving. From a traditional environmental justice standpoint, SAB should de facto be made responsible for change; however, due to the lack of tangibility and visibility, ASC is implicitly pushed to the foreground. An interesting resemblance to Figure 8.16a can be made: Due to the fact that the causers of problems are hard to pin down, ASC as the most visible actor group on the local level is forced into the role of a proxy (Figure 8.16b).

The target of environmental bads, i.e. in this case PEL, does not make – due to lack of actors' visibility – direct claims against environmental bads caused by the source. With PEL's designation of ASC as a proxy, the source of environmental bads is transferred from the environmental to the social space and focused on the inner position. Mentally, the source of bads is condensed and – as with traditional environmental justice research – influences once again the outer circle. To put it bluntly, the replacement of abstract actor clouds with concrete actor proxies has occurred.

Notes

1 At this point it has to be – once again – highlighted, that the following analysis is based on a very narrow, theoretically-driven and deterministic approach, overemphasising the negative effects of short-term research stays in areas where context ought to be vital for understanding local dynamics.
2 As previously highlighted, no social, environmental or socio-environmental NGOs are present in the research area. Thus, it goes without saying that they cannot be included in the above list of actor groups.
3 In order to settle my own doubts, the children were asked what sort of screaming they refer to. Thus the direct connection 'fights' and 'screaming' could be made.
4 During my stay in Las Lajitas in the harvesting season I was in the (un)fortunate position of experiencing the de facto all-pervasive smell of the particulate matter emitted from the soy silo.
5 So far, I have not come across published studies that verify the level of water contamination in Las Lajitas. The main concern of ASC, however, is the content of naturally occurring arsenic. To what extent agrochemicals can be traced back is beyond my knowledge. Nevertheless, there is a common rumour in Las Lajitas that a microbiological study found heightened levels of glyphosate in the local drinking water, but the results were prevented from being published.
6 Of course, it has to be noted that there are still people living off the river, especially those in risky living situations: 'She is going fishing every day, just like we go to the supermarket to get some food' (SOC8).
7 It should be highlighted, that problems of provision with water occur in dangerous settlements, particularly along the railway tracks. However, since a relatively small number of people are affected and due to the fact that informal solutions (e.g. borrowing water hoses from neighbouring houses; PEL8) are in place, these examples are being excluded from the analysis.

References

Baxter, J. and Eyles, J., 1997. Evaluating qualitative research in social geography: establishing 'rigour' in interview analysis. *Transactions of the Institute of British Geographers*, 22 (4), 505–525.
Chapman, G.B. and Johnson, E.G., 1999. Anchoring, activation, and the construction of values. *Organizational Behavior and Human Decision Processes*, 79 (2), 115–153.
Collier, J. and Collier, M., 1986. *Visual Anthropology: Photography as a Research Method*. Albuquerque, NM: University of New Mexico Press.
Crang, M. and Cook, I., 2007. *Doing Ethnographies*. London: SAGE.
Escuela N° 4.510 'Antártida Argentina', 2010. *Memorias de mi pueblo*. Las Lajitas, Argentina.

Fleck, L., 1980. *Entstehung und Entwicklung einer wissenschaftlichen Tatsache: Einführung in der Lehre von Denkstil und Denkkollektiv.* Frankfurt am Main: Suhrkamp.

Fleck, L., 2008. Das Problem einer Theorie des Erkennens. In: E.O. Graf and B. Griesecke, eds. *Ludwig Flecks vergleichende Erkenntnistheorie.* Berlin: Parerga, pp. 63–108.

Goffman, E., 1990. *The Presentation of Self in Everyday life.* London: Penguin.

Hafner, R., 2016. Figures [online]. Available at: http://roberthafner.at/figures (accessed 7 November 2017).

Hall, S., 1997. Introduction. In: S. Hall, ed. *Representation: Cultural Representations and Signifying Practices.* London: Sage in association with the Open University, pp. 1–12.

Krapovickas, J., Sacci, L. and Hafner, R., 2016. Firewood supply and consumption in the context of agrarian change: the North Argentine Chaco from 1990 to 2010. *International Journal of the Commons* [online], 10 (1), 220–243. Available at: www.thecommonsjournal.org/articles/10.18352/ijc.609/

Lefebvre, H., 1991. *The Production of Space.* Oxford: Blackwell.

Mussweiler, T. and Englich, B., 2005. Subliminal anchoring: judgmental consequences and underlying mechanisms. *Organizational Behavior and Human Decision Processes,* 98 (2), 133–143.

Mussweiler, T. and Strack, F., 1999. Hypothesis-consistent testing and semantic priming in the anchoring paradigm: a selective accessibility model. *Journal of Experimental Social Psychology,* 35 (2), 136–164.

Rodaway, P., 1994. *Sensuous Geographies: Body, Sense, and Place.* New York: Routledge.

Rose, G., 2012. *Visual Methodologies: An Introduction to Researching with Visual Materials.* 3rd edn. Thousand Oaks, CA: SAGE.

Rothstein, A., 1986. *Documentary Photography.* Boston: Focal Press.

Schlosberg, D., 2009. *Defining Environmental Justice: Theories, Movements and Nature.* Oxford: Oxford University Press.

Soja, E.W., 1996. *Thirdspace: Journeys to Los Angeles and Other Real-And-Imagined Places.* Cambridge, MA: Blackwell.

Suchar, C.S., 1997. Grounding visual sociology in shooting scripts. *Qualitative Sociology,* 20 (1), 33–55.

Svampa, M., 2001. *Los que ganaron: La vida en los countries y barrios privados.* Buenos Aires: Editorial Biblos.

Vincent, A., 1998. Is environmental justice a misnomer? In: D. Boucher and P.J. Kelly, eds. *Social Justice: From Hume to Walzer.* Hoboken, NJ: Taylor & Francis Ltd., pp. 123–145.

Weber, M., 1988. *Gesammelte Aufsätze zur Wissenschaftslehre.* 7th edn. Tübingen: Mohr.

9   Conclusion

This book may seem unusual to some readers, definitely beyond the realms of a 'classic geography work'. However, how the manuscript has turned out truly reflects my scientific formation, having started in a multidisciplinary surrounding, crossing the borders between humanities and social science, with sneak peaks towards natural sciences.

Throughout the chapters I have argued that context matters, regional, social as well as personal. The major challenge of context, however, is to present as much additional or side information without getting the reader/consumer lost in details that prevent understanding the bigger picture and goal of this book. Hence, this last chapter pulls together those loose threads.

Soy agribusiness, incommensurabilities ...

Why study the soy agribusiness? And why the Chaco Salteño?

One of the main objectives of this book was to visualise the impact that membership in particular thought styles had on the overall research process including its outcomes. Environmental justice was a perfect example to study the power of perspective, since it is used by both researchers and activists; it is highly normative and not (yet) fully conceptualised, leaving room for shaping the concept(ion). Thus, it was necessary to find the gaps of environmental justice research to critically analyse the current models, frameworks and concepts to identify the shortcomings as well as propose a new way of looking at environmental justice research in general.

In so doing, it was crucial to step off the beaten path of environmental justice examples and focus on a topic not widely studied in this realm: soy agribusiness. As observed, one of the major differences between classic environmental justice cases (such as the study of distribution of environmental goods and bads relating to toxic waste sites) and the soy agribusiness lies in the inversion of the relationship between polluter and polluted. Toxic waste sites, for example, have one small-scale point of emission affecting the larger surrounding, while soy agribusiness activities are predominantly carried out in the fields surrounding the recipients of environmental bads. Additionally, due to the nature of the soy agribusiness and the particular organisational setting of the *pooles de siembra* (sowing pools), the visibility of soy agribusiness-related actors is generally low: Landowners rent their fields on a short-term basis (sometimes as minimal as one harvesting season) to investors. They in turn subcontract several companies for the tasks of land preparation, fumigation, harvesting, or transportation, respectively. As a result, for a lay person it is very hard – if not impossible – to identify the actors *actually* working on the soy fields.

Consequently, the two features described here offer particular difficulties for the creation of environmental justice claims making: first, since there is no single point but rather a vague surface of emission of environmental bads, coupled with procedural mid-to-long-term rather than punctual one-off effects, the major local challenge is to actually *identify* effects negatively impacting daily lives. Taking the example of fumigation as a repetitive event, it has been shown that spraying herbicides and/or pesticides once did not generate immediately visible/sensible harm for locals, whereas deforestation as a one-off event encompassed a drastic change of lifestyle for people who had been living in forest areas and (were) – voluntarily or involuntarily – moved to urban areas within the region. Second, even in the case of being aware of causes of environmental bads, the identification of the *causers* and the linking of effects and actors presuppose insight knowledge that is often lacking. Or put in simple terms: if you do not know who to blame for a negative effect, it is hard to state concrete claims against that actor. However, I fully agree with Čapek (1993) or Taylor (2000) that claims making is pivotal for any environmental justice research. Hence, studying the gap between environmental bads distribution and non-claims making is central for understanding the power as well as limitation of applying current environmental justice concept(ion)s.

Where wood is chopped, splinters must fall

Environmental justice research is research based on change. This has been shown in the cases of landfill sites (Bullard 2000; Fan 2012), air (Pearce *et al.* 2006) and noise pollution (Flitner 2007), as well as more abstract topics of global climate justice (Okereke 2010), just to name a few.

Hence, studying the soy agribusiness, the element of change is most likely observed in relatively new areas of production, particularly at the frontiers. Here, Argentina proved to be a particularly interesting frame for a case study. Being the third-largest producer of soy worldwide, the soy agribusiness has grown to become the major sector of revenues over the last 15 years. The most recent expansion of territories have been identified in the north-west of the country, particularly in the Chaco Salteño, a region that is considered as in transition from a traditionally remote and socio-economically disfavoured region to an area of soy production included in a globalised business scheme. Bearing in mind that the term 'environmental justice' is rarely used in Argentina, but rather studied under the term 'conflictos socio-ambientales' (i.e. social-environmental conflicts), previous studies (e.g. Viglizzo and Jobbágy 2011) have envisioned the great potential for such forms of conflict.

Context matters, as I have highlighted on multiple occasions throughout the text. My empirical focus on the municipality of Las Lajitas proved to be the perfect mix of novelty and established frameworks to critically reflect on the state-of-the-art of environmental justice research. Hence, the empirical findings presented here portray one particular context within the soy agribusiness in Argentina. I could have chosen already established conflicts such as the Madres de Ituzaingó, 'Paren de Fumigar', or Desmontar Pizarro located north of my research focus. Working in such openly conflictive situations surely has its benefits: Actors are exposed right from the beginning; discourses are more openly available, including news coverage and external NGO support; resistance is already organised to some degree. Hence, in a broader sense, those conflictive situations are materialised through an almost perfect bi-polarisation of thought styles where the (in-)voluntary causers of environmental bads are opposed by organised groups (of activists) fighting against those – in their opinion – newly created injustices. While those cases are definitely interesting to observe, the starting point for an analysis is located in the materialisation of conflict. Since numerous studies have been compiled on this general framework, I decided to include more context to the studies and focus on the prequel of conflict materialisation. In so doing, I included a broader sense of actors, particularly focusing on the often neglected locals' perceptions of change, effects and conflict (potentials) of the region's inclusion into the globalised soy agribusiness.

Las Lajitas is simultaneously a unique and a classic example. I do not claim that this small-scale example speaks for the great majority of soy agribusiness nor environmental justice cases. It does not have to. The main aim here is to present the fact that universal environmental justice frames have to take context into account, risking the possibility of standardised comparison of cases in favour of a more holistic understanding of local realities, their incommensurabilities and non-formation of conflictive situations. In order to visualise the importance of thought styles and context, I have described three research perspectives on the case study of Las Lajitas: the CLASSIC, the ALTERNATIVE and the COMPLETE.

The CLASSIC approach

Within the boundaries of research on (environmental) justice, this perspective is the one most widely applied. The main characteristics here are the focus on distribution and the heavy reliance on deductive thinking. The shaping of cognition is guided by the researcher's membership in certain thought collectives and subsequently formed by their thought styles. Consequently, the CLASSIC approach relies heavily on the study of previous research results, methods and methodologies in the realms of environmental justice. This, in turn, leads to the application of pre-defined categories and sets of normativity during the fieldwork phase(s). In other words, seen through the glasses of the CLASSIC perspective, the researcher already *sees* environmental goods and bads, change and effects as well as conflict potentials, since s/he is already trained in one particular form of cognition that is dominant in her/his scientific thought collective. I do not argue that this is necessarily a bad thing. However, it is vital to reflexively reveal the underlying frames of thought collective-shaped thinking and acting to the readers/consumers of the research results. Auto-ethnography becomes an interesting tool. Here, it goes without saying that the conclusions of a research project are intrinsically linked to the questions asked. They in turn are shaped by the thought style's pre-set premises and *knowing*.

To put the theoretical considerations into practical examples, I worked through the environmental justice literature to design the first perspective on my case study of Las Lajitas. Based on previous research, the area was likely to suffer social-ecological conflicts relating to the soy agribusiness. The first axiomatic element of the thought style that I here want to call 'environmental justice research' was based on the existence of conflictive situations. Consequently, my research question focused on the 'forms of social-ecological conflicts' rather than asking whether there were any conflicts at all.

Since environmental justice conflicts are always connected to the physical world in one form or another, the first step was to identify conflict potentials within the urban sphere of Las Lajitas. Fifteen different soy agribusiness sites of potential harm for local residents were identified. The main topics were related to agrochemicals, noise and dust/particulate matter. All those issues continue to be studied with an environmental justice focus in different settings, as shown by Guthman (2016), Carrier *et al.* (2016) or Wang *et al.* (2016), respectively. In addition to the punctual representation of conflict potentials, I have presented the areal dominance of soy fields around Las Lajitas. This auxiliary form of virtual-reality presented the soy agribusiness proximity to locals' livelihoods, making it abundantly clear – from the perspective of 'environmental justice research' – that conflicts are present. Having identified the potential locations for conflicts, the next step was to go after the actors involved. However, at this stage, the limitations of the CLASSIC approach became obvious: During stakeholder and expert interviews it became clear that the reality constructed through the thought style 'environmental justice research' did not match the realities of the actors interviewed: None of the concrete conflicts supposed by me were concretely and actively mentioned by the interviewees.

Two conclusions can be drawn from this situation. First, arguing from a universalist perspective, certain principles of justice share worldwide validity. Consequently, injustices are defined by the breach of those global principles. The important feature here is that the actual recognition of such injustices does not play any role in the fact that they exist. To put it more precisely, I identified 15 injustices (and thus conflict potentials) that are backed up by previous research on environmental justice. Even though locals' perspectives do not reflect my results, those injustices still exist; they are based on a universal list of attributes (e.g. fumigation harms health situation; noise has negative effects on locals, etc.). Following this narrow line of environmental justice research/activism, it would then be my task to pinpoint those injustices to locals, making them aware of their 'bad situation' that needed to be fixed. It goes without saying that this approach ignores contextual information, recognition of local ways of thinking and thus continues to be highly criticised by (including) post-colonial studies (e.g. DeLoughrey *et al.* 2015; Kopnina 2016; Milbourne and Mason 2016) for its reliance on hegemonial structures of justice and the environment.

The second conclusion is more based on a social-constructivist and Flecksian argumentation, highlighting the possibility of the co-existence of multiple realities. This way of thinking has far-reaching consequences: Multiple realities also imply the existence of varying definitions of justice, equality and the role of the environment; they all go beyond the definition sovereignty of the researcher, actually redefining the role of the researcher her-/himself. Consequently, her/his main task shifts from the identification of one singular form to the identification of a multiplicity of definitions, perspectives and thought styles. The new challenge, then, is to bring together those different realities to *understand* why they have developed and why they are so different compared to each other. This leads to the second perspective of this study: the ALTERNATIVE.

The ALTERNATIVE approach

While the starting point of the CLASSIC perspective was based on the identification of conflict potentials in the physically tangible (and from the CLASSIC perspective defined as 'objective') sphere, the second approach based its analysis on the social space and the thought styles of four actor groups in Las Lajitas. Hence, the collection of contextual information on change, effects, actors and conflict (potentials) was the first task to be carried out. In so doing, my strategy was to work with direct quotations as much as possible (both in the original Spanish as well as the English translation), allowing the actors to 'speak for themselves' and visualise the construction of four different thought styles:

Thought style I: soy agribusiness actors (SAB)

In a study on the impact of soy agribusiness on the local (social) environment, it goes without saying that the thought style of SAB has to be included. The basic underlying line of thought here is the focus on future growth and development, while being proud of the achievements that have been made in the past. The metaphor of the self-made man thriving under harsh environmental conditions, without substantial support from official entities, is omnipresent.

While it is not denied that conflicts have occurred (particularly in settings of large-scale non-regionally anchored SAB actors), they are considered elements of the past. Nowadays, the discourse of social responsibility has replaced the one of conflict. Consequently, in relation to the understanding of nature and the environment, SAB see themselves as representatives of pliant anthropocentrism, where they are well aware of their power to shape nature; the value of nature is quasi-instrumental, but still has to be taken care of to prevent reckless exploitation and subsequent loss of revenues. To some extent, what Anguelovski and Martínez-Alier called the 'gospel of eco-efficiency' (2014, p. 173) is represented here. Socio-economically, the main discourse revolves around the notions of 'soy production creates jobs', 'soy production reduces poverty' and 'soy production strengthens wealth and development'.

Thought style II: local administration, support and control actors (ASC)

ASC are considered a core group of actors to support and control regional development. Unlike SAB, the regional storyline told by ASC starts before soy production in the region, focusing on the traditional lifestyle of cattle breeding in the *monte* as the cornerstone of regional identity building before the soy boom of the last 10–15 years. Conflicts do play a role in ASC's thought style, but they are mostly shaped by the era of early deforestation and (forced) resettlement of locals from the *monte* to the villages. At the same time, migration has started from the southern provinces to the region: 'Southern (work) ethics' – always positively connoted – have been introduced into the Chaco Salteño, already highlighting the subconscious discontent with the passivity of the local *criollos*. The standpoint on soy production is ambivalent: Considering SAB, major concerns are uttered that many actors are not visible to ASC, making it hard to develop relationships with producers and discuss issues of regional development, particularly in terms of the effects new projects will have on the local community. While GM crops are considered inevitable, ASC consider themselves 'in the middle', having to satisfy the needs both of SAB as well as cater for the health of the locals, without compromising opportunities for monetary influx to the region, directly to PE*, as well as ASC entities.

Thought style III: social actors and schools (SOC&EDU)

The thought style of SOC&EDU is created by the most prominent discontent with the soy agribusiness in the research area. Ecological effects of soy production are predominantly overlooked, while social consequences are put in the foreground. Here, the creation of reality is greatly influenced by the notion of dual-speed development of the region. New processes of soy agribusiness change the regional setting in a time frame of 20 years, while locals would need more time to adapt to those changes. The result is noted by

SOC&EDU as an increase in social unrest and criminal activities, but more so in the form of increasingly unhealthy lifestyles of PE★: Having no work opportunities, but the possibility of collecting social plans from the government, coupled with climatic conditions defined by high temperatures and humidity, PE★ remain inactive, stay indoors and 'get fat' (EDU3). In SOC&EDU's thought style, it has been shown that the activities of SAB are implicitly considered as externalities that just happen; but no real influence can be executed upon SAB by SOC&EDU.

Thought style IV: local perception actors (PE★ = PEL + PEM + PER)

PE★'s thought style is marked by a strong differentiation between the past and the present. Nostalgia towards the old times when people lived and worked in the *monte* is omnipresent. With the arrival of extra-regional (SAB) actors, the story shows an abrupt change, referred to as new 'trouble in paradise': Conflictive situations of (forceful) relocation, land tenure issues and deforestation are the consequences. This break has already been noted in the thought style of SAB and ASC, but is more prominent with PE★: The tangible connection to the physical environment of Las Lajitas becomes detached. The village becomes the new habitat and focus of PE★ livelihoods; environmental change is moved to the background of interest. Regional embeddedness becomes very low, which is not just reflected in PE★ among adults, but even more so represented by local children and young adults. Consequently, the lack of connection to the surrounding environments also fosters decoupling of SAB activities from the lives and thought style of PE★.

Roots for incommensurabilities among the thought styles

All four thought styles create their respective realities in relation to the region's inclusion in the globalised soy agribusiness. Those realities are based on the thought collectives' cognition and learning. In order to approximate the roots of the above summarised thought styles Figure 9.1 puts the thought styles' positions in relation according to their contextual standing, perception of agribusiness activities and benefits. Two particular results stand out: Both the connotation of soy as well as the benefits of the soy agribusiness show an ambivalent position for PE★: Soy is seen as an adversary as well as an opportunity inasmuch as PE★ consider the results of soy production as both highly beneficial and having low positive impact. This oxymoronic situation is explained by the fact that all four thought collectives not only exist in isolation next to each other, but overlap, making PE★ temporarily part of the exoteric circle of the dominant SAB thought style while maintaining its proper structure.

This fluidity of thought collective membership has been shown to be also influential in terms of actors' claims making. Table 9.1 summarises the topics that were used for claims making.

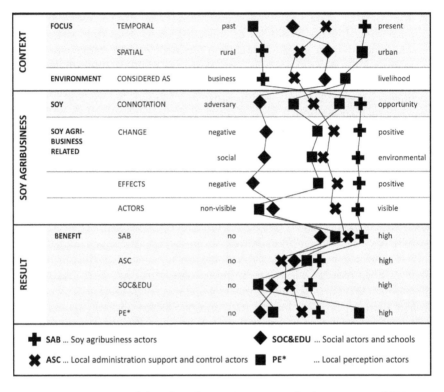

Figure 9.1 Comparison of thought style positions as roots for incommensurabilities.

It was shown that no open conflict materialisation was detected. Consequently, PE★ was chosen as an example to identify four angles of argumentation for this counter-intuitive result:

The first line of reasoning derived from the actors within the region, making cultural elements and the strong embeddedness of the classic patron-peon relationship, i.e. the reliance on the actors above one's hierarchical level. Thus, the self-imposed limiting of PE★'s abilities to materialise discontent and, ultimately, resistance against the negative effects of soy agribusiness activities was observed. The most hands-on articulation here was the phrase: 'You do not bite the hand that feeds you.'

The second argumentation has already been highlighted and deals with the interrelatedness and influence of the four thought collectives. SAB is the overarching thought collective, primarily responsible for shaping local and regional discourses: soy generates jobs, gives work and reduces poverty. Here, it has been shown that the other three thought collectives are part of SAB's exoteric circle and can thus relate to the general framework of soy benefits.

The third line of argumentation is closely linked to the underlying dimensions presented in the environmental justice incommensurabilities framework.

Table 9.1 Summary of claims-making topics and their conflict materialisation

	Thought collectives				Claim articulated against actors	Open conflict materialisation
	SAB	ASC	SOC&EDU	PE★		
Environmental space						
Climate change	+++	+++	+++	+++	No	No
Deforestation		+++	++	++	Yes	No
Water issues	+++	+++	+	++	Yes	No
Pollution				+++	Yes	No
Fumigation		++	+++	+	Yes	No
Social space						
Operational support	+++				Yes	No
Health				++	Yes	No
Work	++			+++	Yes	No
Poverty				+	Yes	No
Social responsibility	++	+	+		Yes	No
Crime		+	++	+++	No	No

Notes
Level of claims making: +++ high; ++ medium; + low; none.

The interrelatedness and fluidity of the thought collectives showed a major influence on PE★'s self-evaluation of their capabilities: The soy agribusiness was clearly positioned as a blocking as well as an enabling factor for PE★. Even though, from an outside perspective, the regional transformation of the *monte* as the basis for locals' livelihoods into exclusive soy monocultures, has directly and swiftly transformed local forms of living (as previously highlighted, unemployment has risen drastically), both indirect benefits in the form of social plans (financed by the soy export-related taxes) as well as dominant thought style-based positive connotations of soy production create an uneasy state of non-materialisation of conflicts.

At this point it has to be stressed again that local hardships do exist, but, as the fourth argumentative result shows, situations with conflict potential against the soy agribusiness experience a decoupling of cause and effect of (environmental) bads. As shown, claims highlighting negative effects within the realms of the environmental space are not directed to the causers of those effects by PE★, but rather deflected to ASC, who in turn act as a proxy of blaming in the social space. Simply put, when locals were re-located from the *monte* to the urban area, they did not make claims against the soy agribusiness actors responsible for their relocation, but directed their discontent against the local government for not providing adequate housing and living arrangements (that were, in turn, financed by the soy export taxes).

Overall, the ALTERNATIVE perspective has shown the importance to understand underlying dimensions that shape the ways of thinking and acting of different actor groups. My task as the researcher was focused less on the interpretation of data collected in the field based on the deductive knowledge obtained by systematically applying categories and lines of thought derived from environmental justice literature. My main assignment was to collaborate with locals and to understand their ways of thinking rather than interpreting it through a narrow perspective of environmental justice.

The COMPLETE approach

Meta-levels are crucial for understanding underlying structures not just in relation to the empirical section, but also with reference to the researchers' positioning within scientific epistemologies. Consequently, the last reading of this book focuses on the contextualisation of the CLASSIC and ALTERN-ATIVE versions above. Simply put, the first is strongly embedded in the theoretical discussion and uses previous environmental justice studies as guidance for the evaluation of conflictive situations *in situ*. Pre-set structures are important, following the axiomatic assumption that the mechanisms of conflict are – to a certain degree – universal and can thus be studied with a basic (generic) tool box. The great advantage of this approach also lies in the more focused research design, since top-down views on the empirical setting already predict conflictive situations. I as the researcher chose the membership of the thought collective 'environmental justice research' and tried to stay within the boundaries of the respective thought style. In order to highlight the central argument that thought collective memberships intrinsically shape the whole research process from choosing a topic via the formulation of a research question and field work to the final results, the aim here was to deliberately avoid thought style expansions towards local *cognition*.

The second version follows a more open form of approaching the empirical setting: In a mixture of the *tabula rasa* approach and elements of Grounded Theory, spiked with pre-attained contextual knowledge from the CLASSIC version, the axiomatic view 'social-ecological conflicts exist' was challenged. Instead of solely *seeing* through the thought collective of 'environmental justice research', I applied forms of ethnographic research to be able to enter the thought collectives of local actors. Hence, the *seeing*-process of 'environmental justice research' was deprioritised in favour of *looking* at the case study and subsequently learning the codes of local thought styles (SAB, ASC, SOC&EDU, PE★). In so doing, I managed to enter those thought collectives' exoteric circles as a lay person and consequently obtain basic cognition of how to *see* the respective realities.

The two different forms of seeing the case study were most visible in terms of thematic identification of environmental justice issues (Figure 9.2). Here it becomes clear that the CLASSIC view was very closely applied according to early environmental justice research, favouring elements of the (physical) environmental space. The ALTERNATIVE, however, has a stronger tendency to focus on the social space and interactions among the actors.

Both perspectives have particular advantages in terms of the researcher's positioning in thought collectives. In the CLASSIC, the researcher has the

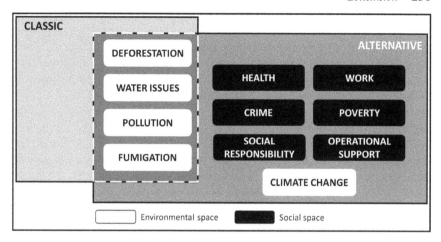

Figure 9.2 CLASSIC vs. ALTERNATIVE perspective – comparison of environmental justice issues.

great advantage of being closer to – if not part of – the esoteric circle of experts in the field of environmental justice research. The codes of conduct and modes of understanding are thoroughly internalised, allowing a more in-depth analysis within the framework of the adherent thought style. Additionally, the results are more likely to be verified by other members of the thought collective, since they are familiar with the methodological toolboxes and strings of argumentation. The ALTERNATIVE has greater potential to go off the beaten path of staying in one thought style and exercising thought style expansions as a main component of doing research. It goes without saying that while the potential of broadening the horizon by understanding other forms of thinking and asking different – more respective reality-based – questions (from the perspective of the researched) are given, the threat of remaining in the new thought styles' exoteric circle as a lay person should not be underestimated. One form of minimising this risk is by following long-term ethnographic research stays to be able to learn as much as possible from the thought collective members.

In conclusion, it has been shown that the differences of seeing and cognition between the CLASSIC and the ALTERNATIVE approach follow similar patterns discovered in the latter. The researcher's contextual embeddedness in particular thought collectives clearly reflect her/his form of *thinking* about and actually *doing* research. While this finding is not new, it is nonetheless vital to actively broach this issue and make the process behind the research more transparent. Consequently, a more-than-mixed methods approach has been applied in this book, summarised under the term 'jazz methodology'.

... and all that jazz ...

Multiplicities of perspectives call for a great variety of capturing them. As has been seen with the CLASSIC and ALTERNATIVE perspective, two approaches towards methods were used. The first relied on an established set of tools within the framework of environmental justice. While the focus was still on the outcome, the thorough execution of the methods – i.e. the methodological/procedural soundness – was a central element there. The second perspective favoured the unearthing and validation of different realities over the full execution of one particular method. Realities are not solely experienced via one sense, let alone focusing only on rationality. Thus, the methodological discussion on viscerality was taken up to show the interconnectedness of rationale and emotion to overcome this artificial dichotomisation (or 'work of purification'; Latour 1993, p. 11) to obtain cognition (via the 'work of translation'; ibid., p. 11) – elements that are also reflected in the meta-theoretical considerations influenced by Ludwik Fleck (1980).

Ethnography – particularly its strands of auto, visual and sensory ethnography – was applied to become a member of the – for me – new thought collectives and to get acquainted with the settings of codes, rules and regulations. The organisation of ethnographic methods adopted the strong metaphor of jazz. This move had two advantages for me. First, understanding the power of jazz, particularly the breaking down of music into small patterns and rearranging those bits and pieces according to the relevant context, gave me a form of structuring my elements of methods that I have applied, always having the focus on the understanding of the different realities in mind. Second, those small structures proved particularly helpful in times when improvisation during the fieldwork became necessary (e.g. when an interview with a headmaster of a school was planned, but the opportunity to build up ad hoc participatory workshops arose). At this point I have to stress that all 16 methods applied (the results of 12 of those were actually used in this book) required intense preparation and familiarisation *before* the actual fieldwork had started (another close resemblance to playing jazz becomes obvious, since improvisation cannot be done on nothing; a base to improvise on is absolutely necessary).

Another reason for the application of a great variety of different methods was to approximate 'authentic representations of experience' (Baxter and Eyles 1997, p. 512) to maintain credibility and confirmability. In so doing, thick descriptions of (non-)events, recordings (where possible), but most importantly auto-ethnographic reflections on my role in applying necessarily subjective methods have become a crucial companion. I want to stress again: the empirical data are – as in any other ethnographic work – dependent on the contextuality of rational and emotional structures and actions. The access to information (i.e. the thought styles), is thus highly dependent on interpersonal relations that unfold due to beyond-rational decisions made by the researcher and researched alike.

... call for environmental justice revisited

A common ground for understanding environmental justice is based on two features: clearly manifested conflict situations and the importance of combining bio-physical variables with social interactions. Both are not the central theme in my work. So, one crucial question arises:

What does this all have to do with environmental justice?

A lot, I argue. I have deliberately used the case of Las Lajitas to evaluate current environmental justice state of the arts to unearth a core blind spot of the application of the concept(ion): incommensurabilities. So far, to my knowledge, no extensive environmental justice study has been carried out to look behind realities' creation process of different thought styles that lead to clearly manifested conflict situations. As observed in my case study, they are, however, pivotal to the researcher's cognition of (non-)conflictivity, giving context to the behavioural patterns of the actors involved.

In order to structure my study, I have described the environmental justice incommensurabilities framework (EJIF) to combine elements of established environmental justice research with a set of tools to work on the conceptual gaps of misunderstandings.

The entry point of this study was manifested in the CLASSIC reading described above. From a researcher's outside perspective, the Chaco Salteño is laden with human-environment relations and resulting conflictive situations: Deforestation and the destruction of natural habitats, subsequent relocations of peasants and *criollos*, anthropogenic influence on regional climatic situations, fumigation of soy fields affecting locals living in nearby villages. Change, effects, actors and conflict (potentials) were identified that had the prerequisites for the environmental justice central manifestation of conflictive situations. The results from the external analysis were then paired with the ALTERNATIVE approach and the perspectives of the four actor groups (SAB, ASC, SOC&EDU, PE★) to show a differentiated picture of the distribution of claims making and non-claims making.

Rather than focusing on the actual claims making, I reapplied elements of seven environmental justice concepts: the pluralistic model of claims making (Davoudi and Brooks 2014), the environmental inequity formation concept (Pellow 2000), policy development monitoring (Fredericks 2011), the actor-oriented concept (Reboratti 2012), the claims-making frame of social movements (Čapek 1993), the focus on robust processes (Elvers 2011), as well as the environmental justice matrix (Flitner 2007). In so doing, the categories of distribution, recognition, participation, responsibility and capabilities were re-contextualised to show the actors' positioning within those categories. In other words, the already existing environmental justice concepts were split up into small patterns (i.e. the categories) to then be rearranged to gain cognition of the underlying dimensions of how and why claims were made or not.

Thus, the strengths of environmental justice concepts were identified and applied not to claims making but to explain the construction of situations of (non-)claims making.

This procedure allowed a hands-on empirical evaluation and analysis of environmental justice situations. Additionally, I argued that a theoretical positioning of justice is vital to obtain a more holistic picture: Thus, the actors' thought style positioning in relation to justice (from universally valid to context-based), the role of the environment (from anthropocentrism via intermediate axiology to eco-centrism), as well as the anchoring of the thought collective were studied as well. This feature offered valid theoretical-contextual information on the respective thought styles regarding their focus on particular situations (ideal, best alternative to negotiated agreement, or non-ideal). A much-needed re-connection to theoretical discussions on justice and the environment could be achieved.

Research on environmental justice is highly normative. Laying bare the structures of how to do research, the theoretical as well as practical positioning of the researcher, particularly in asking questions, are core elements of this field of study. I have shown that four challenges to environmental justice still pertain:

1 *Combining social and environmental factors*: Depending on the weight certain actors put on each factor, the outcome of the research can vary greatly. Unearthing the underlying dimensions of why particular foci are given, has great potential to understanding conflictive social-environmental situations.

2 *Theoretical considerations*: Environmental justice research is divided into two main strands, one being theoretically-driven (predominantly from justice research angles), while the other is case-focused. Combining both perspectives by reflecting actors' perceptions does not make environmental justice research less complex, but allows increased cognition of incommensurabilities.

3 *Focus on actors*: Simply put, most of environmental justice literature focuses on two blocs: the causers of environmental bads and the organised (activist) group resisting. Through my case study of Las Lajitas, I wanted to highlight that the local non-activist population are often overlooked, leaving out perspectives on conflictive situations that can prove vital for a holistic understanding.

4 *Labelling of environmental justice*: Environmental justice is a highly scattered field of different approaches, concepts and conceptions, worked on by researchers from the fields of geography, sociology, political sciences, history, ecology, etc. In addition, there are plenty of other concepts that fall under the term 'environmental justice' but are because of different contexts not labelled as such. The most prominent example here is the Argentine use of social-ecological conflicts instead of environmental justice. Bringing those different approaches under one conceptual roof while maintaining their proper integrity is without a doubt a major challenge here.

Facing those challenges, it is essential to continue working on environmental justice from different disciplinary angles. I have shown that contexts as well as incommensurability are vital to avoid the trap of universal morality without considering other thought styles and local/regional settings. Thus, I consider this book a contribution not just to the environmental justice literature, but see it as a part of critically reflecting debates on geographies of morality (Lee and Smith 2004), ethics (Barnett 2013), or sophistication (Jacobs 2010), while expanding on new elements of visceral geographies (Hayes-Conroy and Hayes-Conroy 2010, 2015) to strengthen geographies between discourse and praxis (Baumann *et al.* 2015). It was highly influenced by post-structural thought from geography, sociology, ethnology, history and philosophy, via critical GIS, hydrology, meteorology and ecology, to – at first sight – seemingly strange fields of musicology and literature.

Finally, why does environmental justice activism/research does not work everywhere? It has been shown that focusing on the respective thought styles leads to the deconstruction of one's own form cognition. One global normative master frame for environmental justice is clearly bound for failure; context matters.

So, ultimately, can there even be justice for all?

Much like the anecdote of Schrödinger's cat, the answer is: yes and no. It depends on your reality.

References

Anguelovski, I. and Martínez-Alier, J., 2014. The 'environmentalism of the poor' revisited: territory and place in disconnected glocal struggles. *Ecological Economics*, 102, 167–176.

Barnett, C., 2013. Geography and ethics III: from moral geographies to geographies of worth. *Progress in Human Geography*, 38 (1), 1–10.

Baumann, C., Tijé-Dra, A. and Winkler, J., 2015. Geographien zwischen Diskurs und Praxis – Mit Wittgenstein Anknüpfungspunkte von Diskurs- und Praxistheorie denken. *Geographica Helvetica*, 70 (3), 225–237.

Baxter, J. and Eyles, J., 1997. Evaluating qualitative research in social geography: establishing 'rigour' in interview analysis. *Transactions of the Institute of British Geographers*, 22 (4), 505–525.

Bullard, R.D., 2000. *Dumping in Dixie: Race, Class, and Environmental Quality*. 3rd edn. Boulder, CO: Westview Press.

Čapek, S.M., 1993. The 'environmental justice' frame: a conceptual discussion and an application. *Social Problems* [online], 40 (1), 5–24. Available at: www.jstor.org/stable/3097023

Carrier, M., Apparicio, P. and Séguin, A.-M., 2016. Road traffic noise in Montreal and environmental equity: what is the situation for the most vulnerable population groups? *Journal of Transport Geography*, 51, 1–8.

Davoudi, S. and Brooks, E., 2014. When does unequal become unfair? Judging claims of environmental injustice. *Environment and Planning A*, 46 (11), 2686–2702.

DeLoughrey, E.M., Didur, J. and Carrigan, A., eds., 2015. *Global Ecologies and the Environmental Humanities: Postcolonial Approaches*. New York: Routledge.

Elvers, H.-D., 2011. Umweltgerechtigkeit. In: M. Groß, ed. *Handbuch Umweltsoziologie*. Wiesbaden: VS Verlag für Sozialwissenschaften, pp. 464–484.

Fan, M.-F., 2012. Justice, community knowledge, and waste facility siting in Taiwan. *Public Understanding of Science*, 21 (4), 418–431.

Fleck, L., 1980. *Entstehung und Entwicklung einer wissenschaftlichen Tatsache: Einführung in der Lehre von Denkstil und Denkkollektiv*. Frankfurt am Main: Suhrkamp.

Flitner, M., 2007. *Lärm an der Grenze: Fluglärm und Umweltgerechtigkeit am Beispiel des binationalen Flughafens Basel-Mulhouse*. Stuttgart: Steiner.

Fredericks, S.E., 2011. Monitoring environmental justice. *Environmental Justice*, 4 (1), 63–69.

Guthman, J., 2016. Lives versus livelihoods?: Deepening the regulatory debates on soil fumigants in California's strawberry industry. *Antipode*, 49 (1), 86–105.

Hayes-Conroy, A. and Hayes-Conroy, J., 2015. Political ecology of the body: a visceral approach. In: R.L. Bryant, ed. *The International Handbook of Political Ecology*. Cheltenham: Edward Elgar Publishing, pp. 659–672.

Hayes-Conroy, J. and Hayes-Conroy, A., 2010. Visceral geographies: mattering, relating, and defying. *Geography Compass*, 4 (9), 1273–1283.

Jacobs, J.M., 2010. Sophisticated geographies. *ACME: An International E-Journal for Critical Geographies* [online] (1), 10–20. Available at: www.acme-journal.org/vol. 9/Jacobs10.pdf

Kopnina, H., 2016. Of big hegemonies and little tigers: ecocentrism and environmental justice. *The Journal of Environmental Education*, 47 (2), 139–150.

Latour, B., 1993. *We Have Never Been Modern*. Cambridge, MA: Harvard University Press.

Lee, R. and Smith, D.M., eds., 2004. *Geographies and Moralities: International Perspectives on Development, Justice, and Place*. Malden, MA: Blackwell.

Milbourne, P. and Mason, K., 2016. Environmental injustice and post-colonial environmentalism: opencast coal mining, landscape and place. *Environment and Planning A*, 49 (1), 29–46.

Okereke, C., 2010. Climate justice and the international regime. *Wiley Interdisciplinary Reviews: Climate Change*, 1 (3), 462–474.

Pearce, J., Kingham, S. and Zawar-Reza, P., 2006. Every breath you take?: Environmental justice and air pollution in Christchurch, New Zealand. *Environment and Planning A*, 38 (5), 919–938.

Pellow, D.N., 2000. Environmental inequality formation: toward a theory of environmental injustice. *American Behavioral Scientist*, 43 (4), 581–601.

Reboratti, C., 2012. Socio-environmental conflict in Argentina. *Journal of Latin American Geography*, 11 (2), 3–20.

Taylor, D.E., 2000. The rise of the environmental justice paradigm: injustice framing and the social construction of environmental discourses. *American Behavioral Scientist*, 43 (4), 508–580.

Viglizzo, E. and Jobbágy, E.G., eds., 2011. *Expansión de la frontera agropecuaria en Argentina y su impacto ecológico ambiental*. Buenos Aires: Ediciones Instituto Nacional de Tecnología Agropecuaria.

Wang, Y., Zha, J., Xu, Y., Ra, K., et al., 2016. Health risk assessment of migrant workers' exposure to polychlorinated biphenyls in air and dust in an e-waste recycling area in China: indication for a new wealth gap in environmental rights. *Environment International*, 87, 33–41.

Glossary

asado   Argentine barbecue.

barrio   neighbourhood.

campesino   person living in the *campo*, i.e. rural space.

comping   active listening, leading and following, action and reaction.

criollos   locally-born people of European, particularly Spanish descent.

esoteric circle   inner circle of a thought collective, often considered the elite.

exoteric circle   outer circle of a thought collective; often considered as comprising lay persons following the esoteric circle's elite.

monte   type of forest, particularly in North-west Argentina.

puesto ganadero   often precarious living area comprising a house, a watering place and farmyard and a fenced area of 2–4 hectares for natural pasture and planting corn.

retenciones   taxation on (soy) exports in Argentina.

thought collective   a group of people with similar backgrounds who share the same codes and rationalities as well as context.

thought style   processes, circulations of ideas and social practices out of which the style-appropriate conditioning of perception, thinking and acting of actors emerge.

Index

Page numbers in **bold** denote tables, those in *italics* denote figures.

For Product Safety Concerns and Information please contact our EU
representative GPSR@taylorandfrancis.com
Taylor & Francis Verlag GmbH, Kaufingerstraße 24, 80331 München, Germany

www.ingramcontent.com/pod-product-compliance
Ingram Content Group UK Ltd.
Pitfield, Milton Keynes, MK11 3LW, UK
UKHW021004180425
457613UK00019B/808